Hiking Snohomish County

—Second Edition—

Ken Wilcox

110 Hikes & Walks

On the coast, in town, in the lowlands and foothills, and in the North Cascades

Plus Parks, Viewpoints, Water Access & Campgrounds

NORTHWEST WILD BOOKS
Bellingham, Washington
2007

Hiking Snohomish County
—2nd Edition

© Copyright 1998 and 2007 by Ken Wilcox.

ISBN: 978-0-9793333-1-6

Designed and published by Northwest Wild Books, Bellingham, Washington.
Printed on 100% post-consumer fiber, processed chlorine-free.
Printed in Canada.

Photography by Steve Satushek and the author. Satushek: pages 49, 53, 60, 84, 101, 120, 125, 126, 128, 149, 154, 155, 157, 167, 170, 172, 177, 180, 184, 185, 187, 195, 196, 198, 203, and 222. Pages 100 and 270 photos by Kris Berger. All other photos and maps by the author.

Front cover: Picture Show Falls and the Boulder River (by the author).
Back cover: Glacier Peak over Image Lake (by Steve Satushek); and wildflowers on Mount Pilchuck, Meadowdale Playfield paths, and North Fork Skykomish River Trail (by the author).

Hiking guides from Northwest Wild Books . . .

Hiking Snohomish County, 2nd Edition (2007)
Hiking Whatcom County, 5th Edition (2006)
Hiking the San Juan Islands, including Whidbey Island (2001)
Hiking Skagit County (coming soon)

We welcome your comments, corrections, kudos, criticisms and/or suggestions regarding current and future editions of these titles. For contact information, please visit www.nwwildbooks.com.

For my parents
. . . and for Jack.

FOREWORD

SNOHOMISH COUNTY, WASHINGTON, is a fine place to hike. I have to admit that I didn't know this during the first few years I lived in the county. On July 4th, 1967, my parents, five siblings, and I crossed the mighty Cascades in a big truck and a little car to make a new home in the amazingly green and drizzly State of Washington. For this happy camper, Utah was history. We settled in at Alderwood Manor the first few months as Dad headed out every morning to build tall buildings in Seattle. But Alderwood was just too urban for this bunch, considering the traffic and subdivisions and all. So in a matter of months we were out on the farm—smack between the north and southbound lanes of I-5, near Stanwood. And despite the sound of it, that was when I-5 near Stanwood was about as busy as a dead-end street in Mukilteo.

Out of school and off on my own by the early 1970s, I still failed to appreciate what there was to see and experience in the lowlands and North Cascades of Snohomish County. I owned a dirt bike and got to know logging roads and cow pastures instead. I took a truck-driving job, built a funky log cabin outside Arlington, then complained about all of the new development and the timber barons taking down so many big trees. The battle for wilderness—an essential ingredient for any civilized society—had begun, and I was headlong into it. The fight for wilderness preservation, strangely enough, carried me deeper into the wilderness than I'd ever been. While I had explored around the edges for a number of years, mostly dayhikes to little lakes and waterfalls, jaunts in the old growth, and up to the alpine meadows, the majesty of it didn't really strike home, I'm embarrassed to say, until a little trip up Mount Baker in Whatcom County in the late 1970s. The view was amazing. I was hooked.

Until then, real hiking, I thought, was something you did at a national park, like in the Olympics or at the Grand Canyon. In 1980 I lept to the realization that hiking—walking really, although that sounds less glamorous—is really what my life was about. In February of that year, my sweetie (at the time) accompanied me to a slide show about a basic mountaineering course being offered by the Everett Mountaineers. We were totally impressed and signed up immediately. And like others who've made the leap, the experience changed our lives profoundly. We learned to "walk" up mountains, with or without a trail. I climbed the ominously subtle Mount Pilchuck the day Mount Saint Helens blew (we heard it go and hustled to the ridge to watch the mushroom cloud a hundred miles away), then Del Campo and Gothic Peaks. Then the big one, Glacier Peak, and Whitehorse, White Chuck, Dome Peak, and dozens more in subsequent

3

years. I must confess to a prolonged peak-bagging phase that has since evolved into more of a fascination with discovering hidden corners, breathing fresh air, and sitting on my duff to watch the world go by. But climbing—that is, hiking with a rope, ice axe, and things that jangle—in no way reduced the attraction of hiking without all the extra baggage. And today, no one could possibly keep me off the trail or out of the mountains. But these are typical sentiments for the hundreds of thousands of Washingtonians who've taken the time to discover and appreciate wilderness in the Northwest.

While life's unpredictableness soon carried me north to Western Washington University and a career as an environmental and recreation planner in Bellingham, the mountains and trails of Snohomish County have remained a forever-important part of my life. After completing a trail guide to Whatcom County in 1987, the notion of writing a similar book for Snohomish County seemed only natural, and a first edition was published in 1998. I hope this new second edition proves to be an even more useful tool for those who would like to discover what Snohomish County really has to offer.

Wilderness, of which the county has a substantial yet insufficient allotment in its share of the North Cascades, is not, by any means, the only kind of place worth exploring. The coast, urban areas, lowlands, and foothills all have something unique to offer, and the walking experiences available are as varied as the landscape—and the people doing the walking. I've tried to include wide geographic coverage, and a range of difficulty levels so hopefully everyone has something to choose from.

While this book catalogues more than 360 miles of trails—over two-thirds of it in the North Cascades—we can expect even more walking opportunities as time goes on if the growing numbers of Americans using trails and advocating for more is any indication. A number of possible trail projects around the county are noted in the Introduction, many of them in lowland and urban areas. For every existing or planned trail, the hard work of trail advocates, volunteers, city and county park staff, state and federal trail planners, trail-minded politicians, trail crews, and others must be commended. So much of what they do is taken for granted, even among many avid trail users. While there's a lot of good energy available to create more trails, inadequate funding presents a typical stumbling block. Nevertheless, as competing interests vie for limited tax dollars, trails will still win out on occasion. Perhaps if more people demand more quality walking opportunities for all the good things they do for families and communities, we can make some serious headway. Instead, we live in a society where, despite broad public support for trails, a lot of couch-potato politicians think we ought to spend less on trails, parks, and the like, and more on paving paradise and subsidizing growth. They seem to have it backwards.

Trails are places to think and feel and communicate with others and with the natural environment, to get clear on priorities, to experience beauty and harmony, to learn some self-reliance, and to appreciate what's so good about this thing called life. Trails are simple, cheap, attractive, and lasting, if they're designed and built correctly. They're something virtually everyone can enjoy—walking or not. As growth and development in the region seem poised to gobble up every wild corner of the lowlands, as single-occupant automobiles and short-sighted politics rattle across the landscape in monotonous shock waves, and as more and more families arrive in their big trucks and little cars looking for a new home, trails offer a step back from it all. And trails, notwithstanding my woeful whining, are just plain fun to walk. I hope this book is most useful in that regard.

Happy trails!

Ken Wilcox
Summer 2007

ACKNOWLEDGMENTS

I'm lucky to have so many good friends to explore the woods with—and for moral support to get this book done. Special thanks to Steve Satushek for his excellent photographic contributions and substantial early work on the book, to Kristin Carroccino, Kris B., Brooke D. and Juliet T. for invaluable editing assistance, and to Jim O., Keith K., Susan K., Sara R., Jana W., Clare F., Jim H., Brad R., Kiko A., Betty P., Steve W., Bill W., David D., and Jim Z., for their support and encouragement. A special group hug also to many others who walked with me for more than a mile or two: Miss Kris (most especially), Mel B., Lorraine B., Floyd B., Joan C., Ginger D., Ed H., Bud H., Jerry H., Steve and Helene I., Tom K., Brandon L., Peter M., Dennis M., Ron S., Steve S., Sue S., John W., and finally to a couple of still missed canine companions, Bean and Si (they were there in the beginning). Appreciation also goes to many agency staff (some of whom have moved on), including Marc Krandel, Doug Dailer, Dianne Housden, Pat Kenyon, and John Tucker with Snohomish Co. Parks & Recreation; Jane Lewis and Daryl Bertholet at Everett Parks & Recreation; Arvilla Ohlde, City of Edmonds; Kathy Johnson with the Lynnwood Parks Dept.; Clark Meek, City of Bothell; Dawn Erickson and the helpful staff at the Darrington Ranger Station and Verlot Public Service Center; Tom Davis and Debby at the Skykomish Ranger Station; Kathy White also with the USFS; and Ralph Radford at Wallace Falls State Park. All were quick to offer the information needed to fill in the gaps.

DISCLAIMER!
This guidebook is intended for use by competent hikers who accept
the inherent and sometimes unpredictable hazards associated with the activity.
Read the introductory material and be sure of your
ability to safely hike any of the trails listed before venturing out.
The user assumes all risks!

CONTENTS

Walks & Hikes   👣 = EASIEST / 👣 👣 👣 👣 = MOST DIFFICULT

THE COAST—

URBAN AREAS—

< *Copper Lake from below Vesper Peak*

Trail Location Map

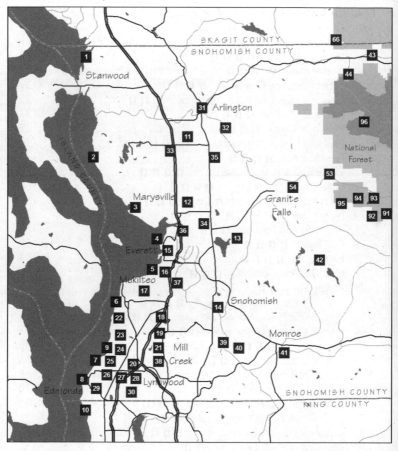

SNOHOMISH

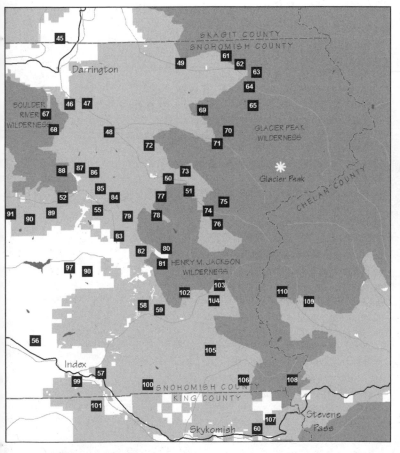

COUNTY

11

Author Recommendations—
(By hike number)

Best for visitors & newcomers
Easy: 4, 7, 8, 17, 21, 28, 35, 36, 37, 38, 47, 60, 86
Moderate: 9, 32, 44, 53, 54, 55, 56, 57, 64, 74, 90, 100, 107
More Difficult: 61, 66, 78, 89, 91, 93, 94, 99, 100, 105, 106, 108, 109
Most Difficult: 65, 72, 73, 76, 80, 81, 82, 83, 84, 85, 95, 96, 102, 110

Best by season
Spring: All lowland hikes plus 44, 50, 56, 57, 59, 60, 107
Summer: All hikes are good in summer!
Fall: All lowland hikes and all spring and winter hikes
Winter: All lowland hikes plus 47, 48, 51, 53, 54, 56

Best by area
The Coast: 4, 5, 7, 8, 9
Urban Areas: 17, 21, 25, 28, 30
Lowlands & Foothills: 32, 35, 36, 38, 40, 43, 44, 47, 54, 55, 56, 57, 60
North Cascades: 61, 65, 66, 68, 72, 73, 74, 76, 78, 80, 81, 82, 84, 85, 90, 91, 92, 94, 95, 96, 98, 99, 100, 102, 104, 106, 107, 108, 109, 110

Best for kids
Easy: 2, 4, 5, 7, 8, 10, 12, 16, 17, 21, 23, 24, 25, 28, 30, 32, 34, 35, 36, 37, 38, 41, 43, 51, 52, 74, 107
Moderate: 9, 32, 40, 42, 44, 47, 48, 54, 55, 56, 57, 59, 60, 62, 64, 75, 79, 86, 88, 90, 94, 100, 107
More Difficult (for older, stronger kids): 61, 66, 78, 87, 89, 91, 93, 94, 98, 99, 104, 105, 106, 109
Most Difficult (for older, stronger kids): 80, 81, 84, 95, 102

Trails with limited wheelchair-access
Paved: 8, 10, 12, 14, 15, 17, 18, 20, 21, 23, 25, 26, 30, 35, 36, 37, 38, 41, 52, 55, 60, 107; see also Parks and Viewpoints
Unpaved: 2, 3, 9, 11, 19, 27, 43, 64, 74, 80, 107

Trail sign, West Cady Ridge (Hike 104).

Introduction

FROM THE WILD BLUFFS AND BEACHES of Port Susan and Possession Sound to the flowery alpine meadows of the Glacier Peak Wilderness, Snohomish County, Washington, is a wonderful place to walk. Hundreds of miles of trails access mountains, glaciers, wildflowers, waterfalls, lakes, rivers, and old-growth forests of the North Cascades, while more than a hundred additional miles lead to lowland forests and fields, more lakes, streams, rivers, and wetlands, urban parks and natural areas, historic communities, and saltwater shores.

Hiking Snohomish County offers a wide selection of walks and hikes—doable in an hour or a day—to all of these destinations, from the easiest half-mile stroll on a scenic waterfront, to a marathon grind to a spectacular North Cascades summit. With the major emphasis on dayhiking, well over three hundred miles of walking is described in this guide, along with suggestions for further exploration. Listings are also provided for dozens of public parks, viewpoints, water access areas, and campgrounds throughout the county.

While many hikers may be content to wander aimlessly and soak up the views, a much richer experience can be expected for those who make the effort to inform themselves of a little history of a particular place, or who learn to identify the rocks and minerals or the more common plant and animal species and their signs and sounds, or who take the time to read or hear what others have experienced about a place (or about themselves) in their brush with the wild. A few resources to help accomplish this are suggested, although sometimes it's enough to hit the trail just to escape the common annoyances of the work-a-day world.

Read on for a short background on Snohomish County, including a brief overview of present and future trails in the region, an environmental and historical synopsis of the county, a bit more on the weather, and suggestions for further reading.

Those who are new to hiking and who could use some extra guidance, turn to page 31, **What to Know Before You Go**. Then see **How to Use This Book** on page 44 for an explanation of the trail listings.

TRAILS IN SNOHOMISH COUNTY

It's clear that Snohomish County has a lot to offer in the way of walking and hiking trails. However, most of these trails—over 80% of the trail miles in the county—are in the North Cascades, on federal (National Forest) and state (Department of Natural Resources or DNR) lands. The rest is generally spread across a number of city and county parks in the lowlands, most notably Lord Hill and River Meadows County Parks. A few urban-style multi-use trails like the Centennial and Interurban Trails, plus several trail-less beach walks, a couple of dike trails, and a few miles within Wallace Falls State Park account for almost all of the balance.

WHAT'S IN THE WORKS

To someone new to the area or one who doesn't get out on the trail often, it may seem as if all our trail worries are over. Yet despite the sound of it, the overall trail system in Snohomish County is far from complete. Perhaps the most obvious trail deficiencies are the general lack of high-quality hiking trails over vast areas of the lowlands, and the near absence of urban trails and greenways in almost all populated areas of the county. Major links between communities are also lacking, with only two notable exceptions: the Centennial and Interurban Trails (and soon, perhaps, the North Creek Trail). The trail system of the future may never rival the sprawling network we've developed to suit our addiction to the automobile, but certainly much can be done to improve on what we have. In fact, much is being done to address these deficiencies.

Thanks to the dedication of many concerned citizens, agency staff, and leaders in the community, a few new trails have materialized, and volunteers deserve much of the credit. Thanks to Volunteers for Outdoor Washington (VOW), Stillaguamish Citizens Alliance, and other local groups, a new 3.5-mile Lime Kiln Trail (*Hike 54*) was opened in 2004 at Hubbard Lake near Granite Falls. The trail may eventually bridge the South Fork Stillaguamish River to connect to the trail at Robe Canyon following the old Monte Cristo Railroad. VOW is also completing work on the Iron Goat Trail (*Hike 107*) that follows an impressive section of an historic railroad grade west of Stevens Pass. The City of Arlington constructed an attractive section of the Centennial Trail downtown, and the City of Snohomish has completed its own downtown Riverfront

Trail to eventually link with the Centennial Trail (*Hike 35*), and perhaps someday, all the way downriver to Lowell. These smaller communities may be outclassing the bigger cities; Everett, for example, has shown only meager support for new trails despite good policies in the comprehensive plan that are meant to address the city's substantial trails deficit.

There is no shortage of good ideas for future trails in Snohomish County. Among the routes under consideration for near-term development are several major rail-trails, nature trails, park-based trail systems, and a range of trail extensions, links, and spurs. Most notable are rail-trail extensions planned over the next several years for the Centennial Trail (from Arlington to Skagit County) and the 27-mile Whitehorse Trail between Arlington and Darrington (*Hike 43*). Some trail improvements within existing parks and natural areas are also in the works in the county and within several cities.

At the same time, other trail opportunities previously identified have stalled, including the idea for a new trail along the Snohomish River between Everett and Snohomish, and various routes linking communities in the western part of the county. Many potential trail projects are long-term prospects that need funding, access, and acquisition issues to be worked out. These include the 13-mile Maltby and 3.5-mile Kruse Junction rail-trails (both of which could connect with the Centennial); dike trails near Stanwood and along the delta of the Snohomish River; other river trail extensions; trail links between communities and between other major trail systems like the North Creek Trail from the Sammamish River-Burke-Gilman Trail in King County to Silver Lake Park via Thrashers Corner and Mill Creek; North Creek Park to Swamp Creek and the Interurban Trail; Stimsons Crossing to link Kayak

Ashland Lakes Trail.

Point Park to the Centennial Trail by way of Lake Goodwin; a link from the Centennial Trail at Hartford to Robe Canyon via the Monte Cristo Railroad grade; and a new route from Everett to Marysville via Smith Island (*see Hike 36*). An interpretive riverwalk trail from Lowell to north Everett and the Port Gardner waterfront is part of the grand vision, as is a Green Lake-style loop trail around Silver Lake (*Hike 18*) in south Everett. Barrier-free enhancements are likely in many areas. To speed up development of these potential trails, citizens should let their city and county representatives know that trails are critical to the quality of life we all want for our communities.

Among the shorter trails and connections within communities that are on the drawing board: linking the Scriber Creek Trail (*Hike 28*) in Lynnwood with Wilcox Park and Meadowdale Beach Park; linking Forest Park (*Hike 16*) to Pigeon Creek; and the development of new trails along several of the ravines between Everett and Edmonds, such as Powdermill and Japanese Gulches, Merrill and Ring Creek, and Pigeon Creeks. Mukilteo intends to extend the Big Gulch Trail (*Hike 22*) to saltwater, while also exploring trail routes along other ravines. New coastal routes could link them all together. A "Tidelands Trail" has been proposed to facilitate better access to the county's 62 miles of marine waterfront. A new link from Harborview Park to Darlington Beach is needed, but the BNSF railroad, as usual, stands in the way like a stubborn reptile. Trails along Terrace Creek, Swamp Creek, Wood Creek, and possibly Lake Ballinger are more good candidates for enhancing the regional trail system, as well as an interpretive trail to Kasch Park bog which drains into Lake Washington, and a trail at Japanese Gulch by way of another abandoned railroad grade. Improving unused street rights-of-way for trail use could further help link schools, parks, and neighborhoods.

In the foothills and Cascades, the emphasis is more on maintaining and repairing what exists and bringing some of the poorest trails up to an acceptable standard. The U. S. Forest Service (crews, contractors and volunteers), for example, has rebuilt several mountain trails in recent years, including the lower wet section of Weden Creek Trail (*Hike 82*) and the trail to Poodle Dog Pass, both near Monte Cristo (*Hikes 80, 81*). Following closure of the road to Squire Creek Pass Trail (*Hike 67*) in 2002 due to a massive slide, the alternative approach via Eightmile Creek (*Hike 68*) has been significantly upgraded. Washington Trails

Association, the Everett Mountaineers, Northwest Youth Corps, the Student Conservation Association, and others have helped improve trails at Perry Creek, Old Sauk, Boulder River, Green Mt., Suiattle River, Heather Lake, Lake 22, Pinnacle Lake, Poodle Dog Pass, Mt. Dickerman, Big Four, Mt. Pugh, Bedal Basin, Sulphur Creek, Ashland Lakes, and Wallace Falls State Park.

Severe flood damage in late 2003 undid some of the good work that's been done, particularly in the Darrington area, creating an enormous backlog of needed repairs which were far from complete in mid-2007. Another big storm hit in November 2006. As a result, <u>some of the trails listed in this guide may not be immediately accessible in 2007</u>, but may be reopened relatively soon. Trails with possible access issues include, by hike number: 55, 61, 62, 63, 64, 65, 67, 69, 70, 71, 74, 75, 76, 78, 89, 102, 103, 104, 105, and 106. Some only require a little extra walking. Check with the Forest Service or **www.wta.org** for current conditions.

Volunteers deserve credit for the thousands of hours of labor donated to dozens of trails in the North Cascades. The Everett Mountaineers (**www.everettmountaineers.org**), has done extensive work restoring and maintaining old fire lookouts and trails in the North Cascades, and recently completed yet another restoration at the Heybrook Ridge Lookout near Index. Trails on DNR lands have also benefitted from recent improvements, much of it by volunteers, including Mt. Pilchuck, Ashland Lakes, and Cutthroat Lakes in the Mt. Pilchuck area, and Greider Lakes near Spada Lake. More great work has been provided through internships and youth programs sponsored by the Student Conservation Association (**www.thesca.org**) and Northwest Youth Corps (**www.nwyouthcorps.org**). Friends of the Trail (**www.friendsofthetrail.org**) has also done much to help clean up Snohomish County trails.

While a number of excellent opportunities exist for new trails on state and federal lands, sensitive ecosystems and the need to protect wilderness values demand a cautious approach to such development. New trails deep in the wilderness are unlikely in the foreseeable future, although some new routes could be justified nearer the edges of wildness, such as day-hiking trails with great views into the wild heart of Snohomish County. Barrier-free improvements are also needed in some locations. Eventually, trails in the Cascades could be linked with lowland trail systems by way of the Whitehorse Trail and other corridors.

SOME THOUGHTS ON FUTURE TRAILS

All of these future trail plans might sound quite ambitious. Nevertheless, the public has consistently expressed interest in substantially expanding trail systems for both recreational use and to serve as alternatives to our sprawling, dreary, and expensive car-based transportation system. The demand for trails is clear. In fact, recent planning efforts revealed a shortage of more than one hundred miles of trails in the Everett area alone, based on accepted planning standards. Fortunately, the county's largest city has an abundance of waterfront around the west, north and east sides, plus much less-developed land to the south which offer tremendous opportunities to help address this deficit. Considering the growing number of people who reside in the region and use trails, we can expect the demand for more trails to rise, probably much faster than we can build them.

That raises at least three interesting questions.

First, can we afford to build and maintain an enjoyable and solidly interconnected regional trail system in Snohomish County? Perhaps we can't afford not to. If a decent quality of life is something we want to keep around for awhile, trails must be an integral component in the ongoing development of our communities. Acquiring corridors for future trails will only get more complicated and expensive over time.

Second, does encouraging people to use trails (or publishing more guidebooks, for that matter) only fill the trails up faster and thereby diminish the quality of the trail experience? Perhaps to a degree, but the upside of building public support for trails is not insignificant. People may have to wander a little farther from home or farther from the trailhead on occasion to find solitude as more good people inevitably come to "our" trails, but the benefits seem to far outweigh the costs. People who walk on trails almost invariably find something valuable in the experience. It might be purely recreational, or personal, or spiritual, or educational, or whatever, but if people value the experience, there's a chance they will also value the place. And what we clearly need more of on Planet Earth is more people who value place—whether it's an old-growth forest, an unpolluted lake, a quiet marsh, or a spectacular mountain vista. If trails take us to places that mean something to us, maybe we'll be inspired to take care of them.

Finally, can the natural environment withstand us all loving it to death simultaneously? Most likely not. We've seen the damage caused by overuse and abuse in the alpine country where thin soils and a short growing season tend to exaggerate the damage from tents, fires, and the like. We hear plenty about the need to protect water quality around sensitive lakes and streams. Many of us have stopped to pick up other people's garbage along the trail, mystified by the mentality of those who might just as easily trash the planet. We also know how humans can interfere with the needs of wildlife. Wolves and grizzlies desperately need a home, not to mention all the other imperiled species whose last refuge may be the wilderness of the North Cascades.

Certainly we can't all rely on the wilderness as one big happy playground dedicated to our weekend whims, nor should we presume that less pristine areas are any less sensitive to our numbers or our carelessness. Yet we can enjoy these areas as concerned humans and learn to explore them in ways that keep them intact and unspoiled. We can learn to coexist with wildlife and the land. We can care about the place. And we can encourage others to do the same.

Logging out a trail in the Glacier Peak Wilderness.

About Snohomish County

FROM SEA TO SUMMIT

Continental glaciers thousands of feet thick carved out much of the Puget Sound region over the past 13,000 to 25,000 years, then melting ice and huge meltwater rivers dumped thick layers of sediment over much of what we call the lowlands of northwest Washington. As the ice retreated and the climate moderated, vast forests gradually reclaimed the land. Wildlife, salmon, and humans followed. The land, free of this enormous burden of ice, went into rebound as if someone took seven thousand years to step off a 400-foot trampoline. But the sea rose almost as quickly, fed by the melting continents. Eroded bluffs along the marine shore offer an easy view of the sand, clay, and rock that were deposited here.

Before, during, and after the "Ice Age" (geologists say it hasn't officially ended), alpine glaciers carved the mountains, as unmelted snow was compressed into ice which, responding to gravity, flowed and still flows like a slow river down the mountain side. Most glaciers are still carving rock from the North Cascades, inch-by-inch, year-by-year. At the same time, the Cascades are uplifting, perhaps as quickly as they're being chipped away. Streams and rivers carry this stony refuse out of the mountains and onto the floodplains where new deposits are made, reminiscent of and intermingled with the vast glacial deposits that characterize much of the lowlands. Hills and foothills of underlying bedrock, like Lord Hill, stand as remnants of a huge and incomplete wearing down of the landscape.

Scientists can watch these natural processes over decades and lifetimes and then extrapolate from their observations what most likely occurred over spans of time that most mortals can hardly imagine. They help us see the natural landscape as the logical result of something dynamic and persistent, such as entire continents drifting around the globe, pieces of oceanic and continental crust colliding ferociously but in ultra slow-motion nearly invisible to human awareness, volcanoes erupting through the weakened rock where one tectonic plate slides hotly beneath another. In the place we arbitrarily refer to as Snohomish County, volcanic Glacier Peak emerged from this sub-earthen waltz to become what is perhaps the region's most dramatic natural landmark.

First climbed in 1898 by Thomas Gerdine, Sam Strom, and three others, 10,541-foot Glacier Peak was called *DaKobed*, or Great Parent, by the natives. Gerdine and his contemporaries called it Glacier, mantled by over twenty square kilometers of ice. The mountain is situated deep enough in the range to be mostly obscured from view from the western lowlands, but it is a dramatic sight from nearby trails and meadows.

Perhaps 700,000 years old, the Glacier Peak volcano produced very explosive eruptions about 13,000 years ago, and several smaller yet powerful eruptions over the past 6,000 years. Many of these events generated huge mud and debris flows, or "lahars," that ran down river valleys all the way to saltwater. At least one buried the Arlington area under seven feet of sediment. More recent activity has been relatively minor, with no significant eruptions for about the last 300 years. Glacier Peak has been very quiet for three centuries, yet no one can predict just when it may wake up from its current snooze. The potential for catastrophic events remains for this and all of Washington's five major volcanoes.

The North Cascades—generally all the mountains between Snoqualmie Pass and British Columbia's Fraser River—are at least several million years old. Their amazingly rugged appearance, best appreciated up close and personal, is largely a result of long periods of stream erosion intermixed with periods of glacial advance and retreat. The frequent occurrence of hanging valleys offer evidence of calamitous ice traffic buzzing across preexisting valleys over centuries and millennia. But whatever the geologists say, the photographers assure us that the result is at least as beautiful as it is educational. Hikers and climbers find literally hundreds of scenic peaks to choose from in the North Cascades for their one- or multi-day adventures.

In the lowlands and foothills the shape and feel of the land is more subtle. Dozens of lakes, streams, waterfalls, forests, wetlands, occasional rock outcrops, and mountain vistas become the prized destinations. Here, there are no rules to say all hikes must end somewhere huge and spectacular. Instead, we look for what's beautiful or unique in nature. And the closer we look, the more there seems to be. To our good fortune Snohomish County has taken great steps to ensure that some unspoiled areas and unique natural features in the lowlands and foothills remain intact for our and future generations to enjoy. Large protected areas, like Lord Hill and the Snohomish River delta (both over 1,000 acres), and other bits of saved land (about ten thousand acres worth), and the mountains, are home to a wide diversity of birds, mammals, fish, amphibians, arthropods, unique plants, and other life forms whose future depends on protecting substantial areas from development, and in some cases, from any human use at all. While wetlands and riparian (or streamside) habitats are turning out to be some of the most valuable places we can protect, we can hope that, some day, viable representative examples of all native ecosystems will be protected. Much work remains.

National Forest lands provide some of this "insurance" for ecosystems, especially wilderness areas. Of the county's 1.3 million acres (2,098 square miles) of land, just under half is National Forest, a fraction of which is designated wilderness. Yet even wilderness areas miss much of the lower forests and streams, and more often protect high meadows, rock, and ice. Nevertheless, Snohomish County is lucky to have several hundred thousand acres of wildlands set aside within the Glacier Peak, Boulder River, and Henry M. Jackson Wilderness Areas. As this book was going to press, the U.S. Senate was nearing its final vote to create a new Wild Sky Wilderness, the first new wilderness area in the state since 1984 and long overdue. (A notoriously anti-environmental congressman from California, Richard Pombo, had blocked the Wild Sky bill for several years from moving forward, despite broad bipartisan support among Washington's best known Republicans and Democrats, as well as the nonpartisan mayors of dozens of cities in the region, not to mention a plethora of businesses and organizations. Pombo also worked to gut the Endangered Species Act and open the Arctic National Wildlife Refuge to oil drilling. Fortunately, California voters gave him the boot in 2006, and advocates are confident of a Wild Sky victory in 2007.)

A small amount of state land is also protected in Snohomish County, most notably around Mt. Pilchuck and Spada Lake. About ten percent of the county is managed by the DNR, albeit mostly for timber production and only incidentally for recreation.

THE HUMAN YEARS

Once inhabited only by wildlife, from salmon and grizzly bear—even bison and woolly mammoth as the ice retreated—to sparrows and butterflies, the land called Snohomish County was eventually occupied by Native Americans. A relatively advanced culture of hunters and gatherers moved into the region, perhaps thousands of years ago, to become the expert fishers, hunters, crafts people, traders, and artists who were encountered during Northwest explorations by Captain George Vancouver in 1792, and others before him and since. In the early 1800s, non-native fur traders passed through, but even by the 1840s no one had seriously confronted the Snohomish tribes whose camps and villages lined the region's rivers and saltwater shores. That would soon change, as pioneers and fortune-seekers began to make their way into the forested frontier. Conflicts arose with virtually all native tribes in the lowland regions, at times escalating into deadly violence. Military forts were established in many areas of western Washington, but from lessons learned in previous Indian wars of the West, a more concerted attempt at pacification, perhaps, led to the signing of the Point Elliot Treaty at Mukilteo in 1855. Territorial Governor Isaac Stevens, his delegation, a number of tribal chiefs, and 2,000 to 4,000 natives assembled for the occasion. In exchange for peace, a few scraps of reservation land, and guaranteed access to hunting and fishing grounds, the natives let go of a vast territory from Seattle to Canada. The treaty, unfortunately, has been violated repeatedly over the years, as much of the Indian land fell into non-native hands, as disastrous attempts were made to forcibly assimilate Native Americans into the white Euro-American culture, and as the salmon catch in particular was unfairly distributed. (The famous Boldt decision in the 1970s helped rectify the latter.)

In 1861, Dennis Brigham homesteaded at the foot of California Street on Port Gardner Bay, and the tiny settlement that would become Everett was born. In the same year, Snohomish County was split off from Island County. On Port Gardner, originally named by Captain Vancouver, the mud, mills, stumps, and saloons of Everett, Washington, would soon develop into of one of the most important timber towns in the nation: Milltown. The West's infatuation with big timber had spread north from California through the Oregon Country and on to the great wilderness surrounding northwest Washington's inland sea. Big timber was exactly what Snohomish County was made of. While the county's first sawmill was just up the shore at Tulalip Creek, it quickly became clear that Port Gardner, at the mouth of the Snohomish River, was the more strategic place. The river was the interior's transportation link to the outside world, as the founders of Lowell, Snohomish, and Monroe had realized in the latter part of the 1800s. Word spread quickly of Douglas fir and red cedar trees over twelve feet in diameter, and a seemingly inexhaustible ocean of timber from the mountains to the sea. It seemed that easy fortunes awaited the barons, developers, and speculators willing to invest in the region's future. Logging camps and sawmills sprouted up by the dozens in every direction. Arlington, Darrington, Granite Falls, Hartford, Edmonds, and of course, Everett rapidly took shape around lumber and shingle mills. In 1889, gold ore was discovered at the headwaters of the Sauk River. The Monte Cristo mines brought a railroad and smelter, adding to the inflated promise of wealth for all who might come to Snohomish County. (For a splendid history of early exploration and prospecting in the North Cascades, see Fred Beckey's *Range of Glaciers*; The Mountaineers, 2003.)

In the 1880s, completion of the Northern Pacific Railroad to Tacoma had enticed a hundred thousand people to Washington within two years. Hundreds of bankers and investors from New York, Boston, St. Paul, and elsewhere took note of the grand potential, and names like John D. Rockefeller, James J. Hill, Henry Hewitt, Frederick Weyerhaeuser, Wyatt Rucker, Charles Colby, Charles Wetmore, and Colgate Hoyt appeared on the scene. They were the economic movers and shakers, determined to see the place grow and prosper as the "City of Smokestacks," while generating more than a tidy profit for their investments. Empire Builder Jim Hill's 1,800-mile Great Northern Railroad reached Everett by way of Stevens Pass, in 1893, but it didn't terminate here as these men had dearly hoped. Hill pushed it through to Seattle, and the dream of Henry Hewitt, "father of Everett," that the city would become the New York of the West, was lost. This turn of events, plus a nationwide financial panic the same year sent the city into turmoil. Over the next several years scores of businesses shut down, unemployment surged, wages fell, and many lost everything they had. A landlord was shot trying to collect ten dollars rent. Thousands of properties went into tax foreclosure and thousands of people left.

Amazingly, where others saw hopelessness, Jim Hill saw a new opportunity. As the nation rebounded from its worst depression to date, Hill struck a deal with Frederick Weyerhaeuser, who bought up nearly a million acres of land from what were the Northern Pacific land grants for the cozy sum of six dollars an acre, then built the world's largest lumber mill on the Everett waterfront. As the city was revived, mostly through the lumber and shingle industries, Hill could expect a vast increase in the use of his railroad to ship wood products and other freight. But industrial capacity rapidly outstripped demand, and markets spiraled out of control. Prices dropped as the supply of lumber increased. Then mills increased production even more to make up the difference. The industry literally collapsed in 1907. Still, by 1908, more than 270,000 acres of land had been logged off in Snohomish County, and a commission was established to figure out what to do about the land. Ultimately, the stumps and slash would be cleared for agriculture and settlement to further the region's economic development.

BOOMING & BUSTING

As workers struggled to survive the winds of boom and bust, many perceived that the greed of industrialists and the politicians they supported were responsible for the poor wages, poor—and at times dangerous—working conditions, mill closures, and unemployment that would plague all the county's lumber towns on and off for decades. Populist sentiments spread among the discontent. Labor unions gained strength. The Industrial Workers of the World, or the Wobblies, became more vigilant, and disgruntled workers flocked to their ranks. Eugene Debs and the Socialists were gaining political ground nationwide, and Washington State had become a veritable hotbed of support. The situation escalated into angry demonstrations and arrests, then beatings and shootings, and ultimately the infamous tragedy known as the Everett Massacre on November 5, 1916. To rally the workers' cause and assert the right of free-speech in Everett, over two-hundred Wobblies boarded a ship in Seattle, steamed north, then were refused a landing by Sheriff McRae and a hundred citizen deputies. A barrage of gunfire broke out, bodies tumbled off the ship, deputies collapsed on the dock. Sixty or more were wounded and at least thirteen were killed, though no one is sure all the dead were ever counted.

In the years following this tumultuous beginning for the City of Smokestacks, conditions slowly improved, and despite the ongoing saga of boom and bust, commerce and industry continued to spread across the county from its social and economic epicenter at Hewitt and Wetmore in downtown Everett. Logging, lumber, pulp and paper, mining,

27

shipping, bargeworks, agriculture, and all the support services needed to keep them going remained the mainstays of the local economy for much of the twentieth century. The land transportation system once consisted of a few meager routes, like the "road" from Mukilteo to Lowell up Edgewater Creek, and the old Turkey Neck Trail from Lowell to the base of Hewitt Avenue. These routes were often impassable because of muck or high water. A modern, all-weather, partly paved road system would emerge by the 1940s. In the late 1960s, the Boeing boom introduced a big-time aerospace manufacturing element to the county payroll, which, along with spin-off development from Seattle and King County, began to change the face of every community south of Everett. What was rural became suburban, and what was urban ballooned outward into strip development, shopping centers, condominiums, and freeways. Similar growth and development is underway in almost every other community in the county. In the 1990s, the U.S. Navy's Everett Homeport opened, promising an annual infusion of millions of dollars more into the local scene.

AN OUTLOOK FOR THE FUTURE

In a few short generations, Snohomish County has become a dramatically different place from what Jim Hill, Frederick Weyerhaeuser, or any other astute industrialist possibly could have imagined a century ago. Between 1980 and 1990, the county was the fastest-growing in the state. During that period, the population increased by nearly thirty-eight percent to 465,642, compared to a statewide increase of only eighteen percent (to 4.9 million). Everett grew almost as fast as the county as a whole. From 1990 to 2000, the county grew by another 140,000 people, a thirty percent increase, then surpassed 655,000 in 2005.

Anyone who's watched this growth take place over the past three decades can scarcely fathom what might transpire over the next few decades. Growth and development shows little sign of slowing down much at all. In theory, the hotly debated Growth Management Act is a potent law that is supposed to help by ensuring orderly and efficient development while protecting the most critical areas from being destroyed. Yet at the rate new subdivisions and shopping centers have been replacing farms, fields, and forests, one can only wonder how or where such growth might possibly stop.

Iron Goat Trail bridge.

In the meantime, it's not just the development or pains of growth, politics, and economics that define what Snohomish County is. The county is, more importantly, a place. It is still a coast, lowland farms and fields, lakes, wetlands, streams, rivers, waterfalls, wooded foothills, and the rock, ice, alpine meadows, and old-growth forests of a magnificent range of mountains called the North Cascades. And, of course it is a community of Northwesterners, some of whom like to hike. The uncertainty is how long we can keep it that way.

CLIMATE & SEASON

Although prospectors and surveyors were blazing trails into the North Cascades a century ago, few roads pierce this stronghold of nature. Development in the eastern half of the county has been limited by precipitous terrain and a lot of precipitation, most of it snow. Except for a few low elevation trails along the Suiattle, Sauk, Stillaguamish, and Skykomish Rivers, most hiking areas are buried in deep snow six months out of the year. More than 150 inches of water, including as much as fifty feet of snow, falls on Glacier Peak annually. This compares to 35 inches in Everett (mostly rain, of course) and 90 or more inches in the foothills.

29

The east slope of the Cascades receives only about half as much rain as the west slope. A warm Pacific High usually rules summer weather over much of northwest Washington, while moist marine and dry continental air masses compete to influence the weather during the rest of the year. The lowlands experience a mild, moist climate and remain reasonably accessible throughout the seasons.

In the light breezes of springtime, lowland jaunts are ideal while the Cascades are still snowed in. Hiking doesn't have to be limited to sunny days, as some might suppose. Beach walks are great any time, but beware of rising and falling tides, especially during stormy periods. The casual hiker, properly clothed and shod, will find that a November sunset stroll along a windy shore can be just as enjoyable as an April day hike to Wallace Falls, or a cool October outing to Lake Valhalla.

In summer, the flowering alpine meadows high in the North Cascades on a warm day are especially inviting and difficult to surpass in their soothing beauty. Mid-July through late-September and sometimes June and October are the best months for good weather and snow-free trails in the North Cascades. In heavy snow years, the higher trails may not even start to open up until late July. Wildflowers and snowfields may have all but disappeared by September, with fall colors peaking by early October. Snowpack in the mid-elevations (2,000 to 4,000 feet) is a crap-shoot year to year. A lake at 3,000 feet may be just as likely to be snowbound in June one year as it is to be snow-free in April the next—that is, unless climate change continues to alter the patterns toward less snow and more rain from fall through spring. Remember, too, that the higher south-facing slopes can be free of snow a month or more before nearby north-facing slopes, so save the latter for later.

In the mountains, the weather can be fast-changing and unpredictable, so good raingear and layers for warmth are essential. Many days of cold rain and/or gusty winds can be expected anywhere, anytime, with or without any warning. Thunderstorms are not unusual, so avoid ridge tops, taller trees, and open water if you think lightning may strike in the vicinity. Snow is possible any day of the year above 5,000 feet. HYPOTHERMIA, therefore, IS A MOST SERIOUS CONCERN, having claimed the lives of more than a few unprepared victims. In the lower elevations, if you're dressed for the weather, the hiking season can last all year.

What To Know Before You Go

PREPARATION

A rewarding trip is usually one with good prep: proper dress, adequate food and water, and a few other basic safety items in the knapsack. Unsolicited advice: tell someone where you're going and when you'll return. Know your limits under the conditions around you. Sharpen your senses before and during your walk. Go at a comfortable pace and make it an enjoyable outing for yourself and your companions. Travel in a small group—three to six is ideal. Anticipate problems that might arise and prepare for them. Is the weather unstable? When does it get dark? When does the tide come in? Will there be snow on the trail?

The shortest walks require little more preparation than what's needed to check the mail at the end of the lane. Some hikes require much more foresight, especially in remote areas. Overnight trips are another matter altogether. This guide is not intended to prepare you for overnight backpacking, though many of the hikes listed offer great overnight potential. Consult libraries, sporting goods stores, outdoor clubs, and knowledgeable persons about furthering your skills in backcountry wilderness adventure. Numerous books are available that address clothing, equipment, navigation skills, camping, weather, ice axe use, hazards and other elements you may or may not be familiar with. Remember that trail conditions change due to any number of factors, so the trail descriptions in this book are not cast in concrete. Carry along a bucket of common sense.

CLOTHING & EQUIPMENT

For convenience, a suggested clothing and equipment list is included below. Volumes have been written on the selection and use of gear for a variety of hiking environments. Outdoor shops are excellent sources of information. Dressing comfortably means wearing loose-fitting layers that can be added or removed as necessary. Just being fashionable won't do. Under typical Northwest skies, the best combination in the mountains often includes a fast-drying synthetic layer against the skin, a light wool shirt or sweater, wool or synthetic durable pants (avoid cotton), a heavy wool sweater or pile or fleece jacket, a wind and water-resistant shell, top and bottom, gloves or mittens, and a wool hat or balaclava. Feet need special attention, and a boot that fits is mandatory. Sturdy, water-resistant lug-soled boots are recommended for mountain trails and on snow. Thick socks over thin absorb friction and can help prevent blisters.

Wet clothes, especially denim and other cotton fabrics, can lead to a rapid and dangerous loss of body heat. Add layers, gloves, a hat and parka in colder weather. Nights in the mountains, even in summer, are usually cold. A wool hat that pulls down over the ears makes a great thermostat. Put it on before you start shivering and remove it before you sweat or overheat. Fashionable sunglasses with UV protection and sunblock (SPF 15 or better) are appropriate for bright days, cloudy days in the snow, and of course, hot tub parties.

For short day trips, a large waist or fanny pack may be useful to carry food and drink, a nature guide, camera, windbreaker, etc. A backpack or rucksack will be required for mountain trips. Some of the higher trails can still be snow-covered in early summer, so an ice axe and the ability to use it may be necessary for safety. Contact outdoor shops or clubs to learn proper ice-axe technique. In remote areas, care must be taken to avoid getting caught in darkness or bad weather without the essentials in your pack. Study the following list and notice what other experienced hikers carry with them. For those who may be hiking by wheelchair (let's hear it for accessible trails), modify the list as needed.

Short walks:

Food, water, proper clothing, footwear, camera, binoculars, guidebook, sunglasses, sunblock.

Short hikes:

Same as above, and sturdy lug-soled boots, small pack, extra clothing (sweater, raingear), pocket knife, whistle, flashlight or headlamp, extra batteries, first aid kit. Some now carry a GPS unit and/or cell phone (cell phones are often unreliable in the mountains).

Longer dayhikes:

Same as above, and extra food and water, more clothes and raingear, sun hat, map and compass (learn to use them), matches, fire starter, foam sit-pad, toilet paper, insect repellent, emergency shelter.

BACKCOUNTRY SANITATION

Cleaning yourself or your food containers and cook pots should always occur well away from camp or water sources. Use common sense if you need to make a nature call. Get well off the trail and a good distance—100 feet or more—from streams or water bodies. Dig a shallow hole then cover it up well with soil, rocks and sticks. Only if it's safe (damp and raining), burn your toilet paper; otherwise pack it out in a special bag with your trash or recyclables. Leaves or snow work well if you forget the TP. Whenever possible, take care of these little duties before you hit the trail.

CONDITIONING

The better shape you're in, the more enjoyable the hiking. And the best way to get in shape may be (surprise!) to go for a hike. If you hike often, each trip better prepares you for the next, each becoming more and more effortless as your condition improves. Most trips require only average physical condition. To cover more miles while avoiding burnout, maintain a comfortable pace. Check with your doctor if there's any doubt about your health or ability to make the trip. If you're not in the greatest shape, start with shorter walks and slowly work up to more strenuous hikes. Don't push yourself to the point that you are gasping for air or listening to your pulse pound in your head. This is supposed to fun. Take plenty of breaks, relax, and enjoy our wild surroundings.

SOME RULES & PRECAUTIONS

In the Cascades, check on park or forest regulations, trail conditions, and other details before arriving at the trailhead. Just because a hike is listed in this or any other book doesn't mean that it will be totally safe when you visit. Conditions can change dramatically over a short period of time. Prepare well, and turn back if trail conditions or the weather are seriously deteriorating, or if you suddenly find you are in over your head.

On federal park and forest lands, a few rules need to be noted: keep the party size small, never more than twelve; practice "leave no trace" hiking and camping; don't trample or destroy vegetation by camping on it or short-cutting trails; pack out your garbage; control your pet (pets are not allowed in certain areas, like the national park); avoid camping or building fires outside of designated areas; carry a small backpack stove for cooking. Northwest Forest Passes (*see p. 39*) and free backcountry permits are required at many trailheads.

Some knowledge of first aid is highly recommended and essential when traveling in remote places. Carry plenty of water. Stream or lake water must always be purified, or you run an increasing risk of catching the giardia bug and other serious health maladies. Beware of changing conditions and unseen hazards. Creek crossings can be dangerous during high runoff periods. Notice that streams often fall during the night and rise in the afternoon. In the early season especially, avoid all steep open snow slopes, due to avalanche danger. If you're unsure, don't chance it. Stay on the trail and don't lose it. At junctions or in places where the trail fades, look back for a moment so the scene is familiar on the return. If you do get lost, calling out, whistling, staying put, and marking your location so it's visible from the air may be your best options. Keep dry and out of the wind, and exercise if needed to stay warm. And know that the vast majority of lost hikers make it out just fine the next day.

On logging roads, watch out for large trucks hauling their heavy loads of timber off the mountain and give them the right-of-way. Washouts, rocks, water, and windfall are common on these roads from fall through spring so keep a sharp eye out to avoid disaster. Be cautious during hunting season (generally in the fall). Wear bright orange when large mammals are in season, or don't go.

WILDLIFE ENCOUNTERS

If a large mammal like a bear or cougar decides, unlikely as it is, that maybe you might be in season, consider the following. Grizzly bears are extremely rare in the North Cascades. In the unlikely event you see one, savor it for a moment then back away slowly. Some say it's unwise to look them in the eye and far worse to run. Running from black bears or cougars also may only encourage them to turn on their predator instincts and come after you (some say play dead if it's a grizzly, a highly unlikely encounter in the North Cascades). Don't panic or scream. Occasionally, a problem black bear can spoil your day by going after you or your food, because careless others have taught them to associate humans with food. Be wise. Cook well away from your tent, and always hang your food, garbage, toothpaste, etc., at least ten feet off the ground when camping overnight. Fortunately, problem bears are uncommon in the Cascades, thanks to bear-proof garbage cans and bear-wise campers. If a black bear seems to come after you (also very rare), drop a bandana or hat to distract it and continue to move away. (See also **www.bearinfo.org**.)

With cougars, use firm language, hold your ground, and make yourself look big. If attacked, fight back aggressively. Climbing a tree is probably moot since both black bears and cougars climb way better than we do. The best defense against these animals may be to not approach them in the first place. Don't threaten their young or get between a mother and her offspring. If you stumble on a partly eaten carcass, move on. Be heard and seen when hiking in the woods or backcountry. With such a low risk of an encounter in the North Cascades, bells and the like are normally dispensed with as more of nuisance than they're worth. Avoid hiking alone, especially if you're a smaller person without a pack. Keep kids and pets close by. And report unusual wildlife sightings or encounters, or any grizzly or gray wolf sighting, to an area wildlife biologist or ranger. Wolves are very rare in the Cascades and will generally go out of their way to avoid you. The vicious attacks portrayed in the movies are far from the reality of wolf encounters, even in Alaska.

Marmot curiosity on Mount Pilchuck.

OTHER DANGERS

If the worst happens (it rarely, rarely does) and you are confronted by a wacko, thieving, trouble-making human on the trail, try to stay cool. Cooperate if it will avoid violence to you or your party. If not, attract someone's attention, scream, run, or fight back as good-old common sense dictates. Give up your valuables if that's what it takes to protect your safety. To reduce the risk, don't travel alone. Trust your instincts when you encounter someone who makes you uneasy. Avoid them or leave. Remember details and descriptions if this is something that should be reported to the police. Report any criminal activity to the proper authorities, and/or **call 911 if there's an emergency**. Fortunately, violent crime seldom occurs on the trail. Common sense suggests that walking alone at night on a deserted city street or unlit trail would be among the riskier scenarios. Hiking with a group during daylight hours, of course, would be a better choice.

Criminal activity, fires, accidents, and lost hikers should be reported to local emergency officials, or just call 911. Search and rescue activities are coordinated through the county sheriff. Call the Sheriff or 911 if you need help with an injured party or to report an overdue hiker. Forest fires can be reported to 911 or to DNR at (800) 562-6010, or to the local ranger. For non-emergency related inquiries, contact the local land management agency.

BUGS

If big and threatening wild animals—whether two- or four legged—haven't frightened you out of the woods altogether, consider, then, the most hideous and terrifying wild beings of them all: bugs. Actually, bugs aren't that bad, rather it's their bites and stings that can spoil an otherwise perfect outing in the hills. For more sensitive folks (you probably know who you are), stings can be downright dangerous and may require immediate care (check with your doctor ahead of time if you think you might have a reaction). However, for most of us, bug bites are just part of the package. The worst tend to be yellow jackets. They nest in rotten stumps and logs or holes in the ground, and once disturbed, they are amazingly quick to react. Sooner or later, just about everyone who hikes regularly will encounter them, although if you stay on the trail when you're below timberline, the odds of stepping on a nest are almost nil.

Mosquitos and no-see-ums are also a pain, but usually only early morning and early evening, although there are exceptions. To ward them off, find a high breezy place to relax, use a little jungle juice (citronella or lemon-eucalyptus seem less intense than DEET, but might have to be applied more often), cover yourself with clothing or mosquito netting, light up a cigar (the smoke deters them—don't inhale, of course), or try moving a few hundred yards and away from moist areas.

Deer flies and black flies (black flies tilt steeply to bite) can be worse than mosquitos and are often intense even in the heat of the day. Similar techniques may allow you to escape their wrath. Horse flies are the big ones that whip around as if on a string. They can bite well, but fortunately, there aren't usually a lot of them buzzing around you at the same time or for more than a minute or two. From May through early August, expect a lot of bugs in the mountains in good weather, and plan accordingly. Happily, their numbers tend to drop off later in summer and in cool, breezy, or wet weather.

HANTAVIRUS

One other pesky life form to be aware of is the hantavirus, a rare but deadly malady carried mostly by a few deer mice. When someone comes into contact with an infected rodent, say, by cleaning, disturbing, or sleeping near one or its nest, it's possible to inhale tiny airborne bits of mouse urine, saliva or feces which could then cause the occurrence of hantavirus pulmonary syndrome. As of mid-2006, thirty-two cases had been confirmed statewide, including Snohomish County. About one in three were fatal. Fever, chills, muscle aches, and other flu-like symptoms develop within a few days or weeks of contact, then rapidly turn into severe respiratory distress. Deer mice, the principal carriers, are about six to seven inches long to the tip of the tail and have a cute white belly.

Prevention is the key. Avoid the mice and their nests, as well as crude cabins, shelters, or other enclosed areas that may be infested or which are not well ventilated, and consider sleeping in a tent rather than on bare ground. Keep food and utensils sealed and protected from rodents. While the odds of contracting the illness are very remote in Washington, reducing the risk to a minimum isn't a bad idea. All in all, there are far more friendly and benign critters in the wild to be appreciated than there are creatures to be feared. So, be wise—not paranoid—and enjoy the wilderness.

BE A CONSERVATIONIST

Finally, take the time to learn about the natural environment before and while you're in the middle of it. Bring your natural history guide to the wildflowers rather than the other way around. Exercise respect for other walkers, wildlife, and the environment. Include a few minutes of trail work on every outing, whether it's just kicking a few limbs off the trail or cleaning out a small ditch or culvert to prevent erosion.

At home, take time on occasion to learn about local efforts to protect our vanishing wild places and make time to speak up for trails and wilderness. Before you and I arrived on the scene, others were doing that for us.

On federal lands, volunteers with Friends of the Wild Sky have worked for years to win wilderness designation for more than 100,000 acres of roadless areas above Index, including spectacular alpine meadows, lakes, salmon streams, high peaks and glaciers, plus much of the old-growth forest that was excluded from the 1984 act designating new wilderness areas statewide. Some hikers may be surprised to know that such familiar wild places as Barclay Lake, Blanca Lake, West Cady Ridge, and Scorpion Mountain are not currently protected (for more, check out the Wild Washington campaign at **www.wildwashington.org**.)

With regard to state and local public lands, Pilchuck Audubon (**www.pilchuckaudubon.org**), the Cascades Chapter of the Sierra Club (**www.cascade.sierraclub.org**), the Cascade Land Conservancy (**www.cascadeland.org**), and others work to protect public lands or acquire private lands having high ecological, scenic, or recreational values. DNR is not doing enough to preserve and protect the best of what's left of the sensitive lands it manages, including the most promising of our maturing second-growth forests. Substantial portions of these lands should be allowed to recover as old-growth forest. The state legislature has also been remiss in failing to understand and act on the need to "protect the best" of what remains.

State Parks could use some advocates for additional funding from the legislature. Budget shortfalls have forced the agency to close some parks and institute (from 2003 to 2006) day-use parking fees. Yet a recent study found that, as the fourth most popular park system in the nation, our state parks generate far more tax revenue from visitors than what it costs to run the entire agency. By slashing the budget, it would seem that the state is only thwarting the revenue potential of an otherwise outstanding park system. Recent attempts to commercialize our parks through corporate sponsorships and the like should be strongly resisted.

A NOTE ON MULTIUSE TRAILS

Many, but not all, of the trails described in this guide are open to nonmotorized multiple use. So it should probably be emphasized that this book is not intended to invite mountain bikers into all the areas described (this is not anti-bike sentiment). As a rule, bikes are best suited to old road grades and more durable trails designated for such use. Mountain biking is a fine activity (I ride one myself), but not when it's to the detriment of a footpath or those who tread more softly upon it. Responsible mountain bikers often work to build awareness around trail issues like these, while also organizing a heck of a lot of trail work in our region. Equestrians, often organized through the Backcountry Horsemen of Washington, are also very active in trail construction and maintenance, and the work of both groups directly benefits hikers. Trail running has assumed some increased popularity of late, and runners should be (and generally are) sensitive to other trail users, especially on steep terrain, blind corners, and on routes that are popular for birding and wildlife watching. Avid hikers should plan to participate in at least one or more trail maintenance work parties each year. For details on how and where you can help, contact any of the land management agencies, Washington Trails Association (**www.wta.org**), Volunteers for Outdoor Washington (**www.trailvolunteers.org**), and the Sierra Club.

NORTHWEST FOREST PASS, STATE & LOCAL PARKING FEES

A Northwest Forest Pass (formerly "Fee Demo Trail Park Pass") is now required in the National Forest. For information or to purchase a pass, contact any ranger district office or information center in the region, including the Verlot Public Service Center and the Skykomish and Darrington Ranger Stations. Passes are also available online through the Washington Trails Association.

Beginning in July, 1997, the US Forest Service instituted a trailhead parking permit system to raise money for much-needed trail and trailhead maintenance on federal lands. Permits were required year-round for nearly all trailheads on the Mount Baker-Snoqualmie National Forest. Since no entrance fee is collected for North Cascades National Park, that agency joined the program. A day pass is $5 and an annual pass $30 (subject to change). Discounts are available for seniors and the less able-bodied among us. Trail maintenance volunteers can earn a pass through their labor. A pass purchased for our region is good at other Northwest Forests as well. If you are a modest or frequent user of our national parks, you can skip the Northwest Forest Pass and instead buy an "America the Beautiful" pass ($80/year in 2007) which not only gets you into all national parks and monuments, it serves as a trail pass on national forests and an entrance pass to most other federal recreational areas. See also **www.fs.fed.us/r6/mbs/passes**.

Are these fees fair? Many recent trail enhancements were paid for by trail pass dollars, and one could presume they may not have happened otherwise. Yet there is debate about what we, as taxpayers, ought to expect from our government in the way of basic public services and what ought to be paid for through user fees. These lands belong to us all. As co-owners, we all have equal access and an equal responsibility to ensure future generations have the same opportunity to enjoy them. We should not have to pay to enjoy what is already ours. Instead of cutting maintenance budgets, shouldn't Congress and the President be insisting that all public facilities are well taken care of first? So while many folks probably don't mind shucking out a few dollars for a nominal fee, many others do, especially if you happen to be among the many living in poverty. But if the money raised is simply replacing what Congress should be providing anyway, that's not a good thing. Some have suggested that the pass is a strategic move toward the commercialization of our public lands—a very serious concern that needs to be watched.

Obviously, there are merits to both sides of the argument, even if the program has become an excuse for axe-happy politicians to duck their responsibility to properly fund public facilities. As the money gets siphoned off for other non-trail-related expenses, public support for the program will surely plummet. That said, the Forest Service in our neck of the woods has at least involved people in the debate, listening to and incorporating ideas. We'll see where it all leads. In the meantime, it's the most reliable source there is for much needed trail improvements.

As noted earlier, the Washington State Parks and Recreation Commission instituted a highly controversial fee system in January 2003 (**www.parks.wa.gov**). The number of park visitors declined significantly as thousands of park supporters (this author included) boycotted the fees. Fortunately, they were scrapped in 2006. Our state and local parks are critically important to our kids, our health, the environment, and the economy. They benefit every citizen of the state, and free access should be a fundamental benefit of paying our taxes, though a few too many electeds seem to think otherwise.

Sadly, Snohomish County also jumped on the parks parking fee bandwagon at Kayak Point, Flowing Lake and Wyatt Parks ($5 daily, $50 annual in 2007) as if to further ensure that families living in poverty have less access to parks. The smaller parks do not require a fee.

Most Washington Department of Fish and Wildlife sites now require an annual Vehicle Use Permit ($10.95) for parking (**www.wa.gov/wdfw**), an approach that is far more palatable than a regressive daily fee, although free access would be an even better idea.

PRIVATE PROPERTY

Veteran hikers in the county may notice that some lowland trails are not included in the book. Some may traverse private lands whose owners might not wish to advertise their use by the general public. Liability for injures, vandalism, and fires are common concerns (although landowners are well protected from liability by state law; RCW 4.24.200 & 4.24.210). A few careless people appear to be responsible for most public access problems being experienced. Check with other hikers or area residents to locate these semi-secret places.

A lot of good hiking country is under private timber company ownership where access is often a bit easier. You can generally avoid trouble with these folks by obeying all signs, closed gates, fences, seasonal fire closures, or other indications that your presence is not welcome. Always assume that camping and campfires are not permitted outside of designated sites. Obtain permission where necessary. Descriptions in this guide should not be construed as permission to violate private property rights.

YOUR VALUABLES

As for your own private property—your personal valuables—don't leave them in your car at trailheads. Way too many brainless thieves have a habit of showing up at the oddest hours to break a window and make off with your goods. Report all thefts or vandalism to the authorities.

BEACH ACCESS

It is often assumed that any old beach is open to the public. That is generally true in Oregon and Hawaii and other coastal states, but it's not so cut and dried in Washington. Regrettably, the State of Washington sold off its best tidelands around our inland sea to private interests over much of the last century. Not only was it an absurd thing to do, it left us with major difficulties in finding good access to more than a fraction of the county's spectacular shoreline. The practice was banned about 25 years ago, but the damage was done. However, there is still a legal argument—and the author agrees—that the public never gave up its right (i.e. the public trust) to use tidelands to access public waters, whether for commerce or recreation or whatever, even though the mud and the crud may belong to an adjacent landowner. That said, private property still deserves some respect.

Private or otherwise, the vast majority of tideland owners are not snobs and couldn't care less whether you and I go for a harmless stroll along a remote beach. However, they are not inclined to advertise these places to the general public due, in part, to the problems caused by a few individuals. Obnoxious behavior, litter, and vandalism are primary concerns, especially where waterfront homes are located close to the shore. Fortunately, remote areas are more interesting to visit and responsible hikers will encounter few problems with anxious landowners. On all beaches, public and private, use common sense: don't take or leave anything; don't start fires; be quiet; avoid large groups; respect wildlife and the marine environment; smile; be courteous to residents; stay off the stairs and pathways leading up to their yards; and avoid walking on railroad tracks.

Beach walks may be good year-round, except during stormy periods. The suggested walks and hikes in coastal areas (*Hikes 1 through 10*) include those with public access, although both public and private tideland ownership may occur. Nevertheless, these areas have been used regularly by the public in the past. While it would take a title company and a survey crew to know for sure which areas are private, there are substantial public tidelands present. It is the user's responsibility to obtain prior authorization if necessary. Plan your visit during lower tide levels (check the tide tables; www.nwsource.com/weather/tides.html), and be aware of rising tides which can surprise, strand, and/or drown you if you're not careful. Walk these and all other areas at your own risk!

FOR MORE INFORMATION

Hiking Snohomish County is the only guide with broad coverage for the entire county, from the saltwater shore to the crest of the Cascades. However, several other guidebooks are available which provide comprehensive coverage of trails in the North Cascades, most notably *100 Hikes in Washington's North Cascades, Glacier Peak Region* (Spring, Manning; The Mountaineers, 2003), Rick McGuire's *55 Hikes Around Stevens Pass: Wild Sky Country* (The Mountaineers, 2003), and several smaller trail guides to the Darrington and Skykomish Ranger Districts published by the Northwest Interpretive Association (www.nwpubliclands.com). The Spring/Manning classic and a number of other titles are available at most bookstores and outdoor shops in the region. Local outdoor clubs sponsor guided hikes throughout the year, usually free of charge. These are listed at the end of the book along with emergency contacts and various land management agencies. Libraries are another excellent source of how-to and where-to hiking information.

USGS and Green Trails™ topographic maps, as well as topographic mapping software for your computer, also deserve mention here as requisite tools for the mountains. These are all generally available at bookstores and outdoor shops. In the cyber world, the Washington Trails Association maintains an excellent Web site (www.wta.org) that is loaded with information, including literally thousands of trail reports filed by users and management agencies, details on volunteer opportunities, and other trail resources and information.

Good guides to the region's natural history include Matthews' *Cascade-Olympic Natural History* (1999), and Pojar and McKinnon's *Plants of the Pacific Northwest Coast* (2004). For more local history, see Norman Clark's *Mill Town* (1970), and *Snohomish County: An Illustrated History*, by Cameron, LeWarne. May, O'Donnell, and O'Donnell (2006).

How To Use This Book

To make best use of this guidebook, first read the Introduction and What to Know Before You Go, then decide on a walk or hike. Check the Trail Location Maps up front for possibilities, read the trail descriptions, then check listings in the back of the book for possible side trips to parks, viewpoints, water access, or campgrounds in the vicinity.

Trails have been categorized, somewhat arbitrarily, into easy, moderate, more difficult, and most difficult hikes, as noted by the " 👣 " (feet) symbols in the table of contents. The easier hikes generally require less than an hour or two round trip, are usually 0.5 to 3.0 miles long, and are often fairly level or at least very short. The rest are more strenuous but vary greatly in length, steepness and overall difficulty. Of course, what may seem to one person to be an easy stroll may be a real workout for the next.

THE LISTINGS

In the description for each hike, round-trip distances to one or more destinations are provided, along with the approximate time needed, elevation gain, best months to visit (varies year to year, of course), and directions from I-5 or the nearest town or highway, including mile-post (MP) notations to the nearest one-tenth of a mile. The estimated times are loosely gauged for walking speeds of one to two miles per hour. Three miles per hour is brisk, and four is almost a trot and difficult to maintain over much distance. Additional time is added where elevation gain is more significant. Read the trail description to see what the times and distances given refer to.

Trips are organized into four geographical areas: The Coast, Urban areas, Lowlands & Foothills, and the North Cascades. Admittedly, some hikes don't fit clearly in one category or another. For consistency, trails that generally stay below 3,000 feet above sea level are listed under Lowlands & Foothills. While these areas can be snowed-in part of the year, they can also be snow-free in the dead of winter if the weather's been mild. A special emphasis has been given to walks and hikes which are not adequately described in other guidebooks, especially between the coast and foothills. A number of other potential trips are mentioned at the end of the numbered trail listings. These are not described in detail for a

On the go near Columbia Peak (Hike 81).

variety of reasons, such as private property concerns, poor maintenance, or difficult navigation. A determined adventurer will soon cultivate the detective skills needed to locate these and other worthwhile trails.

All maps in this book are intended for general reference only, not for navigation. Excellent topographical maps to nearly all areas are available at many outdoor shops. USGS and Green Trails™ maps (and some topographical mapping software) are excellent choices and may be indispensable for most hikes in the North Cascades. Hiking with a handheld GPS unit is gaining in popularity but may be less reliable in steep or forested terrain and is no substitute for a good paper map.

Listings of public parks briefly describe their location and facilities available, and may include short walks not listed elsewhere in the guide. Viewpoints and water access are accessible by car, bike, or a short walk and are self-explanatory. A list of public campgrounds is provided for those who might want to combine one or more dayhikes with a comfortable evening in the woods.

THE COAST

—See note on beach access, page 42—

Big Ditch Slough in winter.

< Mukilteo Lighthouse.

Beach north of Edmonds.>

THE COAST—

1. Big Ditch Slough

Distance: 0.5 - 5.0+ miles round trip   Time: Allow 1 - 3 hours

Elevation gain: None   Season: Best fall through spring

Bring the binoculars and bird guide for this easy scenic saunter along the southeast shore of Skagit Bay within the Skagit Wildlife Recreation Area. The latter encompasses 12,800 acres of sloughs, islands, and tidelands spread across the broad delta of the Skagit River, from Stanwood nearly to La Conner. The dike along Big Ditch Slough, despite the name, offers a fine coastal walk, with good views and good odds of seeing many species of birds and other wildlife, particularly in winter and spring. Harbor seals, otter, beaver, mink, and deer are all possible. There's a catch, though: a fishing license or vehicle use permit is required to use the area (*see page 41*). Paths can be a bit overgrown in summer.

To reach the dike, head west on SR 532 from I-5 and turn right on Pioneer Highway at Stanwood. Drive past pleasant farms and views of Skagit Bay and the lands that embrace it, namely Camano, Whidbey, Fir, and Fidalgo Islands. In 2.7 miles, turn left at the bottom of a hill onto Old Pacific Highway (old U.S. 99). Cross the tracks, but continue straight on a narrow gravel road signed "Big Ditch Access" that leads to the bay and parking area—closed after dark. (An overgrown dike just east of the parking area might be cleared some day for a possible link to Stanwood.) Pass a gate next to the slough and thrash left 0.2 mile for a look south and west across mucky flats to Camano Island. Whidbey's Strawberry Point lies beyond and right. Some wandering is feasible at lower tides, but so is getting stranded—best to stay close to the dike.

The main walk leads north from the gate and tends to be higher and drier with nice views of Mt. Baker and the Twin Sisters Range. Rich, marshy wetlands abut the dike to the west, alive with birds and critters. Watch for eagles, hawks, red-winged blackbirds, great blue herons, ducks, and a variety of shorebirds and upland fliers. Beached logs, rootwads still attached, lie across the flats like fluked whales. Good walking leads past a little colony of beach cabins built on piling, with wooden walkways that have a "don't trespass" look to them. Just beyond, the trail begins to fade, although the dike continues another long mile to Milltown and another access point for more dike walking in Skagit County.

To reach the latter by car, head north on Pioneer Highway 2.4 miles north of the Big Ditch access road and turn left at Milltown Rd. The road climbs over the railroad tracks and bends north to a gate and limited shoulder parking. The dike south to Big Ditch is back where the road crossed the tracks (no parking here). A recently rebuilt dike runs north from the gate and parallels Tom Moore Slough and the South Fork Skagit River to Conway (access there is behind the Conway Ballfield off the west end of Main St.). In less than a mile from the gate, go left at a junction and cross Fisher Slough on a bridge to more wandering on old roads and dikes. A right at the junction leads to an unmarked crossing of the tracks (caution). It is feasible to cross Fisher Slough on a floodgate walkway with railing on the west side of the highway bridge. The obvious dike continues north a long mile to Conway.

THE COAST—

2. Kayak Point

Distance: 0.5 - 2.0+ miles round trip   Time: Allow 1 - 2+ hours
Elevation gain: 0 - 100 feet   Season: Year-round

For some easy beach wandering, nice views across Port Susan to Camano Island, and a chance at seeing an orca whale, try Kayak Point County Park south of Stanwood. There's even a small stand of old-growth forest on the bluff with some giant trees. From I-5, take the SR 531 exit at Smokey Point and go west 2.3 miles to a stop sign, turn right and continue another 6.2 miles to Marine Dr. (where SR 531 goes left to Lake Goodwin, don't turn, but continue straight on Lakewood Rd.). Turn left on Marine Dr., jog right then left at stop signs, and find the park entrance on the right in 2.2 miles.

Grimace at the self-service parking fee station ($5.00/day in 2007) and continue down to the beach. Either head for the pier, hit the beach, or check out the short staircase trails on the bluff. For the latter, look for a path at the foot of the bluff due east of the fishing pier. The first of several large Doug-fir trees (seven feet across) is a few paces up on the left, followed by a big grand fir. Head right at the next junction (more big Douglas firs), and then stay left to return to the parking area less than 200 yards from the start. There are a few other paths in the park,

Camano Island from Kayak Point beach.

including a small network of Boy Scout trails behind the campground, though none are as interesting as the bluff.

Tides, of course, dictate when and where you can walk on the beach, although even at higher tides one can stroll above the drift logs on gravel, grass, or path. The 670-acre park has 0.6 mile of good walkable waterfront, half of it below the high bluff. Picnic shelters crowd the shore north of the pier. At lower tides, say, below five feet or so, it's possible to walk much farther north and south. However, high eroding bluffs shed trees and debris, producing obstacles that are potentially dangerous if you get caught during a rising tide. From the south edge of the park, a 100-foot high bluff quickly gives way to McKee's Beach (homes near the water), then more bluff beyond, rising to 300 feet and higher. To the north, more homes line Kayak Cove, followed again by high bluffs, then the substantially inhabited shores of Warm Beach two miles north. There are no public access points at any convenient distance north or south, so plan to retrace your steps.

The Coast—

3. Tulalip Bay

Distance: 1.1 mile loop   Time: Allow 1 hour

Elevation gain: Negligible   Season: Year-round

Before Captain George Vancouver stopped at Tulalip Bay on June 4th, 1792, native people had already fished and crabbed and lived here for countless generations. When the ship's anchor dropped, JosephWhidbey went ashore, intrigued by the large native village that existed here. The natives welcomed their visitors with hospitality and a parade of canoes. Vancouver, in return, staked his claim for the British Crown. Said he, "I had long since designed to take formal possession of all the countries we had lately been employed in exploring, in the name of, and for his Brittanic Majesty, his heirs and successors. . ." Today, an interpretive sign above the bay wisely acknowledges how tenuous such claims were. "Undoubtedly," it reads, "Capt. Vancouver failed to realize that these lands had been the Northwest coast natives' homelands for thousands of years and were not available as a birthday gift for the King."

To share some of the history of this area with the public, the Tulalip Tribes and Washington Department of Natural Resources developed an interpretive walk along the bay called "A Walk with the Ancestors." Improvements are minimal, but the history is fascinating. The walk begins at the Tulalip Bay Marina west of Marysville. From I-5 Exit 199 head west on Marine Dr. about 4.8 miles and turn left on 64th St. NW, then right in 0.4 mile on Totem Beach Rd. Continue 0.7 mile to the historic St. Anne's Church (1904) on the right; turn left into the Tulalip Bay Marina and grab one of the first parking slots on the left. A big sign with a map of the walk offers a little history of the area. Check out the boats, then walk north past the marina and along a narrow road (paved then gravel) above the beach. To the left, Skayu Point (the Mission Beach peninsula) wraps around half the bay, and Hermosa Point guards the north, forming a "purse" to catch the salmon at low tide. Mt. Rainier is to the south. Pass a road on the right (an optional return route later) and keep going straight until reaching a guardrail and another road (**0.4 mi**). Walk left across Tulalip Creek to an interpretive sign on the left next to what remains of William Shelton's Story Pole. Keep walking left

Tulalip Bay Marina, Camano Island in the distance.

to a grassy area with another sign and a view of the bay over wild rose and blackberry bushes.

Return to the dam and two large interpretive signs and benches across the road. One elaborates on Vancouver's landing two centuries ago. The other tells us that the first sawmill in Snohomish County was built on Tulalip Creek. Walk along the main road 0.2 mile to two more signs, one about the origin of two silos (assimilation of native culture by turning fishers into farmers), and the other a language lesson, including the words for counting one to ten in Snohomish. (Shouldn't all kids know this?) Then either turn right on 36th Ave. NW to reach the road leading out of the marina, or take the next right to find the historic St. Anne's Catholic Church (**1.0 mi**). Cross here to return to the starting point. Sometimes it's possible to purchase fresh salmon at the marina.

THE COAST—
4. Jetty Island

Distance: 0.5 - 3.0 miles round trip   Time: Allow 1 - 4 hours
Elevation gain: None   Season: Year-round

At about two miles long and hardly anything wide, Everett's Jetty Island is barely three dimensional. The north part was once a heap of spoils from dredging to make the city's waterfront (Port Gardner) navigable, while the south part is a more conventional jetty of big rocks piled in a long line that helps break up the waves and swell rolling in from Possession Sound. From this not so glamorous beginning Jetty Island has become a little haven of nature jointly managed by the Port of Everett and the city park department. Views, wildlife, an interpretive trail, and some fine walkable beach make the island attractive to footsters.

The best—or at least easiest—time to visit is in summer when the Everett Park Department runs a foot ferry to and from the island about every half-hour from around the 4th of July through Labor Day (10:00-5:30 Wed-Sat, 11:00-5:30 Sun, no boat Mon-Tue). The ride is a freebie and takes a grueling five minutes each way. The boat can fill up quickly on a nice day, so expect to wait a little, or go on a cloudy day when more folks are home grumbling about the weather. Catch the little cruiseliner at the big public boat launch at Marine Park off Marine View Dr. and the west end of 10th St.

Park staff offer guided walks, or explore a half-mile interpretive trail on your own. 1.5 miles of scenic shore and sandy beach on the west and north sides offer good wandering (don't trample the vegetation).

When the ferry's not running, experienced kayakers have an obvious advantage in enjoying a little island tranquillity (no camping allowed). Always give wildlife a wide berth, and by all means, leave only footprints.

Jetty's west beach.

THE COAST—
5. Pigeon Creek to Point Elliot

Distance: 0.5 - 3.0 miles one-way   Time: Allow 1 - 3 hours

Elevation gain: Negligible   Season: Year-round

For a pleasant stroll on a good beach southwest of Everett, head for Howarth Park just off Mukilteo Blvd. While it's feasible to wander three miles to Mukilteo at lower tides, the best walking is in the first mile where the beach is generally much wider, sandier, and more scenic. From I-5 take Exit 192 and follow 41st St. west a few blocks, cross Evergreen Way, pass Forest Park, and in another 1.5 miles find Howarth Park on the right at Seahurst Ave. Pass the first parking area and park at a viewpoint, then head toward the bluff to find the high footbridge over the railroad tracks. The westerly of two Pigeon Creeks flows across the beach just right of the footbridge.

It's important to time a longer walk with the tide. At higher tides, many areas are impassable, if not downright dangerous. The first mile or so of beach is usually accessible at a moderate tide level of, say, six feet or less. Closer to Mukilteo, unique circumstances present a potential hazard not to be taken lightly, even at this tide level. Be cautious and

Footbridge at Howarth Park, from Pigeon Creek.

don't linger below the rock wall that supports the railroad tracks. If the tide comes in while you're there, you could be trapped. The only escape may be a difficult vertical rock climb. Barnacles six feet above the beach offer a stark clue as to how high the water rises each day. Time your walk with an outgoing tide. The narrow parts toward Mukilteo are best at tide elevations of four feet or less. If you can handle the tide issue, the walk offers a much better chance at solitude than the stretch closer to Pigeon Creeks. Maybe stash a bike at one end, or catch a bus for the return.

From the bridge, descend to the beach and head left for the best walking; right leads toward downtown Everett along a narrow and less appealing shore. The drone of the city's industrial waterfront carries easily across the bay, but so does the musical barking of a sea lion colony that often hangs out at Jetty Island and near the Navy Homeport in fall and winter. To the west, it's about a mile to the far end of the wider beach. Either turn around there, or if the tide's out, continue as far as conditions allow. For the longer trek toward Mukilteo, several streams must be crossed (Glenwood, Merrill and Ring, Narbeck, Powdermill, and Edgewater Creeks) which can be somewhat inconvenient when there's much runoff. But these streams are also significant deposition zones that produce small deltas and better beach to walk on. The upper part of the beach usually offers easier going on packed sand or gravel, although some areas are bouldery and/or slimed with algae. A steep, wild, eroding bluff rises behind the tracks, hiding most homes from view. Drift logs, weathered stumps, scattered boulders, old piling, islands, Mt. Baker, and a curious seal or two add to the scenery. At lower tides in fall and winter, watch for eagles, ducks, herons, and other shorebirds.

The walk to Mukilteo ends at an informal access area off the end of a dirt road east of the ferry (construction activity was a hindrance in mid-2006). To find it from Howarth Park, follow Mukilteo Blvd. 3.3 miles to Mukilteo Speedway. Turn right (not the ferry line), and right again on Front St., across from the ferry terminal. Jog right then left at railroad tracks and continue 0.4 mile to another sharp right; instead, go straight on the bumpy gravel road (if open) to a small parking area at the end of a long concrete wall that shields a former U.S. Defense Department fuel tank farm that is being cleaned up and redeveloped into a new ferry terminal and public transit station. This area may be closed at night.

THE COAST—
6. Point Elliot to Picnic Point

Distance: 0.5 - 5.0 miles one-way   Time: Allow 1 - 5 hours
Elevation gain: Negligible   Season: Year-round

From Mukilteo Lighthouse Park, there's a good walkable beach leading south below railroad tracks and an almost continuous wall of bluffs all the way to Picnic Pt., five miles afar. The problem, however, is that it can only be explored at lower tides, say, three feet or less. The railroad crowds the shore the entire distance, largely built on fill and revetment atop the upper beach and tidelands. There's nothing terribly odd about that, considering that nearly half the county's shoreline has more or less been turned over to the railroad. But it does seem rather unfortunate that so many miles of relatively wild shore are so difficult to access and enjoy. There is no convenient way to access the beach on foot other than at Points Elliot or Picnic, so unless you can time a walk with a lower, outgoing tide, stick to the higher and drier stretches near these two end points. The walk is described from north to south—flip it around if there's a strong wind bounding up Possession Sound.

Morning on the beach at Pt. Elliot.

Find Mukilteo Lighthouse Park—formerly a state park, but turned over to the city in 2003 and soon to be redeveloped—near the Whidbey Island ferry terminal, left off the end of Mukilteo Speedway. One could spot a car first at Picnic Pt., or stash a bike at Mukilteo, then drive to Picnic Pt. for a start there and a bus-bike combo for the return (*see Hike 7 for directions*). The famous beach at Pt. Elliot may be walkable at more moderate tides for a half-mile or more. If not, one is soon forced up onto the railroad tracks which is not something to be recommended here, mainly because there is little room to get out of the way of speeding trains, but also because you might be trespassing. Like with the beach east of Mukilteo, getting caught by rising water below the intermittently steep rock wall that supports the tracks is a hazard to be avoided. Assuming there's still a beach to walk, round a point and continue as far as time and conditions allow. Watch and listen for harbor seals or Stellar sea lions (fall and winter) browsing and blowing along the shore, and perhaps a bald eagle and great blue heron. Thousands of ducks and grebes may feed offshore in winter. Whidbey Island is just a few gull flaps to the west. Possession Sound fills the view north and south.

Ahead, there's an obstacle to negotiate (a possible turn-around point) in the form of a dozen beach cabins perched between the tracks and a big concrete seawall (**1.6 mi**). There's no car access to this idyllic neighborhood. The way continues like before, although some places can only be walked at the lower tides of three feet or less. A few homes appear along the bluff, and a small sewer plant is passed, as well as a couple of small streams emerging from gulches. Another obstacle appears, this time a rotting hulk of something that may have been seaworthy fifty years ago, next to a homestead waterward of the tracks (**4.0 mi**). The beach here is nice, but may be littered with dozens of "private beach" and "no trespassing" signs which might be moot if you stay below the high-water mark. At least we can hope so (*see note on page 42*). Proceed at your own risk, however. Beyond, a few more homes have gravitated toward a small lake perched behind a causeway supporting the tracks, and finally, at its other end, comes the wide beach at Picnic Point and the big footbridge over the railroad tracks (**5.0 mi**).

The Coast—
7. Picnic Point to Brackett's Landing

Distance: 1.5 - 5.6 miles one-way   Time: Allow 1 - 6 hours
Elevation gain: Negligible   Season: Year-round

Walks along the Edmonds waterfront and at Picnic Pt. are among the nicer beach strolls to choose from in the county. If the tide is right (best under three feet or so) the entire six-mile stretch from one to the other is about as wild a walk as you'll find in southwest Snohomish County. High bluffs keep most of the voracious residential development above and out of sight, though there are gaps where homes have drifted close to the beach. The railroad still dominates the upper beach as before, and frequent trains squeal past, but somehow they're more tolerable than a busy highway. The trek is described north to south, but reverse it if there's a brisk southerly kicking up chop.

To reach Picnic Point Park, take Highway 99 to just south of SR 525 and head west on Shelby Rd., which becomes Picnic Point Rd. in a few blocks. Stay right at a Y in 1.4 miles and find the park 1.4 miles farther at the mouth of a small canyon. Scamper across the big footbridge and

A view north from Edmonds.

out to the beach. North (right) leads to Mukilteo (*see Hike 6*). Head south for Edmonds and Bracketts Landing.

Immediately cross the outwash from a small creek, then pass a wharf at Norma Beach (**1.2 mi**), followed by Meadowdale Beach Park (**1.5 mi**). This beach makes a good turn-around for a shorter walk, or maybe stash a car or bike at the upper end of the Lunds Gulch Trail for the return to Picnic Point (*see Hike 9*). Now enter Browns Bay, as Whidbey Island slips into the distance off your right shoulder and the view opens up to bigger water, the Kitsap Peninsula, and Olympic Mountains beyond. Contour around the bay to 162nd St. (**2.1 mi**), the only good public access point between Edmonds and Meadowdale Beach (limited parking). It's 3.5 miles from here to Brackett's Landing in Edmonds.

To continue, skip past the old Haines fishing wharf (big blue and white buildings), leaving Browns Bay behind in another mile. A few small streams are easily crossed, and occasionally the flats grow wide and inviting when the tide is out. This center portion of the walk is great for relative solitude, especially on weekdays, in the off-season, or on less-than-perfect summer weekends. The final stretch to Edmonds seems to arrive too soon, so plan a break accordingly to savor the smells, the sounds, and the beauty of Washington's inland sea. But don't shrug off the time thing altogether, so as to avoid getting forced up on rocks or over the railroad tracks which makes for an unpleasant scurry back home.

The beach walk more or less ends at Brackett's Landing (**5.6 mi**), an Edmonds city park next to the ferry terminal. The park is located at the base of Main Street, just across the tracks. It's a popular place, so if the lot is full, try Sunset Ave. close by, north of Main. This makes a good start for a shorter beach walk as well, maybe combined with a stroll along the city's pedestrian-friendly waterfront (see *Hike 8*), or a gavotte uptown to Edmonds' historic core at 5th Ave.

8. Brackett's Landing to Marina Beach

Distance: 1.0 - 2.4 miles round trip   Time: Allow 1 - 2 hours
Elevation gain: Negligible   Season: Year-round

Easily the best walk on an uban waterfront in Snohomish County, the stroll from Brackett's Landing in Edmonds to Marina Beach and back makes a fine diversion anytime of the year. Although much private development crowds the shore, the city's evolving promenade is nicely designed, especially toward the north where native plantings and beach enhancements have restored some semblance of a natural shore. The rest is mostly seawalls, a public fishing pier, and boardwalks along the boat harbor, with enough public art to make a shutterbug giddy.

Begin at either end of the walk. Follow Main St. through downtown Edmonds almost to the ferry dock; cross the railroad tracks and turn right for Brackett's Landing Park, or go left to Dayton St., followed by a jog right and left (becomes Admiral Way) to the road end and Marina Beach Park entrance. From the latter, a short ramp rises up and over a corner of the boat basin. At the pier (**0.7 mi**) one can add another 0.4 mile out and back; just north of it, step down to a sandy beach (unless the tide is too high) to bypass a short missing link (in 2007) in the seawall promenade.

*Edmonds'
walkable
waterfront.*

9. Meadowdale Beach

Distance: 2.4+ miles round trip   Time: Allow 2 - 3 hours
Elevation gain: 450 feet   Season: Year-round

To while-away the day or catch a sunset at Meadowdale Beach Park's namesake beach, plan on a 1.2-mile walk each way, via the steep, quiet trail through Lunds Gulch. There's a significant loss in elevation involved on the way in (425 feet) so allow plenty of time for the climb back out to the parking area. The trail is wide, a little too wide in places, and can be buzzed at times by fast boys on bikes. An alternative narrow track for hikers that loops back to the start would make a worthy addition to this 105-acre park. A few sets of stairs here and there would help keep the bikes off. For barrier-free access to the beach (0.2 mile path), there is handicap-only access via the service road off the north end of 75ᵗʰ Pl. (reached from Meadowdale Rd.). The rest of us must approach the beach area from the trailhead (*see also Hike 7*).

From 52ⁿᵈ Ave. W. north of Lynnwood, turn west on 160ᵗʰ St. SW (park sign), then right on 56ᵗʰ Ave. and left on 156ᵗʰ St. The park and trailhead are a few blocks ahead (gate may be closed after sunset). The well maintained trail rounds a grassy area and enters a young Douglas-fir forest with bigger trees beyond. The path steepens at stairs, but by the first half-mile most of the elevation loss to the beach is history. Pass several large cedar stumps, then walk easier path among hardwoods closer to the creek to a junction (**1.0 mi**). Either fork leads to a low tunnel under the railroad tracks and the sandy beach beyond (**1.2 mi**). The Olympics are prominent across Possession Sound. Ferries ply the waters—Edmonds to the south, Mukilteo to the north. For strolling north or south, plan for

a tide of five feet or less. Rules posted at the beach are typical of parks everywhere. Almost verbatim: "No-no-no-no-no-no-must be-do not-must be-no." Apparently, some people still need to be told.

Meadowdale Beach Park.

THE COAST—
10. Richmond Beach

Distance: 1.0 - 3.0+ miles round trip   Time: Allow 1 - 2 hours
Elevation gain: Negligible - 200 feet   Season: Year-round

At lower tides, this highly walkable beach at Shoreline's Richmond Beach Park, just south of the county line, offers a mile or more of easy beach wandering, and another half-mile of upland paths for itchy feet. To the south, the walk parallels the railroad tracks; to the north, coast-crowding homes and other obstacles make a longer stroll there not so appealing. But the park's sandy shore is well worth a visit. Upland trails were poorly signed and not well connected in 2007, but easy enough to figure out. With minimal effort, the city could (and should) create an attractive one-mile loop.

From Richmond Beach Rd., turn south onto 20th Ave. W. to find the park entrance just ahead. Park in the upper lot for a longer walk down and back, partly on stairs, or to visit a high grassy viewpoint reached from a path near the entrance (above the road). Or head for the lower lot for more direct access to a railroad overpass and the beach stroll north or south. Restrooms and picnicking are available at the beach. Expect plenty of company on nice summer weekends.

Richmond Beach Park.

URBAN AREAS

Narbeck Wetland Sanctuary (Hike 17).

11. Arlington Airport

Distance: 5.6 mile loop   Time: Allow 2 - 3 hours

Elevation gain: None   Season: Year-round

Joggers and bikers may find the 5.6-mile loop trail around the Arlington Airport appealing, but hikers might prefer to limit their walk to the more interesting portions north and west of the airport. In any case, the trail is easy, uncrowded, and a good place to gander at small airplanes, including ultralights and other creative craft, as well as Cessnas and Pipers. If doing the entire loop, expect noisy traffic along the south side and some minor obstructions (parking lots) along the east margin. The rest is quite walkable, with trail signs marking most of the route. Tread is a mix of gravel and paved paths, roads, and grass.

There are three easy ways to begin, but the trailhead on 188th St. NE, 0.4 mile east of Smokey Point Blvd. may be the best start. The Airport Office on 59th Dr. NE (a half mile north of 172nd St.) may have a trail map posted outside—another possible start. There is also limited parking along 43rd Ave. NE near the corner of 172nd St. From the main trailhead on 188th St., you can head right (west then south) and reach 172nd St. in about 1.4 miles. Or head east 1.7 miles to 59th Dr. and another 1.5 miles to 172nd St. (it's another mile from here to 43rd Ave.). The loop trail could be improved immensely if there was a way to move the south section a few more yards from the road and get creative with some strategic landscaping, a meandering alignment, and better surfacing. A future link with the Centennial Trail to the east has been proposed (*see Hike 35*).

Airport Trail.

12. Jennings Nature Park
Distance: 0.5 - 1.0 mile round trip   Time: Allow 1 hour
Elevation gain: Negligible   Season: Year-round

Saunter through a 51-acre urban park (donated in 1961) with paved and unpaved paths, big rolling lawns, woods, wetlands, historic buildings, and a fuscia garden at Jennings Nature Park in Marysville. This is a good family destination with a lot of room for kids to burn off excess Btus. Head east on 4th St. to 47th Ave. Turn left then right in a few blocks into the park. Or, keep going east on 4th (SR 538) another 0.5 mile to a small parking area on the left (a nice kids' play area here). This side may be less crowded and is the better start. Wander the obvious paved path. Cut left across the lawn to a picnic table perched on a hump for a good view of the wetlands along Allen Creek (bring binoculars in spring for bird-ogling). Where the paved trail ends, head west (left) past a ball diamond and over the hill to a short loop trail around the duck pond. Up the hill to the left is the garden and another path behind it that leads back toward the ball diamond. Figure close to a mile round-trip.

13. Catherine Creek
Distance: 0.5 - 2.0+ miles roundtrip   Time: Allow 1 hour
Elevation gain: Negligible   Season: Year-round

This small wooded park in Lake Stevens has about a mile of walking trails and a link to the Centennial Trail (*Hike 35*) close by, so you can wander as little or as much as you like. The nearest summer access is next to Mt. Pilchuck Elementary School on 20th St. NE near 130th Dr. NE. At other times, park at a Centennial Trail trailhead at 16th St. and N. Machias Rd. and walk a short distance north to a gravelled trail on the left leading into the park. Expect some minor ups and downs, but easy walking overall. The park is good for picnicking and has an 18-hole disc golf course. Downtown Lake Stevens and the lake itself are just a few blocks west along 20th St.

14. Snohomish Historic District
Distance: 0.5 - 2.0 miles round trip   Time: Allow 1 - 2 hours

Elevation gain: Minimal   Season: Year-round

Downtown Snohomish, settled on the north bank of the Snohomish River in 1859, is one of the more attractive historic districts in the state. Fascinating architecture and excellent maintenance of the area's many historic buildings offer a reasonable image of what western Washington's early boomtowns might have looked like, albeit dressed up in fresh paint and an abundance of potted flowers to please the tourists. There are literally dozens of shops in town selling good food, good beer, souvenirs, used books, antiques, and more antiques. Thanks to the Snohomish Historical Society and their fine guide to old buildings, an enjoyable and informative walk awaits the curious wanderer.

Park near First St. and head for the historic information sign and map near First and Ave. B, with a list of sights. The walk up and down First is mandatory, but burn some calories before getting sidetracked by

Historic downtown Snohomish.

all the good eats. Some of the more interesting historic sites on First St. include (west to east) the Northern Hotel (1890), which survived the big fire of 1911, Pioneer Market (1890), the only three-story building in town, the Marks Building (1888) where the town's first flush toilet was installed, old Snohomish City Hall (1927), First National Bank (1907), Princess Theatre (1900), Oxford Saloon (1890), Eagles Hall (1904), and the Alcazar Opera House (1892).

From First St. walk a half-block up Ave. B to find the nicely preserved Blackman House (1878), built by an eminent logging family, and home of the first mayor, now a museum with original wallpaper, and a piano that sailed around South America. Ask for a "walking tour" brochure. Up another block on the right is the Methodist Church (1885) and the county's first church bell. Continue up to Fourth St. to the Stevens House (1887) built for the man for whom Stevens Pass was named. Catty-corner is the Snyder House (1888) with 22 rooms, five fireplaces, and a ballroom on the third floor. All these homes, except Blackman, are privately occupied, so no intruding. Turn east one block then right on Ave. A past other turn-of-the-century homes, including the "Gingerbread" House (1887) south of Third St., then little cottages known as Soap Suds Row (1889), where loggers and mill workers dropped off their laundry. Turn left on Second St., pass the St. Johns Episcopal Church (1893) originally built for $250, then turn right on Union to find many interesting shops across from a City Hall that was designed after Philadelphia's Independence Hall (1938). Head south another block to the site of Snohomish founder E. C. Ferguson's prefab house (1859), the town's first home. Then look for a new riverfront trail just beyond and walk downstream to its end or to steps leading back up to First St.

Other points of interest include a State Senator's home (1889) at Union and Third; the gigantic Iverson House (1908) near Third and Ave. D covering more than 8,000 square feet; Snohomish Hardware (1906) on Ave. C near First St. (has a water-powered elevator); the Odd Fellows Lodge (1886) at Second and Ave. C; and Pioneer Village Museum at Second and Pine with an 1875 log cabin, homes from 1889 and 1892, and a 1910 general store and blacksmith shop. A totem pole stands at Kla Ha Ya Park near First and Ave. C, just east of the American Legion Building (1887). The Centennial Trail (*Hike 35*) begins just east of downtown near First and Maple (a new trail link is planned).

15. Port Gardner

Distance: Approx. 6.3-mile loop   Time: Allow 3 - 4 hours
Elevation gain: 200 feet   Season: Year-round

The possibilities for urban walks in Everett are many, but the following suggested loop offers a variety of natural, scenic, and cultural features that are much more interesting than a pointless jaunt down Evergreen Way. The description begins at Legion Memorial Park at 2nd St. and Alverson Blvd. Park on the west side, or start anywhere on the loop and bump the directions accordingly.

Check out the view of the waterfront then wander northish along Alverson Blvd to Marine View Dr. Cross when safe and walk left, following a sidewalk down the viaduct to sea level, soon picking up the paved path through North View and South View Parks at the water's edge (**1.1 mi**). Maulsby Swamp is across the road. Keep walking south past 10th St. and Marine Park (possible sidetrip). Continuing on Marine View Dr., walk to 14th for the Firefighters Museum (long block to the right), and on to the Everett Marina at 18th St. (**2.1mi**). Head right on walkways and promenade among shops, restaurants, and the boat harbor.

Back at Marine View Dr., continue south up a viaduct with a good view of the Navy Homeport, built for a seven ship battle group, including a nuclear-powered aircraft carrier, four destroyers, and two frigates. The base has supposedly contributed hundreds of millions of dollars to the regional economy. Head up the ramp and take the bridge at 25th St. to Grand Ave. (**3.8 mi**). Turn left and walk a mile to Grand Avenue Park at 16th St., then look down on the route you walked below. Continue north on Grand and Alverson to the start (**6.3 mi**). The route also works well on a bicycle.

Everett waterfront from Grand Ave. Park.

16. Forest Park
Distance: 0.5 - 1.5 miles round trip   Time: Allow 1 - 2 hours
Elevation gain: Minimal   Season: Year-round

One of Everett's more popular parks, 111-acre Forest Park contains a small network of walking paths that require little description. With a little city effort, a signed loop system of a mile or more could be established to enhance the sauntering. Another 60-acre site across Mukilteo Blvd. (gated access) could also use a looped trail that links the bicycle-pedestrian bridge at Forest Park with beachfront at Pigeon Creek, creating a future trail system of three miles or more. In the meantime, just wander the park aimlessly. From Evergreen Way, follow 41st St. a few blocks west and around the bend (becomes Mukilteo Blvd.). The park is on the left.

17. Narbeck Wetland Sanctuary
Distance: 0.5 - 2.0 mile loop   Time: Allow 1 - 2 hours
Elevation gain: Negligible   Season: Year-round

An excellent stroll on fine boardwalk (*photo, p. 62*) and perimeter path awaits urban-weary visitors to the Narbeck Sanctuary north of Paine Field in southwest Everett. Paths wind through 50 acres of natural and constructed wetlands—truly an oasis amid noisy streets and the sprawl of industry and business parks. A creative "mud bank" cave and outdoor classroom with boulders to perch on add interest, although the scant views into the site's largest open-water wetland could be improved. Also, two short sections of perimeter trail follow an unappealing sidewalk

where a needed boardwalk could enhance those views. From SR 526, take Seaway Blvd. to the third traffic light and the signed entrance on the right. A trail map is posted near restrooms at the start.

"Mud cave" at Narbeck Sanctuary.

18. Silver Lake

Distance: 0.5 - 3.0 mile loop   Time: Allow 1 - 2 hours
Elevation gain: Negligible   Season: Year-round

Recent pedestrian improvements along the east shore of Silver Lake, plus short paths at Silver Lake Park to the west and Hauge Homestead Park on the southeast shore allow one to piece together a reasonable three-mile walking loop. It isn't quite the same as a trek around Seattle's Green Lake, but if even a couple of narrow greenway corridors could be located along the north and south shores or among neighboring homes, a circuit of real substance will have been created. But considering how much development already crowds the shoreline, as well as the high cost of acquiring lake frontage, it may take awhile before such an undertaking could be seriously undertook. Nevertheless, a loop trail is a worthy proposition that shouldn't be shrugged off as too costly or ambitious or impossible. The entire 2.5-mile walk can be done briskly in an hour or leisurely in two. Start at Thornton A. Sullivan Park on the west side (off Silver Lake Rd. a few blocks west of 19th Ave. SE) and essentially follow your nose to the most logical paths, roads, and walkways.

If the lake loop is too much, try a short nature trail in the woods across Silver Lake Rd. from the parking lot at T. A. Sullivan Park. A trail sign and white posts mark the beginning (accolades to the Kiwanis Club and Boy Scouts). Several short loops are possible with minor ups and downs. Stay right at junctions on good trail to complete a 0.5-mile loop that returns you to the starting point. The forest is nice, despite screaming traffic on I-5 next door.

Silver Lake at Hauge Homestead Park.

19. McCollum Park

Distance: 0.5 - 1.5 miles round trip   Time: Allow 1 - 2 hours
Elevation gain: None   Season: Year-round

For a short walk in the woods on easy trail, try the little circuit at McCollum Park south of 128th St. SE, just east of I-5. North Creek—a salmon spawning stream—splits the 78-acre park and a portion of the forest. While there is some traffic noise drifting into the trees, the creek's soothing gurgle helps neutralize it. Adopt-A-Stream Foundation and volunteers have worked to enhance the creek and trails for both salmon and people (respectively speaking), also built an environmental education center, and have made interpretive improvements along the creek. A mile-long interpretive boardwalk has also been proposed.

Park south of the pool and aim for the footbridge over North Creek. Go left through woods to begin one of several possible loops with good forested picnic sites (with grills) in the shade of modest-sized Douglas fir trees. Walk past a spur on the left leading to another footbridge and reach a fork just beyond, about 300 yards from the start. The longer loop ends here. Imagine a path around the perimeter of the forest with other paths cutting through the middle, and you will have a sense of where you're headed. To complete the loop, head right (a counter-clockwise start) then generally keep right at major junctions. Or go left to do the opposite. The outer loop is a pleasant half-mile stroll through mixed forest, with a few old stumps and an understory of vine maple, salmonberry,

red huckleberry, Indian plum, wild rose, sword fern, and salal. Gentle terrain offers some wheelchair accessibility for the more ambitious folks on wheels. Find the North Creek Trail nearby (*see Hike 21.*)

North Creek bridge.

20. Interurban Trail

Distance: 0.5 - 12.0 miles one way   Time: Allow 1 - 5+ hours
Elevation gain: Negligible   Season: Year-round

The Interurban Trail between Lynnwood and Everett, much of it along I-5, was a major accomplishment in the 1990s, and we should be grateful that Lynnwood, Everett, Snohomish County, and the local PUD #1 came together to get it built. The paved trail generally follows an old rail corridor for the electric Interurban Trolley that ran from Ballard to Bellingham in the early 1900s. Recent improvements and extensions through Mountlake Terrace and Shoreline in King County have produced a nearly complete route from downtown Everett to north Seattle where the trail ends (in 2007) at N 110th St. Although best enjoyed on a bike, some parts of the Interurban are reasonably hikable as well. If you decide to do it all, expect some noisy and aesthetically dull stretches along I-5. Trail signing is not the best (arrows are tiny and a few signs may be missing).

Despite those not-so-inviting sections, it's important to recognize that the trail is a major urban facility that was designed to provide a significant nonmotorized transportation alternative—not some cozy garden path for the footloose. As further improvements are made, a more attractive urban greenway should begin to emerge for hikers, including new links and sidepaths, pocket parks, traffic bypasses, freeway noise barriers, interpretive facilities, benches, public art, and most importantly, native

Interurban Trail, Lynnwood.

trees, shrubs, ferns, and wildflowers throughout the corridor. Some of these improvements have been happening, like the new separated bicycle/pedestrian path over 196th St. near I-5, which will add much to the trail's appeal once the gaps are filled southward to King County. For a bit of the latter, try the section near Echo Lake south of the county line, just east of Hwy. 99. Common sense suggests not walking alone late in the day or after dark, especially in areas that are more isolated or closed off from public view.

Best bets for footsters include the sections between South Lynnwood Park and Scriber Creek Trail (1.2 miles, *see Hike 28*), and from the small parking lot at 44th St. and Colby Ave. in Everett south 3.2 miles to Casino Rd. (0.8 mile is along Commercial Ave. north of Madison St.). A runner-up is the 1.5-mile chunk between 128th St. SE and Everett Mall, perhaps starting at Thornton A. Sullivan Park on Silver Lake (walk 112th St. west across I-5 to the obvious trail entrance; a trail underpass here allows one to head north or south without having to cross the street above). Trail access and parking are also feasible at the 164th St. Park-and-Ride; at McCollum Park (off 128th St. SE); and just off Alderwood Mall Blvd. between 33rd and 40th Ave. W. Maps of the trail are available on the parks pages of the Snohomish County and Lynnwood websites: www1.co.snohomish.wa.us and www.ci.lynnwood.wa.us. For portions south of the county line, try the City of Shoreline's website at www.ci.shoreline.wa.us.

Sorely needed are links to the North Creek Trail at McCollum Park, a path along Maple Rd., completion of a new bridge at 44th Ave. W. (planned for 2008), and improved links to Everett neighborhoods.

21. North Creek Trail (Mill Creek)

Distance: 2.5 miles one way   Time: Allow 2 - 3 hours (or more)

Elevation gain: Negligible   Season: Year-round

Recent improvements to the North Creek Trail in Mill Creek have turned a skimpy old trail into an excellent choice for a morning saunter—and a good model for other communities to contemplate. While the author still prefers a more sustainable surface of smooth, tightly-packed fine gravel rather than asphalt, the rest of the design features are comfy-cozy and friendly to the environment. Trail extensions south to Bothell and north to Silver Lake and the Interurban Trail could be developed within a few years. About 2.5 miles were complete in 2007.

Access the trail on the north at McCollum Park off 128th St. (near the bus shelter). Or follow 164th St. east of I-5 two miles to Mill Creek Blvd.; go left one block to a wildlife pond and path on the left. For a long-ish seven-mile clockwise loop on paved paths, head right at McCollum Park on Dumas Rd., right at H.M. Jackson High School (**0.7 mi**), left on Trillium Blvd., left on Village Green Dr., left at Cottonwood Dr. (**2.1 mi**; walk up to a crosswalk and more path leading back to Village Green Dr.; a gravel trail on the left offers an optional short loop), and right on Mill Creek Rd (**3.4 mi**). Walk the latter downhill past a nature area to Mill Creek Blvd. and the south end of North Creek Trail one block to the right (**4.2 mi**).

*North Creek Trail
at Mill Creek.*

URBAN AREAS—
22. Big Gulch
Distance: 0.5 - 1.0 mile round trip   Time: Allow 1 hour
Elevation gain: Negligible   Season: Year-round

This short walk along the rim of Big Gulch, a deep forested ravine in Mukilteo, offers a quick breather on a busy day. Future trail extensions are possible (such as a return leg across the gulch), so watch for that. The start is tucked behind the Mukilteo Library on Harbour Pointe Blvd., two blocks west of Mukilteo Speedway. Park near the street so as not to impede the library's patrons, then follow the obvious path along the left side of the building and into the woods. Simply wander until the way ends at the Speedway (**1.0 mi**) where a wide sidewalk offers a longer jaunt with a few landscaping frills. Return by the same route.

URBAN AREAS—
23. Meadowdale Playfield
Distance: 0.5 - 1.0 mile loop (or more)   Time: Allow 1 hour (or more)
Elevation gain: Negligible (at the park) Season: Year-round

When all you need is a short stroll to loosen up, try the mostly paved paths at Meadowdale Playfield in Lynnwood. About a mile of mostly barrier-free trail exists at this multi-agency park and sports complex. From SR 99, head west on 168th St. SW, staying right at Olympic View Dr., then go right on 66th Ave. W and enter the park just ahead. The paths generally meander around and between the ballfields, trees, and

play areas. Go when it's busy and catch a little sports action by some talented youngsters. Any route will do, but don't miss the duck pond on the north side next to a picnic area. Thoughtful rock sculpture adds

Duck pond path near playfields.

a bedazzling touch. An unpaved path parallels Meadowdale Rd. north of the park, becoming sidewalk farther down the hill. If you don't mind the climb back up, it's feasible to wander this walkway all the way to the waterfront. At 75th Pl., nearly a mile from the duck pond, cross to another paved path that leads 200 yards to railroad tracks, a road (caution), and the beach south of Meadowdale Beach Park (*see Hike 9*).

URBAN AREAS—
24. Southwest County Park

Distance: 0.5 - 2.0 miles round trip　　Time: Allow 1 hour
Elevation gain: Negligible　　　　　　 Season: Year-round

Urban wanderers may be surprised to find a limited trail system slicing through pretty forest in what is otherwise a large (120-acre), undeveloped county park near Edmonds. Several good loops can be found, along with some steeper routes in varying condition that don't necessarily lead anywhere interesting. The area makes a suitable destination for a lazy day, and will certainly get better as trails are improved and extended (a new loop trail below the road would help). From Puget Dr. in Edmonds head north on Olympic View Dr. about two miles to a shoulder parking area on the right immediately before 180th St. SW.

Park near the park sign and walk into the woods on the obvious wide path. Stay right in fifty feet to follow a pleasant half-mile loop in Douglas-fir forest. Narrower side-paths offer additional exploring. Or, from the park sign, cross the road and walk left a few yards to another half-mile path running parallel to Olympic View Dr. back to the western park boundary. Inviting spur trails here become steep below. Otherwise, most grades are gentle and easy to walk.

Loop trail, Southwest County Park.

75

Urban Areas—
25. Lynndale Park

Distance: 0.5 - 1.0 mile loop   Time: Allow 1 hour
Elevation gain: Negligible - 100 feet   Season: Year-round

One of Lynnwood's finer parks, Lynndale has a wide range of facilities for everyone, including more than a mile of paths, mostly in a cozy forested setting. About half the trail distance is paved and barrier-free, although the loop described below is mostly unpaved. There are several ways to access the park. The main entrance is off the south side of Olympic View Dr., about 0.3 mile east of 76th Ave. W. Park up the hill near the big log shelter.

Either wander through the park aimlessly, or for a hilly, but easy half-mile loop on good trail, head left on the paved path between the parking area and the log shelter. Cross the access road near the exit from the parking lot to pick up a gravel path. This path leads down 50 yards to a junction. Turn right, climb a little, and follow this path along a narrow wooded ridge, then down steeply a few paces and soon to a four-way junction in a small valley. Head left up the stairs or go straight and take the next left (right goes over a rise and leads toward the park entrance). Stay on the main traveled path through Douglas fir and sword fern to a fork under the power lines. Turn left to reach another junction where one more left heads back to the start. Instead, go right. This leads to a paved

path. A left here returns to the log shelter. Trails around the shelter and several spurs leading to more developed areas of the park are barrier-free.

Forest trail in Lynndale Park.

26. Sierra Park

Distance: Less than 0.2 mile   Time: Allow 1 hour

Elevation gain: None   Season: Year-round

The short paved path at Sierra Park in Edmonds gets a mention for two reasons: a small and informal arboretum has taken hold here that contains a modest variety of native and non-native trees and shrubs; second, the paths were developed specifically for the blind. Low railing, benches, pavement edges, large rocks, and vegetation produce a three-dimensional environment that can be explored quickly and easily by just about anyone. Fragrant pines and flowering plants (spring and summer) add a fourth dimension. Find the park north of 196th St. SW on the west side of 80th Ave. W, but south of 190th St. SW. Parking is off 190th. The walk makes two very short loops through forest and flowers and requires no real description. Interpretive signposts are unique and written in Braille. Benches and picnicking are also available.

27. Lynnwood Golf Course Trail

Distance: 2.1 mile loop   Time: Allow 1 hour

Elevation gain: None   Season: Year-round

Most of us probably wouldn't think of going to the golf course for a hike—at least not without a plaid bag of balls and clubs—but the 2.1-mile loop trail around the Lynnwood Municipal Golf Course actually makes a respectable urban saunter. About two-thirds of the distance is in trees; the rest is neighborhoods and the Edmonds Community College campus. From 196th St. SW, head south on 68th Ave. W. to 204th St.; turn right and follow signs to the golf course (park on the left). The trail is easiest to locate by wandering leftward, or clockwise, around the course. Near loop's end, the route skirts paved parking areas where paint stripes mark the way.

28. Scriber Lake & Scriber Creek

Distance: 0.7 - 2.3+ round trip Time: Allow 1 - 3 hours
Elevation gain: None Season: Year-round

Hidden behind the urban hubbub of noisy cars and rumbling trucks zipping along 196th St. SW in the heart of Lynnwood is a little gem of a lake named for a family who settled here in the 1890s. Like the natives before them, the Schreibers and other settlers found the area rich in game, with good fishing to boot. Later, a resort was developed at the west end, and the lake's name would be phonetically adjusted to Scriber Lake. The area became a park in 1981. A pleasant 0.7-mile loop surrounds the lake and is linked to the Interurban Trail by a 0.8-mile path that generally follows Scriber Creek.

To do just the loop, take 196th St. SW east of SR 99, turn south onto Scriber Lake Rd., then left on 198th St. Park near the restrooms and take the path on the right for a counter-clockwise loop around the lake. Trail surface varies from sawdust and shavings to pavement and

Scriber Lake boardwalk.

boardwalk (some barrier-free). The woods and scrub provide important habitat for wildlife. Bird boxes have been installed to give cavity nesters a better shot at raising a family here. In 0.3 mile, a spur on the left leads to a discreet viewing area with a bench. Just beyond, go left and across a footbridge to continue the loop, or straight briefly to another junction (a left here crosses a second bridge and leads to 196th St.; right heads uphill fifty yards to a grassy picnic spot; go straight to continue on the Scriber Creek Trail). Heading left on the lake loop, several more "duckblinds" are passed before reaching a floating walkway with artistic benches—a fine spot to watch for ducks, beaver, or muskrat. The loop ends shortly beyond (head right to reach the 196th St. crosswalk and Wilcox Park).

Scriber Creek Trail leads from the lake loop to 52nd Ave. and 200th St. SW. Walk left (east) a block and cross 200th St. and 50th Ave. W at the light to pick up the trail at Scriber Creek Park (more parking). Follow either paved or unpaved path (they rejoin shortly) and continue past a park-and-ride lot to a junction with the Interurban Trail near I-5 (about one mile from the lake). A right here takes you another 1.5 miles or so on the Interurban to its end at South Lynnwood Park near 211th St. and 63rd Ave. W.

29. Edmonds Woods Walks
Distance: 0.5 - 3.0 miles round trip   Time: Allow 1 - 3 hours
Elevation gain: Negligible   Season: Year-round

There are three mostly wooded parks in south-central Edmonds that are all within a few blocks of each other, and each offers a little woods walk. Do one or do them all in few hours or less. See the park listings (*page 231*) for directions to Maplewood, Yost Memorial, and Pine Ridge Parks. Maplewood Park is probably the least interesting of the three to walk, although it is a lovely spot for a quiet family picnic. From the northwest side of the lawn-covered hill, find the path across the drive. The trail leads past beauteous ground-cover plants and several large trees as it drops down to a footbridge over a seasonal creek, fading not far beyond. Down and back is about 0.3 mile.

Yost Memorial Park offers a mile of paths looping through woods (mostly red alder), in and out of the ravine containing Shell Creek. Numbered posts refer to interpretive stations that aren't always maintained (check with the park folks for details and/or a brochure). Walk down the service road (handicap parking access) and follow the pavement around a bend a short distance to a good trail on the left. Follow this into the ravine to a junction. Left leads to Main St. near 12th Ave. N and to a minor viewpoint of an old retention dam for a water system downstream. But go right, cross the creek, and follow this awhile, partly on boardwalk; stay left at a junction for more exploring (right returns to the start). There are a number of short trails to wander, including some moderate hills and connections to neighborhoods.

At Pine Ridge Park you can wander an easy, flat trail through Douglas fir-western hemlock forest to Goodhope Pond and adjacent wetlands with a bench to sit and wait for birds and other wildlife to materialize. From the parking area off 83rd Ave. W, walk the wide trail to a small fenced "duck pond" and a larger pond and wetlands beyond. The two paths beyond this point only connect to adjoining neighborhoods. To

do a loop, walk back around the north side of the fenced pond (narrow path next to the fence) and find another good path leading up 100 yards to a junction. Right goes to a partially obscured overlook of the Goodhope Pond (with another bench); left leads back to the start. Figure a half-mile for the loop. Trails in all three parks have been somewhat neglected by the city (as of late 2006), despite potential for some enjoyable walking.

Forest at Yost Memorial Park.

30. Terrace Creek

Distance: 1.0 - 2.0 miles round trip   Time: Allow 1 - 2 hours

Elevation gain: 100 feet   Season: Year-round

Terrace Creek Park in Mountlake Terrace is a 52-acre forested oasis in the midst of a city. The park is not intensively developed and contains one major trail corridor, offering a mostly quiet walk in the woods, about a mile each way. A small parking area and trailhead exists on the west side of 48th Ave. W. near 233rd St. SW. Follow the paved path left around a play and picnic site and large lawn area that makes up part of a unique disc-thrower's "golf course." Unless you brought your bag of competition discs, skip the tee-off and head around a ballfield to where the main path enters the woods.

The hike continues on good trail and old road bed another 0.5 mile, bending right at a small clearing near a service road, followed by a gentle climb up the valley to the trail's end at 221st St. SW. Several narrow paths and boot tracks intersect the main trail at various points and most lead to the numbered "holes" of the disc golf course. A few benches along the main trail allow time to rest and listen for "birdies" (okay, couldn't resist). More short paths can be found across 48th Ave.

Terrace Creek Park.

LOWLANDS & FOOTHILLS

North Fork Stilliguamish River from near the South Fork confluence.

31. Stillaguamish Forks

Distance: 0.5 - 2.0 miles round trip   Time: Allow 1-2 hours

Elevation gain: None   Season: Year-round

On 55 riverfront acres in Arlington, Twin Rivers Park is better known for its ballfields, but there are also a few paths along the South Fork of the Stillaguamish River which lead to summer beaches and extensive gravel bars at the confluence with the North Fork Stilly. Late summer through early spring are better times to visit, since the park can be crazy busy with sun and sports fans. Or go early or midweek to beat the crowds, which happens to be a better time for wildlife viewing anyway. The walk is best during drier weather. If it's raining hard (or just did), you may want to avoid some areas. Several paths are so silty that you may find yourself walking on a trail surface that has the consistency of sauteed slug slime. Both forks can run deep and swift fall through early summer. When the river is high, a flood channel may block access to the big gravel bar. Of course the river can move around too, and trails can simply wash away (best to stand back from any eroding edges).

Find the park on the west side of SR 530 just north of the South Fork Stilly bridge as you head out of Arlington. Drive to the west end and park near the apparent trailhead. Follow the grassy path and continue straight ahead at junctions. The park extends from SR 530 to the confluence with the North Fork about a half-mile downstream and paths will take you there most of the year. Unless the river is running high, you should be able to cross a dry flood channel to reach the big gravel bar. The North Fork rides in from the right. The old railroad bridge, soon to be a new segment of the Centennial Trail, spans the river close by. Various small loops cut through forest between the South Fork and the ballfields, and you can easily reach the river bank at several locations (again, beware of slippery or unstable banks). Another path leads to a popular spot under the SR 530 bridge.

LOWLANDS & FOOTHILLS—
32. River Meadows

Distance: 1.0 - 6.0 miles round trip   Time: Allow 1 - 3 hours
Elevation gain: 0 - 100 feet   Season: Year-round

With one of the better lowland river walks in the county, River Meadows Park near Arlington is well worth a visit anytime, but expect crowds on sunny summer weekends. The 145-acre park is largely undeveloped but nicely maintained. Silt and sand trails follow a long bend in the river and connect with mowed paths among grass and wildflowers, creating a six-mile network of easy walking trails. Many bird species, deer, and other wildlife are often seen. A guide to animal tracks could be useful here. Historic features and interpretive displays also exist and tent camping is available. The park opens early, closes at dusk.

From Arlington follow SR 530 a half-mile north of the South Fork Stilly bridge and turn right onto Jordan Road. Stay right in a mile and continue three more miles to the park entrance on the right. Drive down to the flats and curve right for parking. There is no real need for directions since aimless wandering works quite well here. But if a hint would be helpful, try walking the wooded path on the left near the end

South Fork Stilly at River Meadows Park.

of the gravel drive. Several spur trails access river bars and beaches (some sandy), plus views of a giant boulder and high eroding bluff across the river. The Stilly may be fairly tame by mid-summer, but can be deep and swift much of the year, so keep the young'ns close. The forest includes cedar, fir, hemlock, birch, alder, cottonwood, and many native Northwest shrubs, herbs, and ferns. At some point duck out of the woods and walk the edge of Cove Meadow to Homestead Terrace (orchard, flowers, view). Cross the access road at the base of a hill, walk along Funnel Meadow past an oddly-trunked hemlock tree to a pleasant cedar grove and a giant bigleaf maple with pudgy serpentine limbs. More wandering in almost any direction is feasible. Toss in a checkered cloth and lunch and find a spot to sit and enjoy. Campsites are also available.

Lowlands & Foothills—
33. Twin Lakes Park

Distance: 0.9 mile loop   Time: Allow 1 hour

Elevation gain: None   Season: Year-round

If you can stand the freeway noise (an MP3 player helps), Gissberg Twin Lakes County Park north of Marysville isn't such a bad place for an easy stroll around two artificial lakes. The lakes resulted from the removal of fill material for the development of I-5 in the early 1970s, and while they don't seem too appealing through the wing window at 70 mph, the walk around them is actually kind of scenic.

Just west of I-5 (Smokey Point, Exit 206) turn south on 27th Ave. NE, then take the next left. Follow this past some recent big-box sprawl to the park on the right in 0.7 mile. The walk around the lakes on a grassy path needs no description. Each lake is roughly 400 yards long by 150 yards wide, and they are joined by a narrow channel near the west end which prevents one from walking around just one lake—unless you're up for a short swim or waist-deep wade (more or less). The full loop is just under a mile long. The "peninsula" between the lakes has a rough path leading through cedar and birch trees to the channel. Watch for ducks, geese, other birds, and small mammals. Even a river otter isn't unheard of here. To avoid the heavy decibels, try early Sunday mornings when the big grey ribbon is usually a little quieter.

LOWLANDS & FOOTHILLS—
34. Deering Wildflower Acres

Distance: 1.5 mile loop   Time: Allow 1 hour
Elevation gain: Neglible   Season: Year-round

Thanks to The Nature Conservancy and Western Washington University, this 30-acre nature area was turned over to the City of Marysville for use as a park in 1997. Forested wetlands and a mile-plus trail system are available for exploring, and short loops offer a mini-trek for the kids. It's also a good spot for birding. The park is open weekends year-round, and most weekdays June through September (closed on Mondays). School groups infrequently visit.

Find the park at 4708 79th Ave. NE. From 83rd Ave. NE a few blocks west of SR 9, turn west on 44th St. NE to 79th Ave. and the hidden park to the north. There is limited parking and minimal facilities. Trails are well signed and recent bird and wildlife sightings are noted near the trailhead. A caretaker lives at the site.

Wetland bridge at Deering Wildflower Acres.

LOWLANDS & FOOTHILLS—
35. Centennial Trail

Distance: 0.5 - 15.9 miles one way   Time: Allow 1 - 8 hours
Elevation gain: Neglible   Season: Year-round

The old railroad grade which has become the county's preeminent lowland trail—the Centennial Trail—was originally developed as the Seattle, Lakeshore & Eastern Railway in 1889. The line extended north from what is now the Burke-Gilman Trail in Seattle to Snohomish and eventually to Arlington, then was sold to Northern Pacific in 1892. The line was acquired by Burlington Northern in 1970, but the section north of Hartford was shut down in 1972. In 1987 the line from Hartford to Snohomish and beyond was finally abandoned. The county quickly purchased the land for a trail. Washington State, founded in 1889, celebrated its centennial in 1989, about the same time that trail construction began, hence the name "Centennial Trail."

The original trail from Snohomish to Lake Stevens was just over seven miles long. The grand plan called for a 45-mile trail from King to Skagit County, including the new 10.1-mile section between Lake Stevens and Arlington completed in early 2006. Next on the agenda are completion of a one-mile link south of Arlington and the eight-mile section from Arlington to the Skagit County line. If adquate funding can be secured, work on these should be progressing well by 2008.

Machias Station between Lake Stevens and Snohomish.

The trail has been developed to a "super-highway" standard for trails—wide, paved, landscaped, and embellished with traffic signs, interpretive signs, bollards, gates, benches, bridges, and the like, plus several major and minor trailheads. An equestrian path parallels much of the route. While an expensive trail of this standard seems like a natural in a more urban environment where bicycle transportation is a primary goal, the facility does feel somewhat overdone for a rural area. At the same time, this is a major trail corridor that's intended to serve a lot of needs for a lot of people, and not just the nature walker who might prefer a narrow winding path over a fat straight ribbon of blacktop. Yet it is a remarkable facility, largely made possible by the hard work of the Snohomish-Arlington Trail Coalition, county park staff, the late Mike Parman (the county's trail planner to whom the Centennial Trail is dedicated), and many citizens and civic leaders who worked to make it happen.

Hikers can access the trail at any of the trailheads noted below in bold type (browse www1.co.snohomish.wa.us for a trail map). The more interesting walks head north from Machias Station a few miles north of Snohomish; Rhododendron just south of Lake Cassidy; or south from the new Armar Rd. Trailhead near Arlington. The south terminus of the trail is about one mile northeast of downtown Snohomish at Maple and Pine St. (street parking available). Eventually the path will be extended south to several blocks of paved trail already in place near 1st and Maple, as well as the new riverfront trail along the Snohomish River (*see Hike 14*).

Lake Cassidy dock and float near Rhododendron Trailhead.

Until that happens, a better southern start is at the **Pilchuck Trailhead** (from downtown Snohomish, head 2.5 miles north on Maple St. which becomes S. Machias Rd.). The mileage figures noted below begin at this point. Street crossings are well marked, but use caution.

From Pilchuck Trailhead, walk north to Dubuque Rd. (**1.6 mi**) and a crossing of S. Machias Rd. (**2.8 mi**). **Machias Station**, built in the style of the original rail station, is just ahead (**3.2 mi**; access is off Division St. two blocks west of S. Machias Rd.). The next mile is more pleasant, located back from the road away from some of the traffic noise. Mt. Pilchuck, Three Fingers, and White Horse Mt. (right to left) are visible to the northeast. Cross 16th St. at a ballfield, then pass the **20th St. Trailhead** (**5.8 mi**) located just west of Machias Rd. near downtown Lake Stevens. The trail soon leads beneath SR 92 (**7.0 mi**) and passes the **Rhododendron Trailhead** near Lake Cassidy (**9.4 mi**), where interpretive signs and a dock and float offer a nice respite for lunch. A 195-acre reserve was set aside here for wildlife.

Continuing north, cross 84th St. NE (**10.8 mi**), pass beneath SR 9 (**11.6 mi**), reaching the Quilceda Watershed Interpretive site (**15.0 mi**), and finally, the end of the trail (in mid-2007) at **Armar Rd. Trailhead** (**15.9 mi**; Armar Rd. is also known as 67th Ave. NE). This northern trailhead is located one mile south of 172nd St. NE and makes a good start for a quiet walk in a wooded setting. Expect friendly crowds of walkers, joggers, bikers, and bladers on all but the crummiest weekends.

Itchy feet can head north from 172nd St. (Edgecomb) to walk a less appealing section of the Centennial Trail adjacent to 67th Ave. north to 204th St., followed by a bit of sidewalk and gravel path next to railroad tracks leading to a nicer path through downtown Arlington that ends at the old railroad bridge across the Stillaguamish River. It is approximately 3.7 miles from here back to 172nd St. When the trail is extended to Skagit County, a more northerly trailhead will be established at an historic farm acquired by the county. Most of the grade north of the Stilly in Arlington was overgrown and impassable in 2007, or closed to the public awaiting improvements for drainage, parking, bridge decks, and the like. Skagit County citizens are eager to build a similar trail from the county line north to Sedro Wooley and even brushed out and signed a 3/4-mile section, though further progress could use stronger support from the county commissioners there.

LOWLANDS & FOOTHILLS—
36. Langus Park & Spencer Island
Distance: 1.2 - 7.0+ miles round trip   Time: Allow 1 - 4 hours
Elevation gain: None   Season: Year-round

A fine riverwalk on paved trail close to Everett is found at Langus Riverfront Park on Smith Island next to the Snohomish River. The 2.8-mile barrier-free trail leads to a 3.5-mile looped trail system on Spencer Island, offering strolls of varying length, views of Mt. Baker and Mt. Rainier, and excellent birding in the winter and spring. Spencer Island is jointly managed by Snohomish County Parks and the Department of Fish and Wildlife. Bicycles, horses, and dogs are prohibited to help minimize disturbance to the nesters and feeders, while the north half of the island is open to seasonal hunting. More than 1,000 acres of the rich Snohomish estuary are protected for wildlife and salmon. Reach the park from SR 529 north of Everett. Take the first exit north of the Snohomish River bridge and head south parallel to the highway. Continue south

on Smith Island Rd. to a fork (about 1.5 miles from the SR 529 exit); stay right (left crosses I-5). The park is 0.5 mile ahead on the right.

For a shorter walk, try the stretch from the dock at the north end of the park to the big I-5 bridge and back, a 1.2-mile round trip. Or, from the bridge (**0.6 mi**) continue south along the river to a confluence with Union and Steamboat Sloughs (**1.5 mi**). Benches

Langus Park and trail.

here and elsewhere suggest a relaxing pace and time to sit and watch whatever goes by. A few workboats ply the river and great blue herons reconnoiter the slough's muddy banks. Continue around the bend to the left and up Union Slough to a junction with a gravel road and the old bridge to Spencer Island (**2.2 mi**). The paved trail continues north, ending at a slough view and "keep out" signs (**2.8 mi**). Either retrace your steps or walk the gravel road west 0.7 mile back to the I-5 bridge.

By the time you cross the bridge to Spencer Island, freeway and city noise have diminished considerably. So, look for interpretive signs and a trail map near the bridge. Follow either of two loops: the South Trail (1.5-mile loop) and North Trail (2.6-mile loop). Maybe head south on the boardwalk just left of a dike, passing a cattail marsh overlook and another trail junction in 0.1 mile. Right (South Trail) leads back along the east side of Union Slough, then along Steamboat Slough. Left cuts across the island past freshwater wetlands on the left, and saltwater marsh and intertidal areas on the right—a good place to set up the spotting scope. Not long ago, dikes were breached on the right, allowing natural estuarine conditions to be reestablished, which not only explains all the dead trees, but contrasts nicely with the freshwater system on the left. Watch for waterfowl and shorebirds—nearly 200 species have been observed making use of these valuable habitats. Either complete the south loop or continue along the north loop (but beware of hunters in duck season). A hike on Langus Park's paved trail plus the full loop around Spencer Island and a return via the gravel road is 7.0 miles in length.

Spencer Island wetlands.

LOWLANDS & FOOTHILLS—
37. Lowell Riverfront Trail

Distance: 1.0 - 3.5 miles roundtrip   Time: Allow 1 - 2 hours
Elevation gain: None   Season: Year-round

Enjoy a pleasant stroll along the Snohomish River on an easy paved trail near Lowell, one of the nicer segments of the lowland riverfront trail system slowly developing in the Everett area. The walk is barrier-free in a natural setting and well suited to all ages and abilities. It's a good place for wildlife viewing as well. To find it, cross I-5 on 41st St. (east) and follow the signs to Lowell. Pass Lowell Park, curve left and in a few blocks turn left at a stop sign. The park is just beyond the railroad tracks.

Walk either direction on the obvious paved path. Going upriver (east), the path ends in 0.3 mile at a boat launch (someday a trail may continue upriver from here all the way to Snohomish and the Centennial Trail). Or, go downriver for the longer, more interesting walk along the grassy riverbank past wetlands, woods, and fields. At a big bend, the Mt. Baker volcano near Bellingham is prominent to the north, while several big peaks of the North Cascades scratch the sky to the east. An historic homestead stands quiet on the opposite shore of the river.

The paved path passes good picnic spots but soon fizzles at a railroad crossing and fence (**1.4 mi**), a good turn-around point—trains slither through here fast and frequently. Eventually, the trail will be extended north to Smith Ave. and beyond. To head back, one can follow dirt paths east of the tracks to loop back to the parking area. Or, just retrace the path back along the river. Then imagine how much water it takes for the river to cover a floodplain that's three miles wide in this area.

Snohomish River.

38. Bailey Farm Wetlands (North Cr. Park)

Distance: 0.5 - 1.5 miles round trip Time: Allow 1 - 2 hours

Elevation gain: Negligible Season: Year-round

An impressive one-mile boardwalk trail through extensive wetlands and peat bog south of Mill Creek is the highlight of North Creek Park, developed by the county in 1995-96 on what used to be a dairy farm. The John Bailey Farm was originally homesteaded in 1891, and now, more than a century later, the public can reap the area's natural beauty and diversity. The boardwalk trail is barrier-free, although a small hill must be negotiated at the start. The boardwalk is designed to float when the water rises fall through spring. Bikes can be walked but not ridden on the boardwalk. The trail will eventualy become part of the North Creek Trail connecting Mill Creek to Bothell (*see Hike 21*).

Find the park on the north side of 183rd St. SE a half-mile west of SR 527. A gravel path leads past an overlook and down a gentle grade for 100 yards to the boardwalk. In 0.1 mile go left for the peat bog, pond, and lots of forget-me-nots in summer—plus sedges, rushes, cattails, and hardhack (spirea). From that junction continue 0.2 mile to another junction. Go left 0.1 mile to an obscured beaver pond, or go straight another 0.2 mile to the end of the boardwalk and 0.1 mile of gravel path connecting with 9th Ave. SE (there's no parking at this end of the park). Plans call for additional boardwalk construction to complete a long overdue loop system. Persistent birders may see dozens of species in winter and spring and perhaps a few more in summer and fall. Depending on the season, one can see bald eagles, red-tail hawks, harriers, kingfishers, marsh wrens, swallows, Virginia rail, mallards, canvasbacks, and Canada geese. Also watch for muskrat, deer, rodents, bats, frogs, and elusive pond turtles.

The floating boardwalk.

LOWLANDS & FOOTHILLS—
39. Thomas Eddy

Distance: 1.4 - 2.0 miles round trip   Time: Allow 1 - 2 hours
Elevation gain: Minimal   Season: Year-round

Rivers ought to be simple, right? Water flowing between two banks. There might be a flood once in awhile, but hey, that's just a flood. And a river's just a river. Or is it? In the way so many of us think, it may be that a river is *not* a river at all. At Thomas Eddy, south of Snohomish, it's easy to understand why a river might be more correctly thought of as an entire landscape. Not a static one where the water is over here and the banks and bars are over there, but a dynamic place without any boundaries, where almost everything in sight is linked together in some way, and where things are always changing. Here on the Snohomish River, a broad floodplain of braided channels, islands, and gravel bars offers a natural laboratory in which to ponder the meaning of this word "river." But if the pondering is too much, the wandering is at least as entertaining.

The Snohomish River at Thomas Eddy.

To find the trail to the river, head for the 343-acre Bob Heirman Wildlife Park at Thomas Eddy (named for a local long-time resident and wildlife, fishing, and park advocate). From SR 9 about 2.4 miles south of Snohomish, turn east at the Broadway light, then go left in 0.8 mile on Connelly Rd. The park is on the left in another 0.8 mile; it closes at dusk. There are a few picnic tables on the bluff with a partially obstructed view of the river in the distance and a small lake up close. Lord Hill rises to the southeast. An old road, now a trail, leads down through meadows and pasture to the river bank (**0.3 mi**). Wander downstream (good views) to a junction and stay right (**0.6 mi**). The path may continue 0.1 mile to the edge of the river bed (things change down here). A half-mile or more of wandering may be feasible depending on water level and other conditions. Be sure to memorize the trail's location for the return. At low water in late summer/early fall, it may be possible to walk down a wide dry channel (watch for sun-dried salmon carcasses) about 0.2 mile, then right (clockwise) around a low island between this and the main channel. This adds an easy half-mile loop to the walk.

Maybe check out Shadow Lake on the way back (bring the bird book and binoculars). At the bottom of the hill about 150 yards from the start, one can amble left along one of two paths about 100 yards to the lake. Approach cautiously to avoid scaring off the ducks. Barrier-free improvements to the lake have been proposed (it might be nice to see the two paths joined near the lake and a simple duckblind installed at some point, creating a short loop for wildlife viewing without a lot of disturbance). No dogs are allowed in the park.

LOWLANDS & FOOTHILLS—
40. Lord Hill

Distance: 2.1 - 6.3+ miles round trip   Time: Allow 2 - 4+ hours
Elevation gain: 300 - 700+ feet   Season: Year-round

Named for Mitchell Lord, an original 1870s settler on the hill, Lord Hill has a long history of farming and logging (both state-owned and private)—with virtually all the old-growth eliminated by the 1930s. Of the 4,000 acres that make up this conspicuous volcanic ridge south of Snohomish, the county has acquired over 1,500 acres of emergent forest, farmlands, lakes, ponds, and wetlands which provide habitat for wildlife and a good recreation spot for the not-so-wild humans. Mountain bikes and horses are also frequently sighted. In addition to DNR and private lands that comprised the original park, several acquisitions have been made in recent years, including a 150-acre farm near SR522. More than fifteen miles of trails have been opened up, mostly on old logging roads and along a natural gas pipeline corridor. While the forest is still a bit scraggly in places from excessive timber harvest, it's growing fast and may someday reclaim its former majesty, twig by twig, decade by decade.

In the meantime, Lord Hill offers a quiet walk in the woods, a rest by a marshy lake, an occasional view through the trees, and even a 500-foot descent to the Snohomish River where a mile of riverfront awaits the intrepid footster (best to visit there later in the year during lower

A view from Lord Hill.

water levels). Steep terrain to the southwest offers great view potential, and numerous volunteers have worked to improve those views as well as fix up the trails. Many loops are feasible. For a guide, map, some history, and other details, visit **www.lordhillregionalpark.org** and **www. friendsoflordhill.org**.

To reach the trailhead from Snohomish, follow 2nd St. east to Lincoln and turn right. This shortly becomes the Old Snohomish-Monroe Highway. About 2.5 miles from 2nd St. turn right on 127th Ave. SE and drive another 1.6 miles to the park and trailhead on the left (*map, p. 95*). Check out the trail map at the kiosk to plan a hike that suits the group (map-brochures should be available here), or try one of the hilly loops described below.

The main trail descends more than it ascends to the first junction (**0.4 mi**). Head left for Beaver Lake (bigger than it looks), staying right at two junctions near the lake. Continue up the Pipeline Trail (south) to a four-way intersection (**1.0 mi**). Left adds the Temple Pond Loop (1.2 miles) to your itinerary with spurs leading to two smaller ponds; the loop passes Temple Pond and rejoins the pipeline 0.2 mile south of the four-way. Or bypass this loop and go right at the four-way then left on the "Main Trail" (an old road) just ahead (**1.1 mi**). The return route goes right (it's a mile back to the trailhead). Go left for a longer loop or a descent to the river. For the latter, continue on the Main Trail, staying right at a junction and right again at the River Trail (**2.0 mi**) which descends a canyon another mile and about 350 vertical feet to gravel bars along the Snohomish River (**3.0 mi**). If returning by the Main Trail, figure three miles back to the trailhead. For more wandering, head left on the West View Trail (0.7 mile from the trailhead) and walk this old road grade about 0.6 mile to a junction; continue straight for a short loop with views. Note that trail conditions change and new links are possible, so take a glance back at intersections to more easily retrace your steps if needed.

LOWLANDS & FOOTHILLS—
41. Buck Island & Sky River
Distance: 0.5 - 3.5 miles round trip   Time: Allow 1 - 2 hours
Elevation gain: None   Season: Year-round

On the lower Skykomish River in Monroe, Buck Island offers an easy stroll through a surprisingly beautiliferous forest of bigleaf maple and cottonwood. Walk it anytime, although a sunny day in fall color is especially nice. Several short loops are possible. The island is also known as Al Borlin Park, a big city park more or less hidden behind an industrial area. Directions are circuitous: From SR 2, turn south onto Main St., cross the tracks, then go left on Woods St., left on Fremont, left on Ann, and right on Simon Road. Drive into the park and park near the gated trailhead on the right, across from a picnic area.

Follow an excellent wide trail—the Al Borlin Nature Trail—into the woods. At the first junction go right to a view of a very tame Woods Creek with an interpretive sign, or go straight to continue. Big cottonwood trees, some four feet across, are mixed with bigleaf and vine maple, red alder, tall salmonberry, red elderberry, red huckleberry, snowberry, ferns, and some ever-invasive blackberries, together filling up the understory. At the next junction, a right takes you around the larger loop and left links with the return trail nearby. Stay right and soon reach a large grassy area

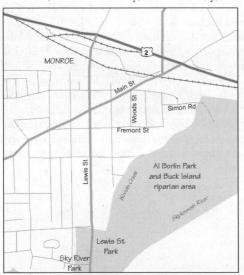

98

(more picnicking); go right to cross Woods Creek (**0.5 mi**) on a bridge built on gabions—intended to survive the next flood. Woods Creek is a salmon spawning stream slowly recovering from severe impacts of decades of logging in the Woods Creek watershed. During Monroe's lumbering heyday, parts of the creek were channelized to facilitate the movement of logs and shake bolts downstream to the mills in town. The footbridge leads to Lewis Street Park (noted below). A left before the creek continues the next leg of an easy 1.5-mile loop with good views as you wander upstream along the Skykomish River. The path soon meets a dirt road that returns 200 yards to the start. Follow it to a path on the left, then go right on another to complete the loop. Watch for a large contorted bigleaf maple tree with ferns growing all the way up the trunk and out the branches.

At Lewis Street Park, amble left across lawns and a parking area to an underpass and a fishing access area beyond. A dirt road leads to a paved path (a half-mile from the Woods Creek bridge) that encircles the ballfields at Monroe's Sky River Park. This park can also be reached from Village Way, a block south of W. Main St. (look for the park sign).

Buck Island cottonwood forest.

LOWLANDS & FOOTHILLS—
42. Explorer Falls

Distance: 2.4 - 5.2+ miles round trip   Time: Allow 1 - 3+ hours
Elevation gain: Minimal - 800+ feet   Season: Year-round

An easy walk to a nice waterfall, this short outing can be extended several miles up a ridge along a Boy Scout trail and old logging railroad grades, although a planned timber sale in the area will likely muck up the possibilities for the near-term. By mid to late-summer, the flow over the brink of the falls has diminished, so autumn (after a rain) through spring may be the better times to visit.

From U.S. Hwy 2 in Monroe, follow Woods Creek Rd. north about 11 miles to S. Lake Roesiger Rd. and turn right, then right again and up the lake to Monroe Camp Rd., 2.5 miles from Woods Creek Rd. Turn right and follow this 2.3 miles to a gate and shoulder parking area. The walk leads straight up the main-traveled gravel road to within earshot of the falls on the right—hidden but close by (**1.2 mi**). Scamper across the creek and clamber upward a few yards to a good view.

To extend the hike, look for an obvious trail downstream that climbs the steep forest via messy switchbacks before crossing the creek above

the falls. At an old grade jog right then left to continue. Despite some rough spots (2006), the trail is reasonably hikable to a ridgecrest where more switchbacks lead past a crude shelter (**2.4 mi**), if logging hasn't obliterated things. The trail skirts a ravine and soon meets the end of an old railroad grade (**2.6 mi**), which leads to more grades (or logging roads), wetlands, and a little lake that might interest the ambitious wanderer with a good map and routefinding skills.

Explorer Falls.

43. Whitehorse Trail & Fortson Mill Ponds

Distance: 0.5 - 7.5+ miles one way   Time: Allow 1 - 4+ hours

Elevation gain: None   Season: Year-round

Snohomish County has had good success acquiring old railroad grades for trails, and the former Darrington Branch line from Arlington will soon become an important link in the regional trail system. Originally developed in the late 1800s, the old grade was abandoned in the early 1990s. Twenty-seven miles was acquired from Burlington Northern in 1993 through rail-banking by Snohomish County Parks. The eastern six miles from Darrington to Fortson were opened several years ago. The rest, now known as the Whitehorse Trail, is being improved in phases and will soon connect with the Centennial Trail (*Hike 35*) near the old railroad bridge across the Stilliguamish River in Arlington. Four miles upriver, the Trafton Farm was aquired by the county to use as a future park and trailhead. Unimproved portions of the corridor are generally overgrown, and signs have been posted by the county closing some areas to public use until they can be properly developed and maintained. For now, the emphasis is on protecting trestles and the grade itself from washing away in the next flood.

Watch for the grade as you drive SR 530 to Darrington. Both east and west of the Cicero Bridge (near MP 29), there are turn-outs where you can explore the railroad bridge over the N. Fork Stilly (deck improve-

North Fork Stilly near Whitehorse Trail.

ments may have been made), plus a half-mile stretch of gravelled path leading eastward to scenic Cicero Pond and a couple of old train cars slowly being swallowed up by the forest. Just before the pond, a right fork leads down 200 yards to a broad gravel bar along the river.

Farther east on SR 530 near MP 39.5, turn north on Fortson Mill Rd. and park at the end of the pavement to hike the Whitehorse Trail to Darrington or to visit the old mill site and its skeletal buildings, historic site of a local railroad station, and two mill ponds—now fish and wildlife ponds—all once utilized by the formerly flourishing sawmill. Old roads and the railroad grade make it easy to explore. The first of two ponds is a juvenile-only fishing area. A small wooden footbridge crosses the pond's inlet stream and a short railroad bridge crosses the dammed outlet. The railroad grade here is the Whitehorse Trail. Follow it rightward (east) a short distance to the second, much larger millpond, which offers better wildlife viewing (**0.3 mi**). The trail may be slightly overgrown for a short distance.

The trail crosses Swede Heaven Rd. (**1.2 mi**) to much better tread, then Moose Creek and Squire Creek (**3.2 mi**), where a future trail link to Squire Creek Park nearby is needed. Pass the Whitehorse Mountain Amphitheater (**4.7 mi**) and the last good views of the river as the trail bends to the southeast for a less interesting finish in a quiet residential area at the end of, yes, Railroad Ave. (**7.5 mi**). You can find this inconspicuous trailhead by car off SR 530 at the east end of Darrington, 0.2 mile north of the main supermarket. Except for the last two miles, the N. Fork Stillaguamish River is often close by and a few narrow paths provide access for fishers, gazers, and sunners. The layered summit ridge of Mt. Higgins is visible downriver and Whitehorse Mt. upriver.

Railroad trestle at Cicero.

44. Boulder River

Distance: 2.6 - 8.0 miles round trip   Time: Allow 2 - 6 hours
Elevation gain: 200 - 800 feet   Season: Almost year-round

This popular, low-elevation, old-growth forest and river walk offers a sumptuous immersion into the North Cascades' Boulder River Wilderness. And that's gratifying when you consider how much of the year the higher elevation forests are buried in snow. Never exceeding 1,600 feet elevation, the Boulder River Trail is sometimes snow-free even in the middle of winter, although ice could make the going interesting in places. If you like waterfalls, do this trip in spring or early summer or shortly after a fall deluge. That's when the river roars and the falls are spectacular. The falls do fall year-round, however, and the walk through old-growth forest is a good plan anytime.

From SR 530 about 8 miles west of Darrington, turn south onto French Creek Rd (USFS Rd. 2010) immediately next to the MP 41 marker. Pass a small campground on the 3.7-mile drive to the trailhead at the

Noisy water enters the Boulder River.

end of the road (*elevation: 900 feet*). The first half-mile is wide and flat (an old road bed) and traverses a long moss and fern-covered rock wall with a modest drop-off. A brief rise leads to the Boulder River Wilderness boundary (**0.9 mi**). Pass a thin streamer of a falls from an unnamed tributary (**1.1 mi**)—a tease for the much bigger one just beyond (**1.3 mi**). Unless you catch it at low water, this gorgeous waterfall, often called Boulder Falls or Feature Show Falls, spreads across the coarse rock face in a thick and lacy apron. Difficult to measure, the nosiy falls are probably more than 100 feet high. Just upstream the river takes a nice drop among cabin-sized boulders.

The trail climbs somewhat over the next quarter-mile, passing giant trees six feet or more in diameter, then finally descends to a not-as-tall-but-lovely-anyway waterfall (**2.5 mi**). A rough trail continues to a ford crossing of the river (**4.0 mi**; *elevation: 1,400 feet*) where an old unmaintained trail once continued up steep forest to Tupso Pass and the summit lookout on Three Fingers Mountain (*see Hike 96*). Obviously, the ford should only be considered by experienced hikers at lower water.

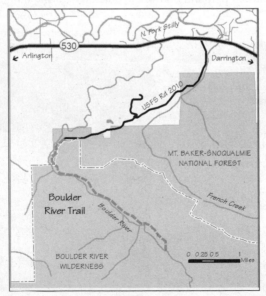

45. North Mountain

Distance: 2.6 miles round trip   Time: Allow 1 - 2 hours
Elevation gain: 400 feet   Season: April - November

North Mountain is not exactly a wicked crag of unmatched beauty, but its mostly wooded and rounded top offers a good perch for wide views into the North Cascades. The other main attraction is a fire lookout that, unlike most, can be reached with minimal effort. In fact, access was a little too easy for some and the site suffered from abuse by a knuckleheaded few. The Forest Service countered by boarding it up and gating the road 1.3 miles from the top. There is no trail here, so the old road is the hike, with views worthy of a visit in all but the snowiest months. An airy catwalk was recently accessible by way of some rickety steps, although the building is old and in dire need of restoration (stay off until repairs can be made). The view: Mt. Baker, Shuksan, the Pickets, Glacier Peak (barely), White Chuck, Pugh, Sloan, Jumbo, Whitehorse, and Higgins, as well as the Sauk and Suiattle River valleys.

From SR 530, 0.7 mile north of the Darrington Ranger Station, turn left on a paved logging road (Rd. 3000) and follow this about three miles to a fork at the end of the pavement; stay right. Continue on the main traveled road as it climbs the west flank of North Mountain to a gate at 12.2 miles. If it's open, you may be able to drive another 1.3 miles to the summit, although the road can be a little rough and you would miss the quiet walk up the road. So park below the gate and hoof it on up.

North Mt. fire lookout.

LOWLANDS & FOOTHILLS—
46. Frog Lake

Distance: 2.0 miles round trip   Time: Allow 1 - 2 hours

Elevation gain: 400 feet   Season: Almost year-round

An old trail, hardly used, and nice enough in the beginning to lure you upwards, then leaving you wishing for more . . . Save Frog Lake for an off-season stretcher, say fall through early spring when the bugs and brush are down, and traffic on the adjacent logging road (also goes to the lake) has diminished or disappeared. Forget it when there's snow in downtown Darrington. To get there from Darrington, head south and east on the Mountain Loop Hwy about three miles to the National Forest boundary and less than a half-mile farther to the trailhead and parking area just beyond the Clear Creek Campground, but before crossing the bridge over Clear Creek (*elevation: 600 feet; map, p. 108*).

Take a gander at the Sauk River parading down-valley to Darrington, then head up moderately steep trail through mature Douglas fir forest. The path quickly rises above Clear Creek and the little gorge that contains it. In a quarter-mile there's a good view off a precipice into

the deep, vertical-walled canyon (hang onto the kids)—perhaps the most interesting part of the hike. For the lake, continue upward, crossing little bridges and a curious footlog (may be slippery), all the while pretending the logging road nearby isn't there. At a narrow old road turn left to find Frog Lake about forty hops away (**1.0 mi**; *elevation: 1,000 feet*). Rising steeply to the southwest is the back side of Jumbo Mt., prominent from Darrington and a close neighbor of the more imposing Whitehorse Mountain.

Frog Lake Trail.

LOWLANDS & FOOTHILLS—
47. Old Sauk

Distance: 1.0 - 6.0 miles round trip   Time: Allow 1 - 3 hours
Elevation gain: 0 - 200 feet   Season: Almost year-round

There are at least two good reasons to put this river walk on your to-do list: this part of the Sauk River is a scenic, low-elevation, mountain river flanked with patches of old-growth forest, accessible almost any week of the year; and, it's a great place to watch for eagles and spawning salmon in the fall and winter. The trail parallels the river for three miles with parking at either end (maybe stash a bike upstream for the easy ride back to the car). Most of the old-growth is along the downstream (northern) half. To start there, drive the Mountain Loop Hwy about three miles south of Darrington to MP 50 and find the signed trailhead on the left (*elevation: 600 feet*); or continue to a paved shoulder parking area at the upstream trailhead near MP 47.5.

Follow the obvious path on the right into an impressive Douglas fir forest with many trees three to five feet in diameter. After the first quarter-mile the path runs close to the river bank and short spurs offer

views up and down. Salmon and steelhead migrate upstream in late summer and fall, then spawn into the winter. Except for a few minor ups and downs the trail is generally smooth and flat, and depending on flows and the location of meandering channels, it may be possible to access gravel bars at several spots. Portions of the area were logged in the 1930s so there are several distinct plant communities and a wide diversity of native species to be seen throughout the corridor. Most apparent are: Doug-fir, western hemlock, red cedar, red alder,

Old Sauk Trail in early morning.

bigleaf maple, black cottonwood, vine maple, salmonberry, thimble-berry, red elderberry, red huckleberry, Oregon grape, salal, devil's club, foamflower, Indian pipe, bunchberry, youth-on-age, bleeding heart, and trillium, plus sword, deer, oak, lady, and maidenhair ferns.

Cross a small stream on a footbridge (**1.0 mi**) with cottonwood and bigleaf maple forest beyond. The trail pulls away from the river bank for a half-mile, then returns to mature forest close to the rushing water. Another bridge crosses the Constant Creek groundwater channel (**2.1 mi**) that was enhanced in 1991 for wild coho and chum salmon. There is a salmon life-cycle interpretive sign here. This could be the best spot to watch for spawning salmon (fall and winter). The way reenters second-growth forest for the balance of the walk, passing a tiny sandy beach before bending up Murphy Creek to another salmon life-cycle sign and the south trailhead (**3.0 mi**; *elevation: 800 feet*).

Perhaps some day another three-mile chunk of the Old Sauk Trail can be reestablished up-river to the White Chuck, more or less follow-ing the route of the Sauk City-Monte Cristo wagon road originally completed in 1891—and later abandoned when it became clear that the Stillaguamish valley from Granite Falls was the more efficient route to the mines. A Native American trail likely predated the wagon road by centuries, if not millennia.

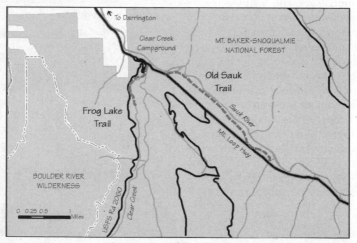

48. Beaver Lake

Distance: 1.0 - 3.0 miles one way   Time: Allow 1 - 3 hours
Elevation gain: 0 - 200 feet   Season: Almost year-round

Following the route of an old logging railroad grade southeast of Darrington, the way to Beaver Lake (a few marshy ponds) and beyond offers a good river walk and off-season wildlife excursion on mostly flat trail. Fall and early spring walks are best for color and views, and for avoiding the worst of the bugs. Note that a large slide area about a half-mile from the east trailhead is difficult and possibly dangerous to bypass (in 2007), but hopefully repairs or a re-route above the slide arc forthcoming. In fact, the Forest Service ought to consider turning this into a loop hike with a new leg back to the start by way of the White Chuck Mt. Viewpoint. In the meantime, access the path at the west end for the longer stroll, or either end once it's fixed. Keep in mind there is a 200-foot descent from the east trailhead.

Follow the Mountain Loop Hwy from Darrington into the National Forest and find the west trailhead on the right at MP 44.8, opposite the USFS Rd. 22 junction (*elevation: 1,000 feet; map, next page*). Walk down slightly then follow a good path along the Sauk River, noisy and tumbling at first, smoother and quieter beyond. A big view of Mt. Pugh fills the horizon upriver before reaching the small marshy lake near the walk's mid-point (**1.5 mi**). Watch for ducks, beaver, deer, and upland birds. Cross a neck of still water on an upgraded trestle. To the northeast White Chuck Mountain's jag-ged summit appears through the canopy. Large cedars are scat-tered beyond the lake. The original grade dis-appears into the broad

Logging railroad trestle at Beaver Lake.

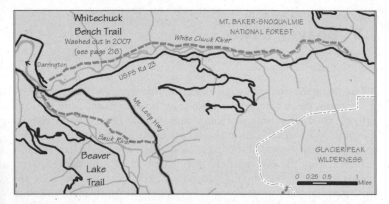

river channel near the big slide (**2.5 mi**)—a good turn-around point (in 2007). Beyond the slide, the way briefly follows a salmon spawning channel then bends to the northeast to pass between two giant cedars. A steep 200-foot climb leads to the finish at the east trailhead at MP 42.2 (**3.0 mi**; *elevation: 1,200 feet*).

LOWLANDS & FOOTHILLS—
49. Buck Creek
Distance: 0.5 - 1.6 miles round trip   Time: Allow 1 - 2 hours
Elevation gain: 0 - 200 feet   Season: April - November

For a short scamper along a rushing whitewater creek important to salmon, try the old trail up Buck Creek, a northern tributary of the Suiattle River (another Buck Creek east of Glacier Peak drains into the Chiwawa River). This sadly forgotten trail (unmaintained in 2006) leaves Buck Creek Campground at MP 15.3 on the Suiattle River Road (USFS Rd. 26). Reach the latter from SR 530 at MP 56.5, seven miles north of Darrington. The hidden trailhead is at the high point of an upper campground loop on the west bank of Buck Creek (*elevation: 1,200 feet*). If it's busy and you're not paying for a campsite, you may have to park near the campground entrance.

The trail stays close to the tumultuous creek, passing bouldery drops and only minimal flatwater, and quickly enters the Glacier Peak

Boys fishing on Buck Creek.

Wilderness (**0.2 mi**). Several large boulders suitable for sunning line the edge of the stream. Expect some rough trail beyond, including down logs, slide areas, and light brush—one of the downsides of turning over management of our public lands to them big corporations.

The trail climbs slightly through a beautiful Douglas-fir forest, passing trees over six feet in diameter. Western hemlock and red cedar add to the canopy above vine maple, huckleberry, salal, Oregon grape, devil's club, gooseberry, salmonberry, boxwood, many ferns (sword, deer, oak, lady, and maidenhair) and flowers. The trail passes a small slide (maybe backup a few steps for a brushy bypass below), and soon climbs several short switchbacks. Tread varies from good to bad and two little streams with delicate waterfalls are crossed, followed by more switchbacks. The old forest and whitewater below beckon further exploration until the trail fades at a steep gully (**0.8 mi**; *elevation: 1,400 feet*). It is unclear whether this trail continued up Buck Creek or was a former route to the long-gone fire lookout on Huckleberry Mt. (*see p. 218*).

LOWLANDS & FOOTHILLS—
50. North Fork Sauk Falls

Distance: 0.5 mile round trip   Time: Allow 1 hour

Elevation gain: 150 feet   Season: April - November

The short hike to North Fork Sauk Falls is a perfect companion to a longer outing elsewhere in the North Fork Sauk River basin, such as the North Fork Sauk River Trail, an old-growth forest hike that starts a few miles upriver (*see Hike 74*). The river can be torrential in spring creating an exceptionally powerful waterfall that literally explodes into swirling mist and a raging pool below (see the photo on the back cover, taken just two weeks after the one below). Yet even at lower water levels, the falls are still beautiful to watch, as is the bending river that rolls through a gorge downstream.

Find it by driving the Mountain Loop Hwy southeast of Darrington to MP 37.8; turn east onto USFS Rd. 49 and head up the North Fork Sauk River 1.1 mile to the tiny trailhead and parking area on the right

(*elevation: 1,600 feet; map, p. 148*). The way down through alder-maple forest is obvious, and the thunder builds as you settle into the canyon. Beware that there is a sheer cliff at the edge of the viewpoint and a narrow exposed ledge that might look tempting—avoid it, though, to increase the odds of making it back up the trail in one piece. The view is excellent, so there's no need to risk limbs, lives, or trampled vegetation for some other imperfect camera angle.

North Fork Falls in spring.

LOWLANDS & FOOTHILLS—
51. Harold Engles Memorial Cedars

Distance: 0.5 mile round trip   Time: Allow 1 hour
Elevation gain: Negligible   Season: April - November

In April, 1981, a friend and I were lucky enough to run into Harold Engles near the summit of Whitehorse Mt. on an early season climb from Darrington (not recommended by this guide). I had read about the man and knew he was legendary, an early Forest Service Ranger with decades of service and one who had been the first to ascend some of the region's more prominent peaks. He and his contemporaries built many of the original trails and fire lookouts outside of Darrington in a time when protecting the woods from wildfire and timber poachers were among a ranger's principle duties. I'll always remember Harold, pushing his eightieth birthday, tearing his shirt off in the high cold air and rolling in the snow at the edge of a glacier 6,000 feet above his home in Darrington. "Invigorating," he said with a glint. Harold was an extraordinary man of the mountains and a strong steward of wilderness. It is only proper that a memorial grove of big cedar trees he set aside for all of us years ago is now dedicated to his memory.

To reach the grove from Darrington, head south and east on the Mountain Loop Hwy to the North Fork Sauk Rd. at MP 37.8; turn left and drive another 3.4 miles to a small turnout and information sign summarizing Engles' life in the Forest Service (*elevation: 1,900 feet; map, p.148*). A short path leads to a gigantic cedar tree fourteen feet across. Wander left to view the river and more big trees, or right to find a nice stand of cedars with so many limbs they create the feeling of a cedar chamber, a refuge from the rain. Watch for wood violet, trillium, bleeding heart, lady fern, vine maple, elderberry, red alder, cottonwood, and Sitka spruce.

Trailhead marker.

LOWLANDS & FOOTHILLS—
52. Youth-On-Age

Distance: 0.4 mile loop   Time: Allow 1 hour
Elevation gain: None   Season: Almost year-round

An easy walk through an ancient forest of giant Douglas fir, Sitka spruce, and western hemlock trees, the Youth-On-Age interpretive trail is particularly good for families, seniors, and those of us who might be a little less mobile. The trail is paved and practically level. The area is named for an unusual plant (youth-on-age) that grows little leaves on the backs of mature leaves. As the older leaves wither and die, the new leaves send roots into the soil and a new plant takes hold.

Find this trail on the south side of the Mountain Loop Hwy at MP 18.7 east of Granite Falls (*elevation: 1,300 feet*). Stroll beneath tangles of vine maple and large Sitka spruce trees. Spruce needles are sharp and the bark is thinner and smoother than other large trees. Sitka is the largest spruce in the world and the principal timber tree in Alaska. Spruce more than eight feet across grow in the Olympic Rainforest and on Vancouver Island, but are far less common in the Cascades. Giant Douglas-firs have deeply furrowed bark and flat, stiff needles—bottlebrush-like, but not sharp. Some of these trees are more than 500 years old and 200 feet tall. Watch for a bird-pecked snag and a spruce with a huge base.

The bank of the South Fork Stillaguamish River seems to move each year and the path has been known to erode and be swept away. Chances are that a good trail remains and you can continue the walk after enjoying the view up and down the river. Pass more big Douglas-fir trees, birch, bigleaf maple, a variety of ferns, spiny devil's club, and another spruce whose mossy branches seem to glow in morning or late afternoon sunlight. The loop ends near the starting point after less than a half-mile of walking.

Douglas-fir and vine maple.

53. Robe Canyon

Distance: 3.5 miles round trip   Time: Allow 2 - 3 hours

Elevation gain: 200 feet   Season: Almost year-round

A lovely stretch of river, tumbling whitewater, and two old tunnels built for the Monte Cristo Railroad in the 1890s are highlights of this unusual trail east of Granite Falls. At less than 1,000 feet above sea level, the area is generally accessible all year, but beware of ice in cold, wintery weather. The trail is managed by Snohomish County Parks and was a favorite for esteemed trail guru and friend, Mike Parman who, most regrettably, left this life just as the trail was being dedicated in the 1990s. Plans call for extending the trail several miles downstream to link with the new Lime Kiln Trail south of the river (*Hike 54*). The Stillaguamish Citizens Alliance and River Network were major players in the county's acquisition of 956 acres here, including the lake, wetlands, forest, and the river gorge. The Alliance also helped develop the trail system. The

Old Monte Cristo Railroad near Old Robe.

route to the river is straight-forward (a crude map of the trail is posted near the trailhead). Note that the trail was severely damaged in a fall 2006 storm and may not be entirely passable nor suitable for kids until it's fixed. Check with Snohomish County Parks for updates on future trail improvements.

To reach the trailhead at "Robe Canyon Historical Park," drive east from Granite Falls on the Mountain Loop Hwy and park on the shoulder at MP 7.1 near the red brick trail sign across from Green Mt. Rd. A good path snakes quickly through a thicket and into an old clearcut where a steep hillside offers a partial view of the river and wetlands below. The trail switchbacks down to pick up the old railroad grade, reaching the river in less than a mile near the site of the old Robe Station. Continue downstream past the now invisible townsite of Robe on the right. Frequent flooding sent the town to high ground near the highway in 1907. Hop over two small streams and suddenly enter the gorge of the Stillaguamish River's South Fork.

A century ago, the steep canyon and moody river from here to a point several miles downstream turned out to be more than the construction engineers had bargained for. Periodic floods and slides ripped the old railroad grade to pieces at many locations, and after several rebuilds the railroad was abandoned in the 1930s. Several tunnels have collapsed, abutments and fills have washed away, so that today only Tunnel 5 and Tunnel 6 may be accessible. Both lie just ahead.

Pass an active slide area (if not repaired, the hike ends here) and find Tunnel 6 just ahead (**1.4 mi**). Imagine rolling and clacking along the rails, nose against the glass, looking straight down at the swirling whitewater just before the lights go out in this tall, curved and nervy tunnel. Once through the tunnel and into the light and sound of the river, comes an alley of sword fern and maple-cedar rainforest. Next is little Tunnel 5 and suddenly the end of the trail at a worse slide area (**1.8 mi**). Unless and until this stretch gets reconstructed (should you be tempted), Tunnel 4 no longer exists and Tunnel 3 is impassable.

LOWLANDS & FOOTHILLS—
54. Lime Kiln Trail

Distance: 7.2 miles round trip   Time: Allow 3 - 5 hours
Elevation gain: 200 feet   Season: Year-round

After years of toil, sweat, mud-caked boots, and crumbled cookies, this great new trail, almost entirely built by volunteers, was finally dedicated in October 2004. (Much credit goes to Volunteers for Outdoor Washington, the Boy Scouts, and trailster extraordinaire Steve Dean for heading up the effort. More than 400 volunteers helped out.) The second half of the route is the best, as it follows the historic corridor of the Everett & Monte Cristo Railway through an impressive canyon of the South Fork Stillaguamish River northeast of Granite Falls. The trail ends where a bridge once carried trains to the river's north wall, about two miles downstream of the Robe Canyon Trail (*Hike 53*), which also follows, in part, the old E&MC grade. The long-term goal is a bridge and trail extension to link the two together.

To find the Lime Kiln Trailhead, head east through Granite Falls, turn right (south) on Alder Ave., then left in three blocks on Menzel Lake Rd. In another mile, angle left on Waite Mill Rd. Pavement ends in a half-mile, but continue straight ahead (slightly uphill) on gravel to the signed entrance on the left. The well-signed path leads into the woods then connects with several old logging roads before descending to the old grade near the river (**1.6 mi**). A mile farther, the namesake kiln stands next to the trail against the hillside (**2.6 mi**). A junction is reached (**3.4 mi**) where a 0.2-mile loop leads to the old bridge crossing, and just downstream, stone steps leading down the river bank.

South Fork Stilliguamish River.

55. Big Four Ice Caves

Distance: 0.5 - 2.5 miles round trip   Time: Allow 1 - 2 hours
Elevation gain: 0 - 200 feet   Season: May - December

*O*ne of the more spectacular views of jagged peaks in the North Cascades is at the viewpoint and trailhead for the Big Four Ice Caves. High snowfields, awesome cliffs, and waterfalls produce a dramatic scene entirely visible from a relatively low-elevation trailhead, and even more impressive near the ice cave viewpoint a mile away. The caves are melting tunnels beneath snow and ice that accumulate when winter snows avalanche down a major gully and pile up at the base of the mountain. Portions of walls and ceilings, literally tons of ice, collapse routinely from spring through fall, thus the wise warnings not to enter. Avalanches are a serious matter in winter and spring, keeping the upper part of the trail closed until things settle down a bit, usually by May or June. (Note that a 2006 storm took out the river bridge, not yet repaired in mid-2007.)

From Mountain Loop Hwy east of Granite Falls, turn right into

the big new parking lot at MP 26 (*elevation: 1,700 feet; map, p. 172*). Either take the board-walk trail (left of the restrooms) through woods toward the South Fork Stilly bridge (**0.3 mi**), or follow the connector trail above wetlands to the old parking lot, a sunny picnic area, great views of the mountain, and the site of the former Big Four Inn which burned in 1949 (next to a 9-hole golf course—it's gone too, of course). Here, a paved path and boardwalk also goes to the river bridge (in 0.2 mile), passing a junction with the first boardwalk

Big Four Mountain from the trailhead.

just before the river. Both routes are barrier-free and together they form a pleasant 0.6-mile nature loop. Stronger wheelchair hikers, perhaps with an assist, may be able to continue up the packed gravel trail to within view of the ice caves (grades are continuous, generally between five and ten percent).

From the bridge, it's a gentle climb to the ice caves viewpoint in a big clearing near the base of the cliffs (**1.1 mi**; *elevation: 1,900 feet*). Some years the caves may be buried in snow into July. The ice was once called "Rucker's Glacier" and may be the lowest perennial ice in the Cascades. Be aware at all times of falling snow, ice, and rock from above. The unusual environment here has produced unique and sensitive plant communities. Don't (need we say?) pick or trample the flowers.

LOWLANDS & FOOTHILLS—
56. Wallace Falls
Distance: 4.0 - 8.0 miles round trip   Time: Allow 2 - 5 hours
Elevation gain: 800 - 1,400 feet   Season: Almost year-round

Probably the most famous waterfall in Snohomish County, Wallace Falls north of Gold Bar also happens to be one of the better hikes in the foothills, especially late fall through spring when runoff is usually higher and the crowd factor has diminished. The place can get a little jammed on sunny weekends late spring through summer. The 265-foot tiered falls of the Wallace River are indeed spectacular, and visible from several vantage points—including SR 2 just west of Gold Bar. The best view, though, is two miles up the trail, or three miles via an old logging railroad grade that winds away from the river. The area was acquired as a state park in 1977. A good trail map is posted at the trailhead.

To reach the trailhead, head east on U.S. Hwy. 2 about thirty miles east of Everett to the town of Gold Bar and take a left at the big park sign near MP 28. Follow signs 1.5 miles to the park entrance (*elevation: 300 feet*). The obvious wide trail heads under transmission lines and reaches a junction (**0.4 mi**): right is the steeper Woody Trail closer to the river; left is the longer, easier, but less interesting railroad grade (the two routes rejoin 1.4 and 2.6 miles ahead). Taking the Woody Trail, descend briefly and pass a connector to the railroad grade above (**1.4 mi**), then

Wallace Falls.

the grade itself just before a bridge over the North Fork Wallace River (**1.8 mi**; *elevation: 700 feet*). Trudge on for a view of the lower falls and scenic pools (**2.3 mi**), then a great view of Middle Falls (**2.6 mi**; *elevation: 1,100 feet*)—a reasonable turn-around point. The worsening trail continues up steep switchbacks to more views from above, and finally an upper falls viewpoint (**3.4 mi**; *elevation: 1,600 feet*). Just beyond, a less obvious path (watch for markers) climbs to old logging roads leading northwest to Wallace Lake, three miles from the upper falls. (Signs to the lake may be scarce, so memorize the route.) The falls, river, and lake up the North Fork were named for a Skykomish Indian woman.

57. Heybrook Lookout

Distance: 2.2 miles round trip   Time: Allow 2 - 3 hours
Elevation gain: 900 feet   Season: March-December

When the mountains are snowed in but the lower foothills aren't, Heybrook Ridge beckons. The hike is short, moderately steep, and close enough to sea level to miss most of the winter snowpack that's normally dumped on the Cascades November to March. In mild years the trail might be accessible in the middle of winter. The ridge's strategic location between precipitous walls of Mt. Index, Mt. Persis, and Mt. Baring means great views of those peaks plus Bridal Veil Falls. After the building deteriorated and was demolished, it was happily replaced in 1999 by a replica built by the Everett Mountaineers in the parking lot of the Skykomish Ranger Station. The building was reassembled piece by piece atop the preexisting tower—in total, a six-year effort. The lookout may become available for overnight rental.

The trailhead's at the west end of a big parking area on the north side of U. S. Hwy 2 east of Index at MP 37.6 (*elevation: 800 feet; see map, p. 193*). A straight-forward, moderately steep woods walk on generally good trail under maturing Doug-fir leads up to the lookout tower. Just as the tower comes into view, a cleared swath offers a nice vista. At the ridge crest, climb the tall tower to an observation deck beneath the closed cabin above (**1.1 mi**; *elevation: 1,700 feet*). Highway traffic noise

*Mount Baring
from the lookout.*

is a little less obnoxious and you can even hear the river. Bridal Veil Falls streams below the hanging valley of Lake Serene to the southwest. Mt. Index is above it, Mt. Persis to the right. Mt. Baring is visible way left, and Puget Sound is thirty miles west, left of Index Town Wall. One can wander the old logging road on top, although it leads to some unsightly transmission lines and more recent clearcuts. Despite serious logging in the 1920s, the forest has retaken most of the ridge.

LOWLANDS & FOOTHILLS—
58. Silver Creek & Mineral City

Distance: 2.0 - 7.0+ miles round trip   Time: Allow 2 - 4+ hours
Elevation gain: 100 - 1,000+ feet   Season: May - October

On the 4th of July, 1889, a lone prospector made his way up Silver Creek to a high pass with a fine view of a ragged range of mountains streaked red and aglitter with the promise of galena, gold, and silver ore. A giddy Joseph Pearsall descended quickly and began to stake the first claims of Monte Cristo on the same day. Within five years a steam train was hauling people, goods, and ore to and from Everett and the new wilderness town of 1,000 people (*see Hike 80*). Prior to 1889, years of prospecting on Silver Creek had led to a gathering of buildings known as Silver City, later reinvigorated as Mineral City upon the discovery of Monte Cristo. But the railroad offered far easier access, thus Mineral City and this southern access were largely abandoned. Today, almost nothing remains but the old road and a few mine shafts (not for entering).

Severe flood damage in 2006 blocked the normal access from U.S. Hwy. 2 (MP 35.7) via Index-Galena Rd. Until repairs are made, one could attempt (bike?) a longer approach from USFS Road 65 off US Hwy. 2 at MP 49.5, taking the upper Index-Galena Rd to just before Howard Creek (2.2 miles past Troublesome Cr.). Turn right, immediately cross the river bridge and turn right in 0.1 mile on the old road up Silver Creek. Most cars will need to park within the first quarter mile (*elevation: 1,200 feet*); high-clearance vehicles might make it a mile farther.

Hike (or drive) to the road end (**1.0 mi**) where the trail begins, generally following what's left of the old grade to Mineral City (a logging road replaced the wagon road in the 1970s). But first, a tenuous crossing of a

Rockslide above Silver Creek.

steep rockslide must be negotiated where the road is no more. A good path led through here in 2006, but conditions do change, so turn back if needed. There is a great view here of the steep whitewater canyon of Silver Creek—a roaring torrent in spring or after a fall deluge. The trail soon improves and passes more canyon views, several historic mine shafts, pretty waterfalls, and a private cabin. Bridges are missing over at least two streams, one of which requires a short, steep scramble (or ladder) that may be difficult for some. Ahead, aging bridges could fail and impede further progress if not repaired soon. Again, turn back if unsure. An old Metro bus is also passed—a surreal reminder of the road's better days. At a fork (**3.5 mi**), dip right for a nice lunch spot/campsite near the creek; or stay left for Mineral City, a wooded flat adjacent to a broad drainage known as Trade Dollar Gulch (**4.5 mi**; *elevation: 2,200 feet*). Beyond, the old trail crossed Silver Creek and climbed another three-plus miles to Poodle Dog Pass (*see Hike 81*). The route is occasionally brushed out, but can be unpleasant and difficult to follow (not advised).

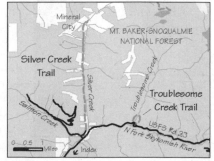

LOWLANDS & FOOTHILLS—
59. Troublesome Creek

Distance: 0.6 mile loop   Time: Allow 1 hour
Elevation gain: 100 feet   Season: April - November

For a great little family woods walk next to a pretty creek in the mountains, try the nature trail at Troublesome Creek Campground northeast of Index. Even if you're not camping at Troublesome, the trail is worth a visit, perhaps combined with other hikes nearby (*see Hikes 58 & 103*). However, beware of slick rocks and dangerous fast water here much of the year (a fatal, off-trail accident occurred in 1997). Note that severe flood damage to the Index-Galena Rd in 2006 may prevent easy access (*see Hike 58 for more, and check with the Forest Service for current conditions*). If access from the east is feasible, take USFS Rd 65 (off US Hwy. 2 at MP 49.5) 15.7 miles to USFS Rd 63 and head left (bike?) 4.7 miles to the westerly campground entrance; keep left to find the trailhead close by (*elevation: 1,800 feet*).

Walk left up the creek and pass under a bridge, continuing upstream in forest past benches to the obvious footbridge ahead. From the bridge

there is a great view of Troublesome Creek crashing through a narrow slot of granite like it can't wait to impale the river a few hundred yards downstream. Once across the bridge go straight on the main trail to continue the loop back to the campground. The trail climbs gently to another junction. A left here loops upslope and back to the bridge. The right fork drops back down to the creek, slides under the road, then reaches a footbridge downstream. Cross and return to the starting point.

Troublesome Creek.

LOWLANDS & FOOTHILLS—
60. Deception Falls

Distance: 0.6 mile loop   Time: Allow 1 hour
Elevation gain: Minimal   Season: April - November

Across the line in King County and west of Stevens Pass is a cluster of beautiful waterfalls all within minutes of the highway. A half-mile loop trail accesses two falls on the Tye River, and a barrier-free path goes to a third on Deception Creek. Park on the north side of US Hwy 2 at MP 56.8, eight miles east of Skykomish (*elevation: 1,800 feet*). Interpretive signs and a map at the trailhead speak to the remarkable railroad history of the Stevens Pass area. Nearby, in the winter of 1893, the last spike was driven for James J. Hill's 1,816-mile transcontinental Great Northern Railway between Puget Sound and St. Paul. The original grade literally switchbacked up the pass until 1900 when the old Cascade Tunnel was opened. In 1929 twelve miles of grade were abandoned with completion of a nearly eight-mile-long tunnel. (Part of that old grade is now the Iron Goat Trail (*Hike 107*).

For the close-up view of Deception Falls, walk the paved path to a bridge where stairs lead to a catwalk under the highway. (South of the highway, a serious mountain trail continues up Deception Creek to the Alpine Lakes Wilderness.) Retrace to a junction for a quick tour of the nature loop. A beauteous Douglas-fir forest and an excitable river make the loop enjoyable anytime it isn't buried in winter snow (generally mid-November through March). In the woods, look for the long needles of one of our less common conifers, western white pine. The first falls viewpoint is five minutes from the car, and a second right-angle waterfall is just beyond. The bedrock's stout resistance to erosion creates a puzzling sight, dramatic when the river is high. The trail continues through a grove of large cedar trees and returns to the parking lot.

Falls on the Tye River.

125

THE NORTH CASCADES

Glacier Peak from the northeast.

61. Green Mountain

Distance: 8.0 miles round trip   Time: Allow 4 - 7 hours

Elevation gain: 3,000 feet   Season: Mid-July - October

Those who keep coming back to Green Mt. in mid-summer return for good reason: views and wildflowers. Most years, from mid-July to early August, the forever-stretching meadows of Green Mt. are saturated with the rich color and sweet smell of mountain paradise. And if you wait for the flowers to fade, blueberries appear, which means this place stays plenty busy virtually every weekend in summer and early fall. To reach the trailhead, take the Suiattle River Rd. (USFS Rd. 26) from SR 530 at MP 56.5, about seven miles north of the Darrington Ranger Station, and follow it 19 miles to Rd. 2680 (signed for Green Mt.). Turn left and drive six more miles to the parking area (*elevation: 3,500 feet*). Note the Suiattle River Road was still closed at MP 12.6 in mid-2007 due to flood damage.

The trail begins steeply and passes through mature, moss-draped forest before entering big meadows (**1.0 mi**). This is a good place to pull out the wildflower guide in mid-summer. Continuing upward, pass two little lakes with campsites and a privy just below (**2.5 mi**; *elevation*

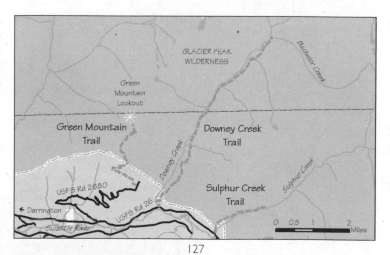

5,200 feet). Beyond, the meadows become more fragile (camping not recommended) and the summit ridge is visible above. Revegetation efforts have helped restore areas damaged by off-trail wandering. Some years, snow fields can linger well into summer.

If the trail is melted out, continue another long, steep, zigging mile to the crest—and the once and future site of the Green Mt. Fire Lookout (**4.0 mi**; *elevation: 6,500 feet*). By the 1990s, the building had deteriorated considerably and an attempt was made to restore it onsite. But damage over the winter led to a decision to helicopter the cabin to a lowland site for reconstruction. If all goes well, the finished building should be back on its scenic perch at the rocky summit in the near future. Before its temporary demise, it was one of only a handful of lookouts in the Cascades that still functioned on occasion as a true fire lookout.

The panorama here is impressive: Sloan Peak, Mt. Pugh and White Chuck Mt. to the southwest, Mt. Chaval and Snowking Mt. to the north-northwest, Mt. Buckindy not far to the northeast, Dome Peak to the east, and the oft-hidden volcanic monarch of Snohomish County, Glacier Peak, thoroughly conspicuous to the south-southeast. The Suiattle River is a vertical mile below.

Summer mist at Green Mt. meadows.

NORTH CASCADES—
62. Downey Creek
Distance: 5.2 - 13.0 miles round trip   Time: Allow 3 - 7 hours
Elevation gain: 800 - 1,100 feet   Season: May - November

This old trail through deep forest leaves the Suiattle River Road near the bridge over Downey Creek and provides access for mountaineers to some of the most remote and precipitous wildland in the North Cascades. Much of the trail was recently improved, but serious brush and many downed trees are likely after crossing Bachelor Creek, 6.5 miles from the start (this creek may be unfordable in early summer). Above this point, the route to Cub Lake is primitive, unmaintained, and more appealing to experienced trekkers with at least three days to burn. However, those first six-plus miles up the lower valley are in generally great shape and well worth a walk.

From SR 530 north of Darrington at MP 56.5, head east on the Suiattle River Rd. (USFS Rd. 26) for 21 miles to Downey Creek. Note that the Suiattle River Rd. was still closed at MP 12.6 in mid-2007 due to storm damage. Find the trailhead on the left 75 yards beyond the Downey Creek bridge (*elevation: 1,400 feet; map, p. 127*). While most of the hike follows easy grades well back from the creek, the first chunk is moderately

steep as you climb to a broad bench and the Glacier Peak Wilderness boundary (**0.4 mi**). A campsite and small creek crossing are passed (**1.7 mi**), then a second creek (**2.1 mi**) before a slight descent leads much closer to Downey Creek. An eroded bank and new boardwalk (**2.6 mi**) make a good turnaround point for a 5.2-mile round tripper. One may be able to scamper down the bank to gravel bars. A campsite is 0.1 mile beyond. It's four more miles from here to Bachelor Creek and the end of the good trail.

Downey Creek Trail.

63. Sulphur Mountain

Distance: 11.0 - 14.0 miles round trip   Time: Allow 7 - 12 hours
Elevation gain: 4,500 - 5,500 feet   Season: Mid-July - October

The 5.5-mile hike (one-way) to Sulphur Mt. is a bit grueling, but there's a big scenic payoff at the end: the icy north flank of Glacier Peak, plus other seldom seen summits of the North Cascades. However, you have to walk most of the trail before you see much of anything. If a hard hike on a sometimes lonely trail is appealing, keep reading. Keep in mind that after the first quarter mile there is essentially no water on the route (carry plenty). Camping on the narrow ridge is impractical, although sites in the woods and near Sulphur Mt. Lake are feasible.

The trail begins a short distance up the Suiattle River Trail from near the end of the Suiattle River Rd. From SR 530 seven miles north of Darrington, turn east on the Suiattle River Rd. (USFS Rd. 26) and drive this 22.7 miles to the parking area near its end, just beyond Sulphur Creek Campground (*elevation: 1,600 feet*). Note that the Suiattle River Rd. was still closed at MP 12.6 in mid-2007 due to storm damage.

Walk the Suiattle River Trail (*Hike 64*) 100 yards to a junction and head left for Sulphur Mt. The Glacier Peak Wilderness boundary is just ahead. The tread is consistently steep but should be in reasonable condi-

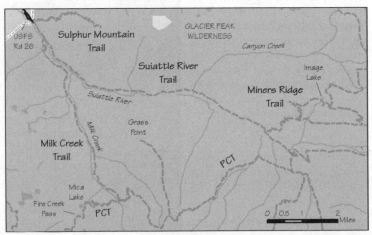

tion (if the trail crew has returned). The only stream is crossed in the first quarter mile after a short descent. After a gain of about 3,500 feet, the trail slips beneath a rock slide (**4.0 mi**; camping feasible just beyond). Enter meadowland (**5.0 mi**) and easier grades before reaching the scenic crest and two flowery high-points where western anemone, valerian, and lupine frame spectacular views of surrounding peaks. The second ridge bump makes a good turn-around (**5.5 mi**; *elevation: 6,100 feet*).

Glacier Peak lures to the south. Tenpeak Mt. is behind and left, Fire Mt. and Lime Ridge are to the right. White Chuck Mt. is visible to the west, obscuring Three Fingers. Whitehorse Mt. and the Suiattle River valley are to the right. Green Mt. and Mt. Baker lie to the northwest, with snowy Snowking Mt. and Mt. Buckindy to the right. The Picket Range is far in the distance. To the northeast is Sulphur Mt. Lake, and toward the horizon, Spire Point, Dome Peak, and Sinister Peak. Rambling Sulphur Mt. fills the skyline from east to southeast. More experienced hikers with some legs left could continue on a less-traveled path southward, losing 200 feet in woods, before climbing to other high points and a 6,735-foot rocky summit after another mile or so. To reach the lake, return to the point where the main trail first hit the ridge crest, then turn left instead of right. It's about 800 feet and nearly a mile down to the lake and good camping.

Glacier Peak and western anemonies from Sulphur Mt

NORTH CASCADES—
64. Suiattle River

Distance: 2.0 - 13.2 miles round trip   Time: Allow 1 - 7 hours
Elevation gain: 100 - 900 feet   Season: May - November

The trail up the Suiattle River, its milky water colored by Glacier Peak's melting glaciers, is a popular route for backpackers with a few days or more to explore wild mountains in the heart of the Glacier Peak Wilderness. Even if you have just a day or an hour to burn, the walk makes a pleasant outing. The entire trail upriver extends half-way around Glacier Peak and dead ends after twenty miles and a gain of 2,500 feet (assuming flood repairs are completed and a critical bridge is replaced in the upper valley). A half-dozen trail junctions offer access to the high country, but to really enjoy these options you'll need at least three days. For a one-day trek, early or late-season, consider hiking all or part of the 6.5 easy miles to the bridge over Canyon Creek. Only got an hour? A short roundtrip to the river bridge described below is a good alternate.

Barred owl.

Find the trailhead (*elevation: 1,600 feet*) at the end of the 23-mile Suiattle River Road (USFS Rd. 26) which leaves SR 530 just east of the Sauk River bridge at MP 56.5 (*map, p. 130*). This road was damaged and closed by floods in 2003 and 2006, but may be reopened by 2008. Walk the wide path along an old roadbed through beautiful old-growth Douglas fir. Some trees exceed eight feet in diameter. At a junction (**0.8 mi**), stay left to continue upriver on the main trail, or head right briefly on the Milk Creek Trail (*Hike 65*) to the bridge over the river (washed out in 2003, but hopefully replaced by 2008). Look down the brown river to spot a green mountain, appropriately named "Green Mt." In good light the fire lookout on top may be visible (*see Hike 61*). Back on the Suiattle River Trail, the route leaves the old road grade behind and rises and falls with the terrain, staying close to the river for miles. Several streams are crossed and small clearings offer occasional glimpses of the surrounding high country. Scenic Canyon Creek makes a good turn-around point for a longer day-hike (**6.5 mi**; *elevation: 2,300 feet*).

65. Mica Lake & Fire Creek Pass

Distance: 6.0 - 23.0 miles round trip   Time: Allow 3 - 4 hours (or 2 days)
Elevation gain: 700 - 4,700 feet   Season: Mid-July - October

Fire Creek Pass is a high and wild place on the northwest flank of Glacier Peak, where big meadows encounter the rock and ice of Washington's most remote volcano. Not far below, colorful Mica Lake lies in a stark rocky basin at the southeast end of Lime Ridge. Visiting the area in a day may be unthinkable for most mortals, but a good view or two of the mountain from the lower valley makes a shorter daytrip worthwhile. Or pack for an overnighter and see it all. The upper four miles of the hike follow a segment of the Pacific Crest Trail (PCT), so the possibilities for extended trips are endless. Check with the Forest Service for status of the PCT—it was rerouted after the 2003 flood and a critical bridge over the upper Suiattle River may not have been replaced yet. The lower bridge at Milk Creek was also unfinished in 2007.

From the end of the Suiattle River Road (*elevation: 1,600 feet; map, p. 130; see Hike 64 for directions*), walk an old roadbed—the Suiattle River Trail—to a junction (**0.8 mi**). Head right and descend to the new bridge over the river (if completed). The trail climbs about 400 feet over the next two miles and breaks into open meadows with a good view of Glacier Peak (about **3.0 mi**; *elevation: 2,300 feet*). The trail gently ambles along for several miles before climbing more steeply across

Glacier Peak from Fire Creek Pass.

avalanche chutes and forest to a junction with the PCT on the left (**7.5 mi**; *elevation 3,900 feet*). Stay right to cross Milk Creek on another new bridge (if completed) and climb another mile to meadows and a gaggle of switchbacks leading to lovely Mica Lake (**10.5 mi**; *elevation: 5,400 feet*); good camping nearby. A steep stroll up open slopes (may still be snow-covered in mid-summer) leads to Fire Creek Pass where Glacier Peak's summit can be seen peering over a ridge (**11.5 mi**; *6,300 feet*). Toward the left skyline is Frostbite Ridge, rising above the upper Kennedy Glacier. From the pass, the PCT descends nearly 1,000 feet before traversing the wild western flanks of the volcano and regaining the altitude on the way to Pumice Meadows and Kennedy Ridge (*see Hike 71*), then descending to the White Chuck River, and rising again to White Pass, 20 miles from Fire Creek Pass (*see Hike 74*).

66. Mt. Higgins Lookout & Myrtle Lake

Distance: 2.0 - 9.2 miles round trip   Time: Allow 1 - 6 hours

Elevation gain: 600 - 3,500 feet   Season: June - October

One of the most westerly summits of the North Cascades is Mt. Higgins, a distinctly layered, mile-high summit visible to the north of SR 530 between Arlington and Darrington (good view at MP 40). While the true summit is best left to experienced mountaineers, the slightly lower west summit can be reached by a fairly good trail and offers an equally dramatic view of the North Fork Stillaguamish River valley and ragged skyline of the North Cascades.

From MP 37.9 on SR 530, about 5 miles east of Oso, turn north on a gravel road (DNR Road 5500, signed "C-Post") and cross the North Fork Stilly in about a half-mile. Continue on the main road (stay left just past the bridge, then right); ignore the less traveled spurs. Find the trailhead parking area at the road end, three miles from the highway (*elevation: 1,400 feet*).

The path climbs moderately through a regenerating forest then suddenly breaks out into a steep clearcut in the first mile with an excellent view of Whitehorse Mt. to the southeast. This is a good turn-around for an off-season trek. Or, climb more steeply through some tight switchbacks among rocky outcrops, passing a little memory carved into the rock by Sam Strom, a Norwegian immigrant in

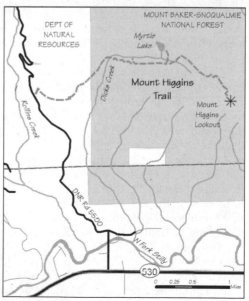

Mt. Higgins and Round Mt. (left) from the old fire lookout site.

the late 1800s and one of Darrington's more illustrious gun-totin' pioneers. He was also among the first team of climbers known to ascend Glacier Peak (in 1897).

Leave the steep clearcut on DNR land and enter old-growth forest at the National Forest boundary (**1.2 mi**). The grade moderates a little and continues up through woods, crossing Dicks Creek twice before topping out in a gentle subalpine meadow and a junction 200 yards past the second creek crossing (**3.4 mi**; *elevation: 3,700 feet*). A left descends slightly to Myrtle Lake, 0.3 mile away. For the old lookout site, go right to skirt lovely wetlands and to climb the last steep mile in woods, rocks, and meadow to Higgins' west summit (**4.6 mi**; *elevation: 4,849 feet*). Remains of the fire lookout are visible, built in 1926 and flattened by heavy snow in the mid-1960s. The panorama (clockwise): Glacier Peak in the distance, Darrington and the North Fork Stilly, Whitehorse Mt., Three Fingers, Boulder River, Mt. Rainier, Puget Sound, the Olympics, the Twin Sisters Range (reddish rock), Mt. Baker, Mt. Shuksan, and close by, the sharp middle and east peaks of Mt. Higgins. The hike is attractive in early summer if the lower meadows are melted out, but skip the summit, if necessary, to avoid avalanche danger.

67. Squire Creek Pass

Distance: 10.6 miles round trip   Time: Allow 5 - 8 hours

Elevation gain: 2,800 feet   Season: Mid-June - October

Until a major rockslide took out the road two miles short of the trailhead in 2002, the hike up Squire Creek to its namesake pass was one of the best dayhikes in the Darrington area, replete with classic North Cascades scenery. There is always the risk of further rockslides, so if the trail is closed, it's best to oblige and try something else, like the scenic Eight-mile Creek Trail which also leads to Squire Creek Pass from the opposite valley (*see Hike 68*). As of 2007 the trail was not officially closed and access across the slide area was not difficult. However, the trail had not been maintained for several years and hikers may encounter much brush, downed trees, and other obstacles. It is possible that trail repairs could be made in the not-too-distant future. In the meantime, the trek is not recommended for less-experienced hikers. Check the Forest Service website (or ranger station) for current conditions before heading out.

To reach the trailhead, take SR 530 to the west end of Darrington and turn south on Fullerton Ave. In several blocks turn right at Darrington Ave. which becomes Squire Creek Rd. (USFS Rd. 2040). Leave the pavement behind in 1.6 miles and stay on the main traveled road for another 1.9 miles to the current trailhead (*elevation: 1,300 feet*). On the drive in, Whitehorse Mt. appears like a spire.

Walk the road to the obvious slide area (**0.2 mi**) where a boot track leads more or less level across this open disturbed area

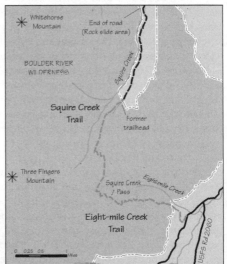

Squire Creek Wall from near the old trailhead.

beneath several gullies. Do not linger here in case something else decides to tumble down! As you reach the opposite end of the slide area, the boot track leads up a short, steep slope to the old roadbed which can be followed to the former trailhead (**1.9 mi**; *elevation: 1,900 feet*). Watch for the immense 2,000-foot high granite face of Squire Creek Wall. From here the trail follows abandoned road bed through an old clearcut for the first half-mile then crosses a small creek and enters old-growth forest near the Boulder River Wilderness boundary (**2.5 mi**). The grade passes some big cedars, then steepens at switchbacks for a 500-foot gain. Cross a steep boulder wash with views of waterfalls and the mammoth wall of mountains across the valley. Three Fingers is toward the left end. Just after the trail flattens out, enter a large rockslide area with giant flakes of scattered granite and unobstructed views of smooth high walls on both sides of the valley (**3.8 mi**). This is a good early-season turn-around (in June, the trail is likely to be under snow near the pass).

The path continues up through talus to the base of another wall, followed by a stand of dead trees, more forest, bright granite slabs, subalpine meadows, and finally, the gentle, slabby pass (**5.3 mi**; *elevation: 4,000 feet*). Glacier Peak's snowy cone is visible to the east between trees. Mt. Pugh is closer and to the left, and White Chuck Mt. is east-northeast. The entire subrange of Whitehorse, Bullon, Three Fingers, and Big Bear Mt. looms above, particularly impressive in morning light. Once the snow has retreated one can wander south a half-mile through open meadows and granite, perhaps some snow, up to an excellent ridge crest view.

68. Eight-mile Creek

Distance: 5.6 miles round trip   Time: Allow 4 - 6 hours
Elevation gain: 2,300 feet   Season: Mid-June - October

The old Eight-mile Creek Trail was resurrected from its near-forgotten state after a major rockslide in 2002 obstructed the more popular northern approach to Squire Creek Pass (*see Hike 67*). Prior to the big slide, Eight-mile was in notoriously bad shape, but has since been improved considerably now that is serves as the primary approach to the pass. It isn't perfect, but it's a reasonable trek to a relatively low pass with high-country views. At just 4,000 feet, the winter snowpack can melt out a little more quickly than most places with this much scenery.

To reach this trailhead by car, drive the Mountain Loop Hwy about two miles south of Darrington to just past the National Forest boundary and turn right on Clear Creek Rd. (USFS Rd. 2060) across from the Clear Creek Campground. This road may be rough in places. Stay right at a fork in 5.6 miles; the signed trail is on the right 0.6 mile beyond (*elevation: 1,700 feet; map, p. 137*).

Three Fingers Mt. from Squire Creek Pass.

The path initially follows an old logging grade, passing giant cedar stumps, and soon reaches old-growth forest and the Boulder River Wilderness boundary (**0.7 mi**). The path steepens then breaks into the open at the base of a big rock face known to climbers as Three O'Clock Rock (**1.1 mi**). After a bit more climbing, the grade eases and the landscape changes to gentle rock slabs, small streams, and subalpine meadows. Three Fingers and Whitehorse Mts. appear above. The way may be marked by rock cairns for a short distance across rocky slabs to the scenic pass (**2.8 mi**; *elevation: 4,000 feet*). Rock walls and craggy summits dominate the view. The now uncommonly hiked Squire Creek Pass Trail descends to the northwest. Camping is feasible, but good sites are scarce. Expect lingering snow near the pass in early summer.

NORTH CASCADES—
69. Meadow Lake & Meadow Mountain

Distance: 15.0+ miles round trip   Time: Allow 8 - 12 hours
Elevation gain: 1,500+ feet   Season: July - October

Meadow Mt. was once a favorite for locals, not only because the meadows and views are great, but because access used to be a breeze. But that easy access was taking a toll on the meadows. To reduce the impact, the USFS closed the logging road (some years ago) leading to the main trailhead on the west end of the mountain, thus requiring a five-mile road

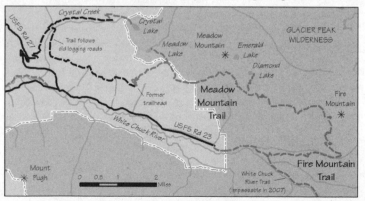

Tiger lilies.

walk to reach the trail, followed by a 1.3-mile hike to the first good meadow. Meadow Mt. thus became more practical as an overnight hike. But if you're leggy and ambitious you could still make a long day of it to the high country and to Meadow Lake 2.5 miles from the road end—a 15-mile round trip. Note, however, that there was no road access to the trailhead from either the Suiattle or White Chuck River roads in 2007 due to severe flood damage in 2003. However, the Forest Service expected repairs to the Suiattle River access to be completed by 2008. Check with the agency on current conditions before heading out.

Until late 2003 there were three good ways to access the area: White Chuck River Rd. (closed indefinitely by the 2003 flood); the Fire Mt. Trail (also accessed from White Chuck and cut off by the same flood; *see Hike 70*); and Rat Trap Pass Rd. via the Suiattle River. Assuming the latter has reopened, head north of Darrington on SR 530 to MP 56.5 and turn right on the Suiattle River Rd. (USFS Rd. 26). At MP 10, turn right on Rd. 25 and follow this a bit over three miles to Rd. 27; stay right and continue another nine miles to the trailhead at an old logging road (2710) on the left. Park here and walk this spur (staying right at a fork) to its end at the former trailhead (**5.0 mi**; *elevation: 3,900 feet*). Mt. Pugh towers across the valley to the southwest.

The trail climbs 1,000 feet in a mile, passes through meadow, then reaches a junction (**6.8 mi**; *elevation: 5,100 feet*). Go left for Meadow Lake, a 300-foot descent north and west from the crest (**7.5 mi**). The lake is nestled in a pocket of meadow, trees, and cliffs. Keep right to wander the meadowy ridge beneath Meadow Mt. with many ups and downs and good views of Glacier Peak and other high summits of the North Cascades. From the junction it's about six miles to Fire Mt.

NORTH CASCADES—
70. Fire Mountain

Distance: 14.0+ miles round trip   Time: Allow 7 - 12 hours
Elevation gain: 3,200+ feet   Season: Mid-July - October

The trail to Fire Mt. may or may not be hikable due to blocked access and trail damage in 2003. However, there is a reasonable chance that repairs could be made by 2008, so the listing from this book's first edition remains. If access to the White Chuck River is not restored, it may be possible to reach the area from Meadow Mt. (*Hike 69*). The connecting route makes a good backpack and mostly traverses scenic high country northwest of Glacier Peak. That trek includes several miles of easy walking, with some nicely spaced flat stretches to break up the grunty parts. Once repairs are made, the Fire Mt. Trail will again be an appealing day-hike. (*see Hike 71 for directions; map, p. 140*).

Assuming the new trail is built in the same location, leave the road-end parking lot (*elevation: 2,300 feet*) on flat trail and enter the Glacier Peak Wilderness (**0.7 mi**) before finding the Fire Mt. Trail on the left **1.5 miles**), 200 yards past the footbridge over Fire Creek. Head left (right goes to Kennedy Hot Springs—or what's left of it from the 2003 flood). After a half-mile of easy walking, some minor muddy spots, and a half-dozen switchbacks, rise to an unusually large forested bench. Here begins another mile of easy wandering in nice woods (possible muddy spots), followed by a half-mile of steepish and a half-mile of flattish trail adjacent to Fire Creek. The route crosses the creek on a hewn, maybe slick, footlog (**4.5 mi**; *elevation: 3,700 feet*).

The trail steepens up several switchbacks with peek-a-boo views through openings left from an old burn. At a left hairpin (*elevation: 4,600 feet*), Glacier Peak makes a stunning appearance. The best views of the mountain are found along the next 0.2 mile of trail, but you either have to stop to enjoy it or hike backwards (not recommended!). Lighting for photos is best late afternoon till sunset. The trail reenters thick woods, then shortly reemerges in patchy meadows with views of Fire Mt. above. Pass an inconspicuous trail junction (a hard right leads to more meadows, views, and a possible route to the 6,591-foot summit for the more seasoned hiker), but stay straight to pass the remains of an old log shelter and a small stream with campsites nearby (**6.5 mi**). Just

Glacier Peak from Fire Mt. Trail.

beyond are beautiful rocky meadows with good views and lots of big boulders for sunning if the bugs are tolerable.

One can continue across the meadow and follow the trail a short distance toward a wooded crest (**7.0 mi**; *elevation: 5,500 feet*) where another opening affords a good view of Glacier Peak's icy summit. Views reach around Black Mt. above Lake Byrne to White Chuck Mt. and beyond. This is a good turn-around point. Or, walk a few paces down the other side for a good look at Meadow Mt. The trail descends about 200 feet to cross a large subalpine basin, then climbs gradually to the 6,000-foot ridge top in about two miles. From there it's another six miles to the west end of the Meadow Mt. Trail, followed by a five mile walk on an old logging road to the west trailhead (*see Hike 69 for directions*).

NORTH CASCADES—
71. White Chuck River & Lake Byrne
Distance: 10.5 - 15.5 miles round trip   Time: Allow 6 - 12 hours
Elevation gain: 1,000 - 3,600 feet   Season: May - November

The White Chuck Trail was a popular access to the Pacific Crest Trail for many years, and the principal climbers' access to Glacier Peak, as well as the busy route to Kennedy Hot Springs. But that all changed with the big storm of October 2003. Much of the trail was obliterated, along with the hot springs and USFS Rd. 23 leading to the trailhead. The springs were murky, often crowded, and not exactly hot, but now certainly missed by many. The easy hike through old-growth forest close to the White Chuck River was worth a jaunt by itself—and may be again by 2008 if repairs are completed. Trips beyond to Lake Byrne or Kennedy Ridge and the PCT invite backpacking adventures. Check with the Forest Service for current conditions before heading out.

If the road has been fixed (it may not be), take Mountain Loop Hwy from Darrington to MP 44.7 and turn left on the White Chuck Rd. (Rd. 23) that leads 10.4 miles to the trailhead near its end (*elevation: 2,300 feet*). There's a good view of the volcano from the last half-mile of road. Once rebuilt, the trail will likely enter the Glacier Peak Wilderness in less than a mile and pass the Meadow Mt./Fire Mt. Trail on the left (**1.5 mi**), and Pumice Creek beyond. The old trail climbed moderately past Glacier Creek and a junction with the trail to Kennedy Ridge (**5.0 mi**; *elevation: 3,300 feet*). Here, a 1,000-foot climb leads to the ridge and PCT in under two miles. The White Chuck Trail continued 0.2 mile

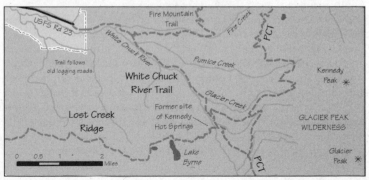

Lake Byrne.

across Kennedy Creek, past another link to the PCT (at Sitkum Creek), and across a river bridge to the now-hidden springs. The iron-rich (not sulphur) spring formerly had good flow with temperatures in the low-90s. A few remnants of the campground survived the flood.

Once across the White Chuck (assuming there's a bridge), a 2,300-foot trudge over 2.5 miles leads to Lake Byrne, great views of the volcano (look for climbers' tracks on the Sitkum Glacier toward the center of the mountain), and Lost Creek Ridge. The higher ground is only accessible later in the season when the winter snowpack has had a chance to melt, usually by mid or late-July. To continue up Lost Creek Ridge, head right over a hump then up through heather and huckleberry to a viewy crest north of the lake. A trail continues up the crest a half-mile to a rocky basin, and over a meadowy rise toward Camp Lake (below). Mt. Baker's white cone is above the horizon to the northwest, Sloan Peak juts to the southwest, and White Chuck Mt. rises to the northwest. An intermittent path continues west along the ridge for seven scenic miles to Round Lake (*see Hike 73*). Take care not to lose the trail on the return. High camps are feasible on Kennedy and Lost Creek Ridges and at Lake Byrne, and possibly good sites near the springs as well. Anticipate nosy bears and hang your food.

NORTH CASCADES—
72. Stujack Pass & Mount Pugh

Distance: 7.0 - 9.5 miles round trip   Time: Allow 6 - 10 hours
Elevation gain: 3,800 - 5,300 feet   Season: July - October

If you're an experienced Class 2-3 rock scrambler up for an exposed climb to a 7,201-foot summit, Mt. Pugh can be one of the more enjoyable hikes you'll find in the North Cascades. The trail to the site of an old fire lookout follows the crest of a sheer and narrow ridge in one section, and was literally blasted out of the cliffs in another. However, if that kind of thing is not your pod of peas, or there's still a lot of snow up high, the more moderate hike past Lake Metan to Stujack Pass is also a worthy objective. Mount Pugh is conspicuous from SR 530 and the Mountain Loop Hwy near Darrington and was known as *DaKlagwats* to natives, then was named for an area settler. The original fire lookout was built in 1919 but was destroyed many years ago. Old cable marks the lookout site.

From Mountain Loop Hwy out of Darrington (good view of Mt. Pugh dead-ahead near MP 45.3), turn left near MP 40.8 onto USFS Road 2095 and drive about 1.5 miles to the trailhead just around a sharp bend (*elevation: 1,900 feet*). Note: this road may be gated from mid-October through May to protect wildlife. The trail climbs moderately through woods the first mile (some big trees), then steepens with switchbacks to the sudden appearance of little Lake Metan (**1.6 mi**; *elevation: 3,200 feet*); stay left. The trail keeps climbing and finally reaches open

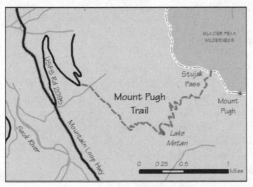

meadow at a campsite among boulders (**3.2 mi**); the path is to the right. Stujack Pass is clearly visible above as a deep notch in Pugh's northwest ridge (**3.8 mi**; *elevation: 5,700 feet*). The views are excellent: Three Fingers and Whitehorse Mt. to the west, White

Near the summit of Mt. Pugh

Chuck Mt. and the Mt. Baker volcano to the north-northwest, Sloan Peak to the south-southeast, and Mt. Rainier beyond and to the right.

Above the pass, the way is less defined, unmaintained, and may be snow-bound well into July. Steep snow—not to be taken lightly—requires an ice axe (and the skills to use it), and scrambling on steep rock with huge drop-offs suggests only the more experienced scramblers even consider it. Wait for August for a better shot at dry rock and a snow-free summit ascent. The scariest part of the hike may be a short steep section above a tiny glacier and not far beyond the knife-edge ridge with a natural 'sidewalk' that seems perfectly placed. Remember, too, that coming down is always more difficult than going up. The summit (**5.0 mi**; *elevation: 7,201 feet*) is broad and rounded and littered with the remains of the old fire lookout. Glacier Peak is a real loomer to the east. The sheer, 2,000-foot east wall of Mt. Pugh drops into the Pugh Creek basin. Round Lake is three miles to the southeast, and Mt. Forgotten is across the Sauk River to the southwest. Carry extra water if continuing beyond the pass.

NORTH CASCADES—
73. Round Lake & Lost Creek Ridge

Distance: 9.5 - 14.0 miles round trip   Time: Allow 7 - 12 hours
Elevation gain: 3,600 - 4,400 feet   Season: July - October

Near the west end of Lost Creek Ridge is a jewel of an alpine lake sunk in a bowl beneath a craggy skyline, appropriately named Round Lake. The trail leading to it links with the Lost Creek Ridge Trail and Lake Byrne, five crow-miles to the east (*see Hike 71*). Good overnight possibilities are feasible along the scenic ridge route, although water could be skimpy. To find the trail, drive the Mountain Loop Hwy from Darrington to MP 37.8 and turn left on USFS Rd. 49 which climbs into the North Fork Sauk River valley (*see Hike 50 for a short side-trip to North Fork Falls*). The trailhead is on the left 3.1 miles ahead (*elevation: 1,900 feet*). At a clearing a half-mile past the trailhead, Lost Creek Ridge, Bingley Gap, and steep-walled Spring Mountain are visible from the road.

The trail begins as an easy forest walk, sometimes wet, then becomes increasingly steep and switchbacked in the first two miles. Look south for glimpses of Sloan Peak's summit spire across the river valley. After a

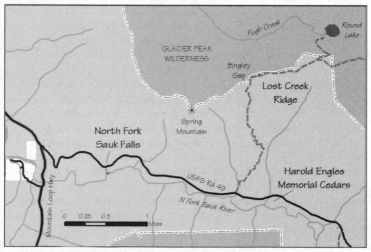

Round Lake.

stiff 2,500-foot gain, reach wooded Bingley Gap and the Glacier Peak Wilderness boundary that runs the ridge southwest to Spring Mountain (**3.0 mi**; *elevation: 4,400 feet*). A half-mile beyond is the first good view north to Mt. Pugh, White Chuck Mt., and Mt. Baker.

The incline soon moderates as the trail traverses Lost Creek Ridge in broad meadows (blueberries in late summer), with excellent views of Sloan Peak. At a junction, stay left for the nearby saddle (**4.5 mi**; *elevation: 5,500 feet*) and Round Lake in the basin below (**5.2 mi**; *elevation: 5,000 feet*). From the saddle, a steep boot track leads eastward, gaining 200 feet to a rocky knob with a great panorama from Mt. Pugh to Glacier Peak. To reach the lake (good camping) settled in the west-facing cirque below, follow the trail left and downward from the saddle. Or skip the lake, return to the junction before the saddle, and wander the meadows eastward along Lost Creek Ridge as far as time allows. Just around the next spur ridge (0.3 mile) is another great view of Glacier Peak. Beyond, the trail deteriorates on the way to Lake Byrne and may be hard to follow, so memorize the terrain for the return.

NORTH CASCADES—
74. North Fork Sauk River
Distance: 1.0 - 18.0+ miles round trip   Time: Allow 1 - 12 hours
Elevation gain: 100 - 4,400 feet   Season: May - November

If a terrific old-growth forest hike on mostly level trail far from civilization sounds appealing, check out the trail up the North Fork Sauk
River valley, southeast of Darrington. Two miles in you might even see
a mountain goat grazing the cliffs high above the trail. If that seems too
easy, there's an abrupt 3,000-foot climb from the valley floor for great
views and a strenuous workout. Longer multi-day back-country trips
into the heart of the Glacier Peak Wilderness and along the PCT or
Pilot Ridge (*Hike 76*) could also start here, although the higher trails
aren't normally snowfree until mid-July or later.

From Darrington, follow the Mountain Loop Hwy to the North
Fork Sauk River Rd. (USFS Rd. 49) at MP 37.8. Turn left and drive
6.6 miles to a junction; stay left again to reach the trailhead just
ahead (*elevation: 2,100 feet*). Giant Douglas fir and western red cedar trees up to nine feet in diameter line the first mile or so of trail,
with some of the biggest ones near the wilderness boundary (**0.5
mi**), a possible turn-around point for an easy stroll. A short stretch
may be wheelchair hikable. Other lowland tree species like western
hemlock, bigleaf maple, and red alder seem to have bumped into the
lower limit of Pacific silver fir, producing an exceptionally diverse

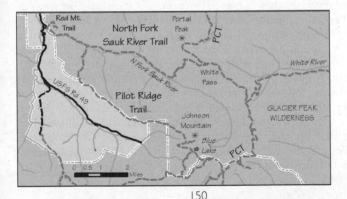

North Fork Sauk Trail.

forest. Red huckleberry, vine maple, several ferns, and the dreaded, but easily avoided, devil's club add to the mix.

Often close to the river, the wide path wanders along, a little up and down, past more big trees, several openings, and an avalanche slope and creek crossing (**1.3 mi**). Just across the creek look back over your right shoulder for a great view of the 7,835-foot summit of Sloan Peak and the Sloan Glacier to the west. A junction is reached (**2.0 mi**; *elevation: 2,400 feet*) where the trail to Pilot Ridge heads to the right and across the river. Just past the junction, pan the cliffs above for mountain goats. There's a high, multi-tiered waterfall here, although it peters out later in summer.

After a gain of only 900 feet, the Mackinaw Shelter (primitive) and campsites near the river are reached (**5.4 mi**; *elevation: 3,000 feet*). Just beyond, the trail begins an abrupt climb of 3,000 feet in under three miles to join the PCT in steep meadows (**8.2 mi**; *elevation: 6,000 feet*). A right here leads easily (if snow-free) to the sprawling wonderland of White Pass (**8.9 mi**). A left at the junction climbs 500 feet in 1.7 miles to Red Pass and beyond. Views improve rapidly about two miles above Mackinaw, but only the strongest hikers may have the legs for a day-trip to Red or White Pass. Allow plenty of time for the long, knee-pounding descent.

NORTH CASCADES—
75. Red Mountain Lookout

Distance: 1.8 miles round trip   Time: Allow 1 - 2 hours

Elevation gain: 800 feet   Season: May - October

The hike to the old Red Mt. lookout site above the North Fork Sauk River is short, steep, and scenic—a good place for an early season jaunt, or a fall one too if the snow hasn't started to pile up. Maybe combine the walk with a stroll up the North Fork Sauk River (*Hike 74, same trailhead; map, p. 150*), or with North Fork Falls (*Hike 50*), and the Harold Engles Memorial Cedars trail (*Hike 51*). The trailhead is south of Darrington off the North Fork Sauk River Rd. (*see Hike 74 for directions*).

From the trailhead (*elevation: 2,100 feet*), walk less than a hundred yards up the North Fork Sauk River Trail and turn left on the Red Mountain Lookout Trail. The narrow path among giant trees quickly finds steeper terrain, then switchbacks up the lower west slope of Red Mountain. Sloan Peak comes into view at a small clearing (**0.5 mi**). The trail forks near the remains of a shed, and the lookout site is a few paces to the right (**0.9 mi**; elevation: *2,900 feet*). The building is gone, but there is a good view of Sloan Peak and the Sloan Glacier to the southwest across the North Fork valley. Bedal Peak's summit rocks jag to the right. To the south, the Monte Cristo peaks tower above the Cadet Creek valley and Pride Basin six miles away.

It may be feasible for expert hikers to continue three miles up Red Mt. on steep, intermittent trail all the way to tiny Ruby Lake and meadows 2,600 feet above. From the lookout site, the old trail heads up and

right to a switchback, then a short, steep, rock scramble with an okay view. Confident route-finding and scrambling skills are mandatory, especially for the descent (a few old blazes). Carry extra water.

Sloan Peak and Glacier.

NORTH CASCADES—
76. Pilot Ridge

Distance: 10.0 - 13.0+ miles round trip Time: Allow 7 - 12+ hours
Elevation gain: 3,300 - 4,300+ feet   Season: Mid-July - October

Pilot Ridge above the North Fork of the Sauk River is best hiked as one leg of a multi-day loop, but can also be enjoyed by stronger hikers in a longish day (minimum 10 miles round trip). A steep climb leads to great views of the Monte Cristo range and Glacier Peak. The hike also requires a ford or log crossing of the river which, of course, is not advised during higher flows (a fat footlog was available in mid-2007).

The hike begins at the North Fork Sauk Trailhead (*see Hike 74 for directions; map, p. 150; elevation: 2,100 feet*). The Pilot Ridge Trail begins two miles up this trail (**2.0 mi**; *elevation: 2,400 feet*). Head right at the junction past a nice campsite and look for a good footlog over the river a few yards upstream—or turn back if there is no safe crossing. The trail is in good shape and heads up steeply with many switchbacks to a trailside trickle in rocks—possibly the last water after mid-summer (**3.0 mi**; *elevation: 3,500 feet*). Pass a good campsite, then finally reach a saddle followed by a steep ridge ascent to a rounded meadowy knoll (**5.0 mi**; *elevation: 5,400 feet*)—a good destination for a moderate dayhike with a good view of Kyes Peak (left), Monte Cristo Peak, Pride Glacier, The Cadets, and Sloan Peak (closer to the northwest), and Glacier Peak.

The trail descends 400 feet in woods then regains it all to more meadows (**6.5 mi**; *elevation: 5,600 feet*) and the start of a spectacular 4-mile stretch of high (and dry) country leading to Johnson Mt. and Blue Lake for an extended backpack. A 3-4 day circuit to the PCT, White Pass, and back down the North Fork Sauk makes a superb outing.

Monte Cristo Peaks from Pilot Ridge.

NORTH CASCADES—
77. Bedal Basin

Distance: 5.0 miles round trip   Time: Allow 4 - 6 hours
Elevation gain: 2,300 feet   Season: July - October

This is a more difficult hike on a rough, unmaintained trail into the upper basin of Bedal Creek, a modest tributary of the South Fork Sauk River. The trail is remote and doesn't normally see a lot of use, although it was once the principal climbing route to Sloan Peak, one of the more striking summits in the region. Harry Bedal built a small trapper's cabin in the meadows here, most of which has been reclaimed by the winds and whims of nature. When the snow recedes, some limited wandering is feasible above tree line, but routefinding skills are needed both to keep it safe and to find the way back home. Best to save this trek for better weather. And even then, it may be better left to more experienced pathfinders.

From Darrington follow the Mountain Loop Hwy to Bedal Campground and the bridge across the North Fork Sauk River. Continue another 0.7 mile (MP 36.6) and turn east onto USFS Rd. 4096. Drive this road three miles to the trailhead (*elevation: 2,800 feet; map, p. 156*). The old road is blocked beyond this point (but is walkable to Elliot Creek Trail; *see Hike 78*). Expect steep and rough sections on the drive in, as well as good views about two miles up of, right to left, Mt. Pugh (due north), White Chuck, Forgotten, Stillaguamish, Vesper, Sperry (to the southwest), and Morning Star Peaks. The trail climbs moderately from

Sloan Peak from Bedal Basin.

Monte Cristo Peaks from the ridge above Bedal Basin.

the start and steepens higher up. Anticipate a little mud, rocks, windfall, and thick brush in places.

The trail begins in pleasant old-growth forest, with some open areas, before reaching a junction (**1.5 mi**). The right fork crosses Bedal Creek on logs and rocks, but the left fork may be easier. The latter enters a rocky creek bed higher up, then follows this channel for several hundred yards, eventually climbing out the opposite side to resume progress on the old trail. Remember the entry and exit points along this section for the return (cairns may help). The tread climbs briefly then traverses south to a small flat meadow strewn with large boulders (**2.5 mi**; *elevation: 5,000 feet*). The disappearing remnants of the Bedal cabin are near a giant over-hanging rock. The immense rock wall of Sloan Peak looms above. One could continue up a partly wooded ridge to more openings with views of Mt. Baker, Three Fingers, Whitehorse, Bedal (north), Sloan, and the Monte Cristo Peaks (south), as well as the Sauk River valley below. Keep an eye trained for mountain goats. Retrace your steps for the return. In 2003, the Bedal Basin Trail was considered to be an "endangered" trail by the Washington Trails Association. If trail improvements are made, its primitive character should be maintained.

NORTH CASCADES—
78. Elliot Creek & Goat Lake

Distance: 9.0 miles round trip   Time: Allow 5 - 7 hours
Elevation gain: 1,300 feet   Season: June - October

The almost five-mile hike up Elliot Creek to Goat Lake can sometimes be done as late as November and is often snow-free by June, making it a good early-summer hike when many other mountain trails are still buried. Until the 2003 storm blew out the Mountain Loop Hwy (repairs should be completed in 2007), this was a popular hike in summer and fall. Pick a weekday or an imperfect weekend to better avoid the crowds. It seems hard to fathom, but in the 1890s an eight-mile puncheon wagon road from Monte Cristo to the lake was constructed via Elliot Creek (the old puncheon is still visible along the creek trail and near Mountain Loop Hwy). A number of cabins, a hotel, and other buildings existed near the lake's outlet, most of which were destroyed by fire.

About 3.5 miles north of Barlow Pass on the Mountain Loop

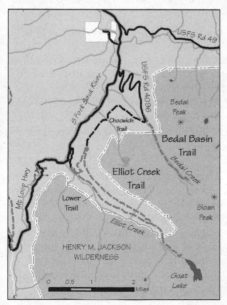

Hwy, turn east on USFS Rd. 4080 (MP 34.2) and drive another mile to the trailhead (limited parking; *elevation: 1,900 feet*). At the trailhead, there are two options: one trail immediately descends (briefly) from the parking area to the creek, then follows the pleasant and historic wagon road up-valley before reaching a junction (**3.2 mi**; *elevation: 2,800 feet*) with a second trail that leaves the parking area to the left of the first trail. This upper trail follows an old logging road and passes a junction with another old road on the left

Goat Lake and Cadet Peak.

about a mile from the trailhead (this spur, also called the Chocwich Trail, leads north about 2.5 miles to the Bedal Basin trailhead with a gain of just a few hundred feet, passing a small waterfall on Chocwich Creek; *see Hike 77*). The main path to Goat Lake stays right and meets the junction with the lower trail at 3.5 miles from the trailhead. The two trails offer an attractive loop. The distances noted below assume you hiked in via the lower route along the old wagon road. Above the upper junction, the old logging grade fades and the trail passes huge cedar trees near the Henry M. Jackson Wilderness boundary (**3.8 mi**). The last half-mile to Goat Lake steepens to switchbacks where McIntosh Falls makes a headlong tumble to the right.

At the lake (**4.7 mi**; *elevation: 3,200 feet*) one can wander the lakeshore toward a waterfall (gets brushy) while watching for fish, or gaze up-basin toward snowy Ida Pass and Cadet Peak for signs of the determined prospectors who roamed these craggy mountains in search of the mother lode. Trails once led to Ida Pass and the Foggy Mine near the base of Cadet Peak, 1,500 feet above the lake. The extensive mining bustle that occurred here a century ago has almost entirely disappeared.

NORTH CASCADES—
79. Barlow Point

Distance: 2.2 miles round trip   Time: Allow 2 - 3 hours
Elevation gain: 900 feet   Season: June - November

At the headwaters of the Sauk and Stillaguamish Rivers near Barlow Pass, a low ridge with a rocky top affords reasonable views of the upper basins of both watersheds. Depending on snow conditions, the Barlow Point Trail can open by mid-spring and makes a nice early season jaunt when higher trails are snowbound. Although it's just one long mile to the top, expect a steep workout with plenty of switchbacks. Barlow Point is also a good place for a summer sunrise (or set). There is no water on this trail. From Granite Falls head east on Mountain Loop Hwy to MP 30.6 and park up the hill on the left just before the pass (*elevation: 2,400 feet; map, p. 159*).

The trail leaves the parking area and bounces up and down through woods, over a rocky hump, then downward beneath large rock outcrops. Just past a clearing the trail splits. Left drops 50 yards to the old Monte Cristo Railroad grade. Stay right for Barlow Point. At another junction close by (**0.3 mi**), a left follows the hardly used Old Government Trail leading down-valley to the highway near Sunrise Mine Rd. Instead, go right and climb to the ridge crest (**0.6 mi**). More switchbacks lead past an occasional glimpse of Sheep Mountain to the southeast. Finally, the top arrives (**1.1 mi**; *elevation: 3,300 feet*). Trees prevent a full panorama, but views are good nonetheless. To the west Big Four and Hall Peak rise above the South Fork Stilly. Twin Peaks and Mt. Dickerman are to

the north and northwest; the South Fork Sauk valley extends northeast toward Mt. Pugh; and Sheep Mt. stands close by to the southeast. Drop-offs along the crest deserve some respect.

Sheep Mt.

80. Monte Cristo & Glacier Basin

Distance: 8.5 - 14.0 miles round trip Time: Allow 5 - 10 hours
Elevation gain: 400 - 2,300 feet Season: June - October

The popular hike to the old mining townsite of Monte Cristo east of Granite Falls follows an old road along the South Fork Sauk River and is an easy four-mile stroll with two river crossings on bridges. The longer hike past Glacier Falls and up into Glacier Basin, two miles beyond the townsite, is more challenging with a harder, steep section near the end that may not be for everyone. The historic townsite was developed in the 1890s after a promising discovery of rich gold ore high on the ridge southwest of Glacier Basin. Millions of dollars were invested in mines, trams, a railroad, and infrastructure for a city of 2,000 people in this wild and remote setting, yet the effort never broke even and was mostly abandoned by 1907. The townsite is a fine destination, but for the big-

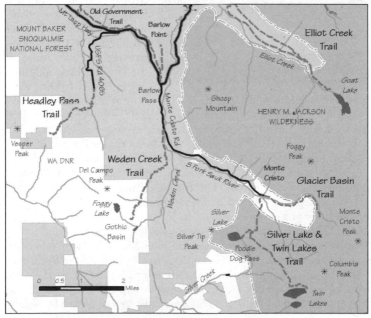

Glacier Basin and Monte Cristo Peak (left).

ger scenic payoff you'll have to trudge up to Glacier Falls or Glacier Basin (may still be under snow in early July).

From Granite Falls head east on the Mountain Loop Hwy to MP 30.6 and the trailhead at Barlow Pass (*elevation: 2,400 feet*). Cross the highway and walk or mountain bike the obvious gated road leading to Monte Cristo (bikes are banned beyond the townsite). Cross the Sauk River on a bridge (**1.1 mi**). Flood damage in 2006 impacted the crossing here, although experienced hikers were getting through in mid-2007 (turn back if unsure). Trudge on awhile, pass a few private cabins, then a campground before crossing a good bridge leading into the townsite (**4.0 mi**; *elevation: 2,800 feet*). The U.S. Forest Service and the non-profit Monte Cristo Preservation Association help look after the townsite. In its heyday Monte Cristo supported at least five hotels, three saloons, a newspaper, and the railroad. Most miners, amazingly, lived on the higher slopes close to the mines.

Wander past a railroad turntable, historic cabins, and the site of an old lodge at a grassy clearing. The lodge operated until it burned in 1983. Cross Seventy-Six Creek on a good footbridge (left) and follow Dumas St. past Peabody's Garage and Kyes Memorial (a WWII Navy commander who, as a boy, planted this tree in front of the Royal Hotel). At a junction follow the signs (left and right) to Glacier Basin (or wander right to see the sites of a schoolhouse, assay office, hotel, and blacksmith shop on the way to Sunday Falls; *see also Hike 81*). Nearby are the remains of the large Boston-American Concentrator that prepared the mined ore for shipment to a smelter in Everett.

The main trail merges with the old Mine-to-Market Road (**4.9 mi**) and continues to the brink of an eroding slope above the creek with good views of surrounding peaks, Glacier Falls, and other waterfalls up-valley, lacy and thundering in early summer. Either turn around here or head for the basin above the falls. The trail climbs straight up the mountainside right of the falls and enters the Henry M. Jackson Wilderness. Pass a rock outcrop next to crashing water then keep climbing the steep bedrock path (tougher coming back down) until the trail finally eases off at Mystery Ridge and the entrance to the basin (**6.3 mi**; *elevation: 4,500 feet*). The creek meanders peacefully through fragile meadows. Look for the old mine road, cables, clutter, and waterlines upslope in talus. A half-mile ahead, Ray's Knoll is a good perch to admire Monte Cristo Peak rising from the head of the valley. Cadet Peak is to the northeast, and the huge maze of rock walls and towers known as Wilmans Peaks and Spires is to the south and west. The highest mine in the area—the 3,000-foot long Comet Mine—was 1,000 feet up this ridge, although it too has collapsed.

NORTH CASCADES—

81. Poodle Dog Pass, Silver & Twin Lakes

Distance: 12.5 - 18.0 miles round trip   Time: Allow 6 - 12 hours
Elevation gain: 2,000 - 3,800 feet   Season: July - October

The Silver Lake Trail to Poodle Dog Pass begins at the old mining town of Monte Cristo east of Granite Falls and climbs two miles to the subalpine meadows around Silver Lake (*see Hike 80 for directions to the townsite; map, p. 159*). For backpackers and marathon dayhikers, a continuation to Twin Lakes adds another 5.5 miles roundtrip and 2,000 feet of climbing (in and out), although you can trim more than a mile and cut a third of the elevation gain by zipping over for the view and not dropping down to these latter lakes. Silver Lake, on the other hand, is an easy walk from the pass. There's good camping at both lakes.

Walk or bike (if passable) from the Mountain Loop Hwy at Barlow Pass to Monte Cristo (**4.0 mi**; *elevation: 2,800 feet*). Continue through the townsite to Seventy-Six Creek, but don't cross and head right instead

Columbia Peak from the trail to Twin Lakes.

(follow signs). Continue upward on steepening path, passing the commotion of Sunday Falls before entering the Henry M. Jackson Wilderness. The path sets aim for Poodle Dog Pass and soon merges with remnants of a former trail from the townsite. Before the pass, openings offer good views of Foggy and Cadet Peaks and Addison Ridge. Pleasant Poodle Dog Pass (**6.0 mi**; *elevation: 4,400 feet*) was named by early prospectors for the furry marmots commonly seen here and throughout the western slopes of the North Cascades. Silver Lake is an easy 0.2-mile walk to the west (left goes to Twin Lakes). The pretty lake is enclosed in the meadowed arms of Silvertip Peak rising 1,800 feet above the shore. From the lake, a miners' trail once descended Silver Creek to more old mining claims, Mineral City (*Hike 58*), and the road to Index and U.S. Hwy. 2.

If the snow is mostly gone and a longer hike beckons, head up from the pass on a generally good trail through woods and meadow, climbing to the crest in less than a half-mile with more good views that get better as you go. The gold rush of Monte Cristo began nearby on July 4, 1889, when Joseph Pearsall spotted iron-rich deposits on Wilmans Peaks and Spires to the northeast across Seventy-Six Gulch (named by Pearsall). The trail traverses open slopes then descends to bypass a large rock face before climbing a short distance to woodsy Wilmans Pass. Follow the trail to the next rocky hump on the ridge for an excellent panorama (**7.5 mi**). Seventy-Six Gulch, spectacular Wilmans Spires, and Columbia Peak (the close one) and its waterfalls dominate the view. Sheep Gap Mt. and the Crested Buttes scratch the sky to the west. Ahead, lingering snow fields may prevent safe passage without an ice axe until mid-July or later. Expect minor brush and rock scrambling as the route runs the ridge another half-mile then ducks right around the high point to reach a fantasmical view of Twin Lakes set in Columbia Peak's huge western cirque (**8.0 mi**; *elevation: 5,400 feet*). Classy mountain hemlock trees frame the view. An interesting isthmus separates the two lakes. It's less than a mile but almost 700 feet down to the lakes from here, which may be more than most sane hikers are apt to try in a dayhike from Barlow Pass. If biking the road to Monte Cristo, however, the hiking distance is a tad more feasible.

NORTH CASCADES—
82. Weden Creek & Gothic Basin

Distance: 8.0 - 13.0 miles round trip   Time: Allow 6 - 10 hours
Elevation gain: 2,800 - 3,300 feet   Season: Mid-July - October

With all the great trails and spectacular mountains clustered around the headwaters of the South Fork Sauk and South Fork Stillaguamish Rivers, one might think there would be at least one easy route to the alpine zone. If there is, the old miners' trail to Gothic Basin isn't it. Stronger hikers should expect a longish climb on steep trail to the little lakes, tarns, meadows, and rocky terrain that beautify the basin. The lower half of the trail is in national forest, but the upper half traverses land managed by the Washington Department of Natural Resources (DNR) as the Morning Star Natural Resources Conservation Area. In fact, 6,610-foot Del Campo Peak at the head of the basin, and one of the region's most striking and dominant summits, is within this NRCA—representing the highest point of state land in Snohomish County.

The trail is reached from Barlow Pass and the old road to Monte Cristo (*map, p. 159*). Park near the pass east of Granite Falls at MP 30.6 on the Mountain Loop Hwy (*elevation: 2,400 feet*). Walk the gated gravel road to the signed trail on the right (**1.1 mi**) immediately before the

Three Fingers and Whitehorse Mt. from Gothic Peak.

bridge over the South Fork Sauk. If flood damage from a 2006 storm has been repaired (as expected), an easy half-mile of trail will cross an unnamed creek then head steeply up a ridge west of Weden Creek. The route traverses several basins, skipping over plunging streams with waterfalls and mountain views—and possible snow bridges, avalanche danger, and high runoff in early season. Keep an eye out for old mining relics, an old cabin site (**2.5 mi**), and a nice waterfall (**3.2 mi**). After a gain of 2,700 feet, the trail reaches a ridge crest (**4.0 mi**; *elevation 5,200 feet*), then rocky meadows and the first little lakes and tarns just ahead. The twin summits of Sheep Gap Mt. rise to the south.

Hang out at the tarns or wander ice-carved rocks (remember the route back to the tarns), or head northward over a rise about 0.3 mile to fishless Foggy Lake (also called Crater Lake), an icy jewel beneath Del Campo Peak. The lake can hold ice in August. From near the outlet it's possible to hike/scramble up the rocky slopes of Gothic Peak for a great view from the ridge (for climbers the summit is a short class 3 scramble). Tin Cup Lake is the puddle east of Foggy. A few old inconspicuous mine shafts and adits and other traces of the area's mining history are visible south of the tarns and along the trail. O. N. Weedin, from whence the name comes, apparently got in a fight over water with four neighbors on the Sauk River. He killed them and then himself.

83. Headlee Pass

Distance: 4.8 - 6.0 miles round trip   Time: Allow 4 - 7 hours
Elevation gain: 2,300 - 2,600 feet   Season: Mid-July - October

If steep and scenic suits your wilderness hankerings, an ascent of the old miners' trail to Headlee Pass and beyond may be a perfect candidate. Views are great from the start and only get better with elevation. And the elevation comes quick. After an easier first half-mile, expect a 2,500-foot climb in less than two miles more to the pass. But steep is good in this instance, or this would be a much more popular place. (Experienced climbers can also look forward to a Class 2 or 3 scramble up Vesper or Sperry Peaks, but lingering snow in summer may require an ice axe.) This rough trail may not be the best choice for beginners.

The scenic trailhead is west of Barlow Pass at the end of the Sunrise Mine Rd. (USFS Rd. 4065). Leave the Mountain Loop Hwy at MP 28.8 and drive Rd. 4065 2.2 miles to the parking area (*elevation: 2,400 feet; map, p. 159*). To the south the layered slabs of Del Campo Peak rise up the valley beyond Morning Star Peak. Sperry Peak is the giant pyramid to the southwest. Follow the trail a short distance up a small creek and boulder-hop or cross on a bridge (if it hasn't washed away). Cross another on rocks, then a bigger stream—the veritable South Fork Stillaguamish River (**0.5 mi**), which can be tricky or dangerous without a footlog if the water's high. It's usually low enough to cross by mid-summer. Turn back if uncertain. Just before the "river" watch for a spur to the left leading to the collapsed Manley miner's cabin.

The path quickly enters open avalanche slopes and climbs several switchbacks before rounding a ridge to enter rocky Wirtz Basin between Sperry and Morning Star Peaks. There are forty switchbacks in the upper basin, many of them short and steep over loose rock. Glimpse Glacier Peak to the northeast just before the craggy wooded pass, named for Sunrise Mines prospector F. M. Headlee (**2.4 mi**; *elevation: 4,700 feet*). Note that hard snow may persist in the chute below the pass into mid-summer, suggesting the need for an ice axe (and the skills to use it) even in July. Forget it if it's questionable. Take care not to dislodge rocks onto other hikers.

Beyond the pass, the route briefly traverses a wooded slope to steep,

Steep, short swithbacks below Headlee Pass.

loose scree and talus. There are a couple of tricky spots, although the path is generally distinct. Head westward to a little cascade (Vesper Creek) then northwest into a scenic snowy basin with a little icy lake between Sperry Peak to the northeast and Vesper Peak to the southwest (**2.8 mi**). From the cascade, a steep climbers' path ascends a meadowed ridge to Vesper's snowfields and bigger views. (Experienced climbers with an ice axe should be able to find their way up either peak without difficulty. There are sheer drop-offs at both summits. Avalanches can be a concern early season.) To see the Sunrise Mines, look across the valley of Vesper Creek from the east edge of the scree slope near Headlee Pass.

84. Mount Dickerman

Distance: 8.6 miles round trip   Time: Allow 6 - 9 hours
Elevation gain: 3,700 feet   Season: July - October

Few trails lead to the summit of a mountain in the North Cascades of Snohomish County. Happily, the Mt. Dickerman Trail is one of them. And that suggests two things: one, great panoramic views, and two, a long haul up. With regard to the first, the views are indeed splendiferous, from Glacier Peak, Mt. Baker, Mt. Rainier, and the Olympics in the distance, to Stillaguamish Peak and Mt. Forgotten, neighbors to the north. Sloan and Bedal Peaks rise to the east (right of Glacier Peak), the Monte Cristo peaks to the southeast, Del Campo and Morning Star

Peaks to the south, Sperry and Vesper Peaks, Big Four, and Hall Peak to the southwest across the South Fork Stillaguamish River valley, and Three Fingers and Whitehorse to the northwest. Way down Dickerman's northwest face—3,000 feet below—Perry Creek tumbles through its lush valley. With regard to the up part, there's definitely a lot of it. The trailhead, at 2,000 feet, is not 100 feet above the river, which puts the 5,723-foot summit 3,700 feet higher. Go early to beat the heat and the crowds. Beware of cliffs below steep snow in early summer (turn back if unsure).

The trailhead and parking area are east of Granite Falls on the north side of the Mountain Loop Hwy at MP 27.4 (*map, p. 169*). The route immediately heads up through an attractive forest of Douglas fir and western red cedar. The smaller trees attest to a big forest fire here in the early 1900s. Dozens of switchbacks and a couple miles later the route begins traversing northward past big cliffs and crosses a stream (**2.4 mi**; *elevation: 4,400 feet*); steep snow here and beyond may force a retreat in early summer. Pass a tarn and expanding views, especially to the southwest. The trail wanders to ridge crest views, and bends east to climb through rock garden meadows of heather, huckleberry, and wildflowers. Good trail and maybe some lingering snow lead to the final summit hump and the 360-degree view (**4.3 mi**; *elevation: 5,723 feet*). Water can be scarce in late summer.

*Big Four Mt. from
Mt. Dickerman Trail*

NORTH CASCADES—
85. Perry Creek Falls & Mt. Forgotten Meadows

Distance: 3.8 - 8.0 miles round trip   Time: Allow 3 - 8 hours
Elevation gain: 1,100 - 3,200 feet   Season: June - October

By late spring the trail up Perry Creek may be snow-free and passable to Perry Creek Falls, as a half-year of winter relents and the low to mid-elevations of the Cascades begin to open up. The route to the meadows, however, will likely be under snow until July. Although a May or June hike to the falls has some appeal, avalanche danger can persist during these (and prior) months, particularly below the huge gullies coming off Mt. Dickerman. The trail has some rough sections and is moderately steep overall, but easy to follow. Unique plant communities make this a fragile area and botanists will appreciate the diversity of ferns and flowers in the lower valley. To ensure its protection and to further ongoing scientific study in the valley, the Forest Service established a Research Natural Area at Perry Creek in 1997.

The trailhead (*elevation: 2,100 feet*) and a skinny parking area are

Montane residents, more often seen hanging out in the woods.

a mile up the Perry Creek Rd. (USFS Rd. 4063) which heads north from the Mountain Loop Hwy at MP 26.4 east of Granite Falls. Stay left at a fork in 0.6 mile. Big Four Mt. is visible down-valley. The trail is easy at first, then quickly enters open slopes and abundant fern gardens below the imposing northwest face of Mt. Dickerman (*Hike 84*). High waterfalls tumble down big rock walls in spring and early summer. Stillaguamish Peak rises above the north side of the valley. Look for a variety of ferns, wild ginger, trillium, meadow rue, fringe cup, and miner's lettuce among the wild bouquets of the lower valley.

Perry Creek Falls (**1.9 mi**; *elevation: 3,200 feet*) is reached about an hour from the trailhead—a good turn-around early in the season. The trail passes near the brink of the falls, so be cautious peering into the chasm below. Perry Creek is crossed just ahead and may be your last reliable water later in summer. Traverse a giant rotten log and pass a couple of campsites, then continue up more steeply through old-growth forest and switchbacks until a high meadow and trail fork are finally encountered just below the crest of a ridge (**3.6 mi**; *elevation: 5,000 feet*). A nice campsite is perched on the ridge. The path climbs rightward briefly in trees to a large open meadow, then ends at a drop-off (**4.0 mi**; *elevation: 5,300 feet*). The views of snowy peaks and rocky summits are excellent—and so are the blueberries which should be pickable by mid-summer. A steep climber's path drops below a crag then contin-ues up the south and southeast flanks of Mt. Forgotten close by, with views of Glacier Peak between Sloan Peak (right) and Mt. Pugh (left). Steep snow and rock make the final ascent of the 6,005-foot peak suitable only for experienced mountaineers. From the earlier ridge crest campsite, a wandering boot track heads west toward Stillaguamish Peak a mile and a half away.

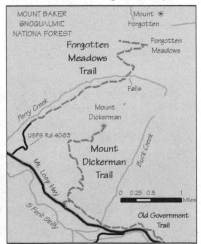

169

NORTH CASCADES—
86. Coal Lake & Pass Lake

Distance: 0.5 - 1.0 mile round trip   Time: Allow 1 - 2 hours
Elevation gain: 0 - 300 feet   Season: June - October

When all you need is a quick dip in a cool mountain lake a stone's throw from the car, Coal Lake might just do it, but expect to bump elbows with fellow lake-lovers on nice summer weekends. Weekdays or off-season will give you more room to thrash. The lakeshore is a little rugged, but loungeable. If Coal Lake is busy, look for peace and serenity at Pass Lake, still a short walk and accessed from the same parking lot. From Mountain Loop Hwy east of Granite Falls turn north onto the Coal Lake Rd. (USFS Rd. 4060) just before the east entrance to Big Four Ice Caves (MP 26). Drive this road 4.5 miles to the parking area on the left (*elevation: 3,400 feet*). Several very short paths across the road lead to Coal Lake and the narrow valley that contains it. For a bit of privacy try the talus on the north shore or paddle, row, or swim up-lake as desired.

Walk up the road 0.1 mile to find the Pass Lake Trail on the right. After 0.3 mile of moderate climbing in woods, skirt right of a meadow, then rise briefly to the lakeshore beyond. A brushy, unmaintained trail descends to North Fork Falls Creek.

Pass Lake.

NORTH CASCADES—
87. Independence Lake & North Lake
Distance: 2.0 - 7.0 miles round trip   Time: Allow 2 - 7 hours
Elevation gain: 200 - 2,300 feet   Season: July - October

The hike to Independence Lake has some ups and downs, but is only 0.7 mile each way so it's plenty popular. North Lake, on the other hand, is a grind, requiring a steep climb of 1,200 feet beyond Independence Lake followed by a drop of nearly 800 feet to the seldom visited lakeshore. Views are excellent and the hike to the ridge is worthwhile even without descending all the way to North Lake. A lake-sized tarn (not shown on some maps) and many small pools add some pizzazz to the trek. If you're lucky, you might see an osprey take a fish from one of the larger lakes. Listen for its high-pitched chittering.

The trailhead is at the end of Coal Lake Rd. (*elevation: 3,600 feet*), 0.3 mile beyond the Coal Lake parking lot (*see Hike 86 for directions*).

The path climbs out of a 1961 clearcut past monkey flowers, pearly everlasting, grass of Parnassus, foamflower, fireweed, and cow parsnip. Enter old-growth forest then descend on a moderate grade over the next quarter-mile, before regaining the elevation plus 100 feet or so. A big rock wall east of the lake comes into view just before reaching the lake. The trail crosses the outlet stream and passes above the west shore, then descends to a lovely meadow at the north end (**1.0 mi**; *elevation: 3,700 feet*). Find good campsites in trees with a privy nearby. Here the trail heads right to steep switchbacks in woods and flowery avalanche slopes. After a brief descent to a small clearing, the path climbs to a crest with a view (**2.0 mi**). Walk left a few yards for a look, but to continue go right 0.1 mile to an inconspicuous junction just past a little tarn. The North Lake trail heads left up a small rockslide (yellow paint marks the spot), or go straight another 0.1 mile to pass between two lovely tarns. There are good views of Whitehorse Mt., Three Fingers, and Devil's Thumb nearby.

Heading up from the rockslide junction, enter woods again and cross a saddle (**2.2 mi**; *elevation 4,900 feet*) with views of North Lake and Glacier Peak just beyond. White Chuck Mt. and Mt. Pugh (left of Glacier Peak) are also prominent. The trail to this modest-sized lake descends almost 800 feet in a circuitous route in meadows, rock slabs, and trees. The path goes well left, then right, passing numerous tarns and pools and some good campsites on the mile-plus descent to the lake (**3.4 mi**; *elevation 4,100 feet*). One could also just hike down 0.2 mile for a better view of the lake and stop there, avoiding the long climb back to the ridge.

Independence Lake.

88. Deer Creek Pass & Kelcema Lake

Distance: 1.0 - 2.2 miles round trip   Time: Allow 1 - 2 hours

Elevation gain: 0 - 300 feet   Season: June - November

A short, level walk to a pretty mountain lake, this one sees a lot of use since it's so easy to get to. The trail seems like a good candidate for reconstruction to a barrier-free standard for the less mobile among us. That might increase use somewhat, but the payoff for kids, seniors, and others may be worth the cost. For now, expect mostly good trail with some rough spots and a little mud. From MP 23.4 on the Mountain Loop Hwy, east of Granite Falls, turn north on the Deer Creek Rd. Beyond, the highway is often closed and under snow in winter; the large parking area accommodates skiers and snowmobilers (the latter are banned from Deer Creek Rd. in winter to protect wildlife). To reach Kelcema Lake, drive the Deer Creek Rd. 4.2 miles to the trailhead and parking area on the left (*elevation: 3,100 feet*). Walk the trail easily to a big campsite that's obviously a tad too close to the lakeshore. Wander left to a log jam and a nice view, then go right along the shore to a giant boulder with a scrabble path up the backside (**0.5 mi**). This perch makes a good destination, with deep water for a swim close by.

From the same trailhead, wander up the road fifty feet to the Deer Creek Pass trail on the left. This old unmaintained trail climbs through minor brush to slightly better trail in the woods, then attains the ridge just above the pass (**0.6 mi**; *elevation: 3,400 feet*). Contour around to a west-facing avalanche slope and a good view of Three Fingers, Big Bear, and Liberty Mts. Poke around the trees some to find a view of Whitehorse Mt. right of Three Fingers. The trail continues down and northward a short mile to the Clear Creek logging road, perhaps not quite worth the trouble.

Kelcema Lake.

NORTH CASCADES—

89. Cutthroat Lakes & Bald Mountain

Distance: 7.0 - 9.4+ miles round trip   Time: Allow 4 - 7+ hours
Elevation gain: 1,100 - 1,800+ feet   Season: July - October

Impressive views from the summit ridge of Bald Mt. and the enchanted meadows around Cutthroat Lakes are main attractions of this moderate hike into the state-owned highlands between the South Fork Stilly and Spada Lake in the Sultan River basin. The mountain's six-mile ridge is part of the Mt. Pilchuck Natural Resources Conservation Area. Just east of the mountain's middle, a craggy granite summit rises to 4,851 feet near Cutthroat Lakes. Two trailheads allow access from the west and north, creating options for moderate to strenuous dayhikes or overnight treks. To visit the lakes—and a veritable galaxy of tarns and pools that surround them—head for the Walt Bailey Trail beginning at Mallardy Ridge. Then either hike up and back for a seven to ten-mile roundtrip, or spot a car at the Ashland Lakes Trailhead (*see Hike 91*) for a one-way 15-mile trek. The hike could also begin at Ashland Lakes.

Tarn near Cutthroat Lakes.

Expect some rough or brushy sections along the ridge, but mostly good trail otherwise.

To reach the Mallardy trailhead, head east from Granite Falls on the Mountain Loop Hwy to MP 18.1 and turn right on USFS Rd. 4030, just west of the South Fork Stilly bridge. Follow this one-lane paved road 1.4 miles and turn right on Rd. 4032 (pavement ends here). The trailhead is another 5.7 miles ahead at the end of the road, but since there is very little room to park or turn-around, it may be easier to stop at shoulder parking areas 0.1 mile or 0.4 mile from the road end (*elevation: 3,200 feet; map, p. 179*). Note that a washout blocked the road 4.2 miles from the trailhead in mid-2007 (may be repaired). There's a good view of Mt. Pilchuck about 0.8 mile back down the road. The trail climbs the bank and soon enters old-growth forest, then a few small meadows. Pass a much larger meadow at the foot of Bald Mt. before crossing a narrow brook (**1.6 mi**). Although the trail tread is sometimes good and sometimes not due to slippery roots and occasional mud holes, the quality of the work that's been done to improve this trail is excellent. Much progress has been made to upgrade the worst parts and it will surely get better over time. Kudos to CCC-veteran Walt Bailey and other volunteers for much hard work over the years.

Some minor ups and downs lead to an open basin and meadowy talus with a waterfall close by. The trail reenters forest (**2.0 mi**), climbs to another broad flat, then switchbacks up more talus and woods to big subalpine meadows and the first tarn (**3.0 mi**). There are views here of Big Four Mt. and Sperry Peak. Reach a much larger tarn just ahead then several more beyond, each one prettier than the last. Pass above lower Cutthroat Lake, then cross the cascading outlet of the upper lake (**3.5 mi**; *elevation: 4,200 feet*). Spur trails lead to a number of good campsites. Either relax near the lake, take a dip, and head back from here, or wander the meadows (unless wet) around the upper lake. Take note of local landmarks—like this lake's small rock island and peninsula, each with a single tree, and the summit crag of Bald Mt. to the south—to lessen the odds of ending up somewhere down Boardman Creek, discouraged or lost. The main trail runs along the south shore of the lake and climbs in trees and meadow, with views of Three Fingers and Whitehorse Mt. to the north, to a hidden junction with the official Bald Mt. Trail (**4.0 mi**). If you miss the junction, you'll cross the ridge in another 0.1 mile and begin descending an old trail to logging roads above Spada Lake. From the junction, take the less-used path down slightly, then across gentle rocky meadows 0.2 mile to the ridge crest south of the summit crag. There's an amazing view here of Spada Lake, Mt. Rainier, and dozens of other peaks.

For the summit or a longer trek to Ashland Lakes, keep walking. The next stretch swings west around the summit and climbs to an even better view from a ridge leading directly up to the top (**4.7 mi**). Everett, the Sound, and the Olympics are all visible. Experienced rock scramblers can follow a faint boot track and possible cairns up and right to an easy class 2-3 route to the summit (may be a loose block on top). The seldom-hiked trail winds along the rocky-wooded crest of Bald Mt. for the next six miles with a few major ups and downs, and occasional views of the lakes and tarns that characterize the region, and the mountains beyond. The path finally descends 1,000 feet in two miles to the Ashland Lakes Trail, two miles from that trailhead.

NORTH CASCADES—
90. Boardman Lake & Lake Evan
Distance: 0.5 - 2.0 miles round trip   Time: Allow 1 - 3 hours
Elevation gain: 0 - 300 feet   Season: June - October

Lake Evan, while just a hundred easy yards from the parking lot, hardly counts as a hike, but the setting is pleasant and surely worth a visit. Via the same trail, the hike to Boardman Lake is still an easy trek for most of us, and is far more interesting. Not only is the lake more dramatic, but the forest walk getting there winds through beautiful old-growth Douglas fir, red cedar, western hemlock, and silver fir, all perfectly placed among huckleberries (usually pickable by August). Note that some years the area may be accessible in May. The hike can also be combined with Ashland or Bear and Pinnacle Lakes nearby (*see Hikes 91 & 92*).

From Mountain Loop Hwy east of Granite Falls, turn right at MP 15.8 onto USFS Rd. 4020, signed for Ashland Lakes. Stay left at a fork in 2.7 miles and drive another 2.2 miles (some views) to the obvious trailhead just beyond a sharp bend (*elevation: 2,800 feet; map, p. 177*). The trail rounds the marshy shore of Lake Evan, climbs slightly

Lake Boardman.

through big trees, then eases off before climbing again to a low ridge north of Boardman Lake (**0.8 mi**; *elevation: 3,000 feet*). Descend to a little gravel beach and log jam at the lake's outlet, Boardman Creek. If the water isn't too high it should be easy to cross here, climb steps, and follow paths to nearby campsites or to a good resting perch along the rocky shore. When the lake's busy, try the quiet cove about 0.2 mile down the east shore. Bald Mt. rises steeply to the south.

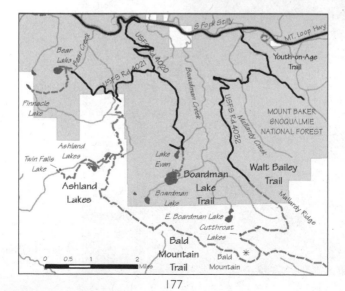

NORTH CASCADES—
91. Ashland Lakes & Twin Falls

Distance: 5.8 - 10.4 miles round trip   Time: Allow 2 - 6 hours
Elevation gain: 400 - 1,000 feet   Season: May - October

I believe it was a dayhike with the Pilchuck Audubon Society in the late 1970s that introduced me to Ashland Lakes. The trail, including much boardwalk, was newly built and we were eager to see what was there. The lakes were quiet, mysterious, and thoroughly inviting, despite a morning of drizzle and mist permeating our raingear. On a visit years later, the clouds and mist hung just as stubbornly as before from a dripping tarp sky. Then just as we were leaving, the clouds parted, confirming that a sunny day at Ashland Lakes is quite possible after all.

To reach the trailhead from Mountain Loop Hwy east of Granite Falls, turn south on USFS Rd. 4020 at MP 15.8. Stay right in 2.7 miles (Rd. 4021), then left 1.4 miles beyond. The trail and parking area (*elevation: 2,400 feet*) are 0.2 mile up this steep, bumpy road. The route follows an old logging road and crosses Black Creek in the first half-

Lower Ashland Lake.

178

Twin Falls Lake.

mile, then leaves the road and enters old-growth forest (**1.0 mi**; *elevation: 2,600 feet*). The tread varies from dirt to mud to single and double-plank boardwalk to log rounds to rock steps to whatever it takes to get a hiker through the woods on generally wet ground. Improvements are ongoing, although most of the trail is quite walkable. Gain 400 feet to the first lake, then easier grades to the next two.

At a junction (**1.6 mi**), a left leads 0.1 mile to Beaver Plant Lake (*elevation: 2,800 feet*). A former half-mile boardwalk loop around this scenic lake/bog has rotted away, exacerbated by some eager beavers whose dam building habits caused periodic inundation followed by dam failures. From the last junction, stay right 0.2 mile to reach the Bald Mt. Trail on the left (**1.8 mi**), which climbs 1,000 feet in two miles to the top of a six-mile long ridge, then runs its entire length to a link with the Walt Bailey Trail and Mallardy Ridge to the east (*see Hike 89*). For upper and lower Ashland Lakes, keep right to reach another fork in 0.1 mile. The left fork leads around the south side of Upper Ashland Lake. The right fork is in better condition and follows the north shore. The two rejoin at the west end of the lake (**2.3 mi**). This is a good turn-around point for a shorter hike. Or, continue on the main trail to one more junction (**2.6 mi**). Left drops a short distance to Lower Ashland Lake and more boardwalk on the west shore (an abandoned trail, rough and overgrown in 2006, continues all the way around). The right fork descends rough trail about 400 feet in 1.6 miles to upper Twin Falls, a beauteous waterfall crashing into Twin Falls Lake (**4.2 mi**; *elevation: 2,300 feet*). A short path leads along the right side of the lake to a perfectly lunchable slab of granite. Note that the lower Twin Falls is audible below but not visible due to dangerous cliffs. Good campsites are at Twin Falls Lake and at upper and lower Ashland Lakes.

NORTH CASCADES—
92. Bear Lake & Pinnacle Lake

Distance: 0.6 - 4.2 miles round trip   Time: Allow 1 - 4 hours
Elevation gain: 100 - 1,200 feet   Season: May - October

The easy walk to Bear Lake is a good choice in spring when the higher trails are still snowbound, and in the fall when nature pencils in some color along the lakeshore. Like anywhere else in the Cascades, early to mid-summer can be buggy at times around the lakes. And if a 0.6-mile roundtrip adventure to Bear isn't quite the workout you had in mind, continue on to Pinnacle Lake, not quite two miles farther, but almost 1,100 feet higher. This lake usually needs more time to melt out in the spring than Bear Lake, but the latter's lower elevation means the trail to it can be snow-free in some years by April. The hike to these lakes can also be combined with an easy trek to Ashland Lakes or Evan and Boardman Lakes close by (*see Hikes 90 & 91*).

To find the lakes from Granite Falls, leave the Mountain Loop Hwy at MP 15.8 and head south on USFS Rd. 4020. Stay right at a fork

Placid Bear Lake

in 2.7 miles (Rd. 4021), and right again in 1.4 miles (Ashland Lakes Trailhead is to the left). Reach the trailhead near the road end 1.6 miles beyond (*elevation: 2,700 feet; maps, p.177 & 183*). The trail climbs moderately then eases off as it winds through an attractive stand of old-growth hemlock and big cedars with gnarly tops. The trail to Bear Lake is well maintained. Reach a junction (**0.2 mi**) and stay right to find the lake about 0.1 mile beyond. A rough fisher's path leads along the shore, but mud and brush make a circumnavigation unappealing. Horsetails and meadow patches rim the lake in soft layers of green.

A left at the junction leads to Pinnacle Lake. The tread worsens as the trail climbs to a ridge crest, passing a very large western hemlock tree before gaining a view of Bear Lake through the woods (on the right). As the grade lessens, water and mud make the going slightly cumbersome in places, but worth the effort. Patchy meadows appear and a large tarn with two rock islands is passed on the left where scattered boot tracks can confuse the route. The main trail heads down a draw to Pinnacle Lake only two hundred yards past the tarn (**2.0 mi**; *elevation: 3,800 feet*). The lake is narrow and settled in a steep basin below the eastern ramparts of Mt. Pilchuck. Big boulders make good sundecks near the lake's outlet, and a cool cascade drops to another small tarn below.

Pinnacle Lake.

NORTH CASCADES—
93. Lake Twenty-Two

Distance: 5.5 miles round trip   Time: Allow 3 - 5 hours
Elevation gain: 1,400 feet   Season: May - November

A good early season hike in the North Cascades, the modest climb to Lake Twenty-Two is not unpopular. Big trees, lovely waterfalls, and nice views from the cliffy carved basin that holds the lake are the treats. The trail ends at the 2,400-foot level where winter snows usually vanish long before the higher alpine country has seriously begun to release its heavy snowpack. Probably best to go early in the year, possibly even April if it's mild, when the falls are up and the crowds are down. In July, watch for marbled murrelets, a smallish seabird (a federally-listed threatened species) that nests in old-growth forests. The birds are sometimes visible from the lower trail.

From Granite Falls take Mountain Loop Hwy to MP 13.1; the trailhead is to the right (*elevation: 1,000 feet*). The trail is an easy stroll the first half-mile, then begins to climb steadily, but moderately. Soon pass the first low falls on a footbridge. Big western red cedar trees are scattered up and down the hillside. An-

Puncheon, Lake 22 Trail.

other falls, somewhat hidden from view, is passed but sheer cliffs make it difficult to see (an invitation to trouble for those who can't stand not seeing every square inch of every waterfall). More impressive waterfalls are passed higher up, about half-way to the lake (a short path at a switch-back leads to a double falls nearby). Savor an earful of water music, then continue the climb to Lake Twenty-Two (**2.7 mi**; *elevation: 2,400 feet*).

The steep cirque surrounding the lake is a half-mile deep, and just a mile east of the summit of Mount Pilchuck. Happily, a great new loop trail around the lake, including much boardwalk, was completed in 2006. The lake (it's deep, too), the trail, and 790 acres of land that contain them comprise the Lake Twenty-Two Research Natural Area, established in 1947. A mere postage stamp in size by today's National Wilderness standards, it's a pretty big deal that an area like this was set aside a half-century ago just to keep it wild. By designating such areas, foresters could evaluate the effects of logging on a forest ecosystem. Imagine what the watershed might be like had we held the experiment to 790 acres of logging, and left the rest wild. To help keep this natural area natural, camping and fires are not allowed.

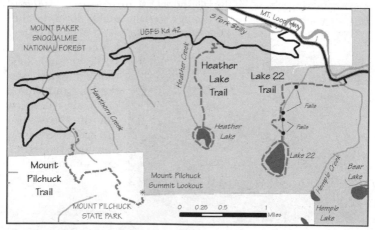

NORTH CASCADES—
94. Heather Lake

Distance: 4.0 - 4.8 miles round trip   Time: Allow 2 - 4 hours
Elevation gain: 1,000 feet   Season: May - November

The hike to Heather Lake is just a moderate trek, but the scenic payoff at trail's end is heavy-duty. The lake lies at the base of a deep cirque carved from the north face of Mt. Pilchuck by a glacier that only "recently" disappeared. The setting is remarkably comparable to that of Lake 22 (*see Hike 93*) and its deep cirque immediately east of Heather Lake. On a quiet day in early summer, big trees, high cliffs, snowfields, and streaming waterfalls are reflected in the cool still water. From the Mountain Loop Hwy east of Granite Falls take the Mt. Pilchuck turnoff (USFS Rd. 42) at MP 12 and drive 1.4 miles to the trailhead (*elevation: 1,400 feet; map, p. 183*).

The first half-mile bypasses the former route up an old logging road. Giant cedar stumps suggest a magnificent stand of trees here not so long ago. The trail climbs moderately and rejoins the old road briefly before the tread narrows and enters old-growth forest (**1.0 mi**). Hike through brushy talus on good trail, followed by a small cascade and more rocky tread above. The final quarter-mile descends slightly through big trees, with Heather Creek close by, lamming noisily down the mountain. Cross footbridges to reach the lakeshore (**2.0 mi**; *elevation: 2,400 feet*). In spring and early summer a dozen waterfalls tumble down the cliffs as in a scene from a Chinese painting. A scenic, 0.8-mile loop trail circumnavigates the lake and should not be missed. A few campsites exist near the lake where snow sometimes lingers into early summer.

Heather Lake.

NORTH CASCADES—
95. Mount Pilchuck

Distance: 6.0 miles round trip   Time: Allow 4 - 7 hours
Elevation gain: 2,200 feet   Season: July - October

*O*f the hundreds of peaks in the North Cascades that are climbed each year, Mt. Pilchuck is one of the most popular, especially on decent summer weekends. A good trail and a short easy rock scramble (optional) near the top make the ascent feasible for almost anyone in average or better shape. The old fire lookout up top, one of only a few that remain in the state, was restored beginning in the late 1980s by the Everett Mountaineers in cooperation with Washington State Parks. Oddly enough, Mt. Pilchuck is not on federal land like most peaks in the Northwest, but is part of Mt. Pilchuck State Park which supported

*Mt. Pilchuck
summit lookout.*

a small downhill ski area from 1957 to 1980. A small walk-in picnicking and tent camping area exists just above the trailhead.

To bag the summit of this prominent peak (highly conspicuous from the west county area), wait for the weather to clear and the snowpack to recede then drive east from Granite Falls on the Mountain Loop Hwy. The peak is quite visible near Robe, and with a sharp eye you can see the lookout on the summit. Turn right on the Mt. Pilchuck Road (USFS Rd. 42) at MP 12. Follow this road seven miles to the wide parking area and viewpoint (*elevation: 3,100 feet; map, p. 183*); the road may or may not be recently graded. Much of the last two miles is paved. The trail was reconstructed in the late 1990s, including relocation of about half the distance. There is much rocky tread after the first mile, but the trail is generally in good shape. Old-growth forest gives way to a thirty-year-old clearcut and views open up the second mile amid granite rock gardens and stone stairs. Above timberline, lingering snow patches in early summer may require an ice-axe (and the skills to use it). A slip on firm snow can send even the most winsome biped careening into rocks or over cliffs, and the steeper snowfields can be an avalanche hazard earlier in the season. If you aren't sure, don't chance it. By mid-summer the upper half of the hike ascends scenic bouldery terrain and can be very warm and bone-dry, so carry extra water. Finally, a short scramble up boulders to a stout ladder take you to the summit lookout (**3.0 mi**; *elevation: 5,324 feet*). A fine array of interpretive exhibits gives a brief history of the place, while the views in all directions offer a raptor's insight into the North Cascades' magnificence.

NORTH CASCADES—
96. Saddle Lake & Goat Flat
Distance: 5.0 - 14.0 miles round trip   Time: Allow 3 - 10 hours
Elevation gain: 700 - 3,800 feet   Season: July - October

The hike to Goat Flat, in the heart of the Boulder River Wilderness, is one of the region's more coveted treks, and understandably so. The view across meadows and glacier to the three towering summits of Three Fingers Mt. is a true North Cascadian alpine scene. This locally famous mountain is widely visible from the western county and beyond, and

Three Fingers from Tin Can Ridge.

along highways near Granite Falls and Darrington. Amazingly, a fire lookout was constructed on the higher south summit in the early 1930s. Before it was ever climbed, the top fifteen feet of the summit was blasted away by Harry Bedal and Harold Engles (*see Hike 51*) to accommodate the little building which has since been restored and maintained by the Everett Mountaineers. Unfortunately for some, an ascent to the lookout requires basic mountaineering skills, like sure proficiency with an ice axe. Still, there's plenty to look at from the meadows below—including many other people looking, though not always. Along the way, Saddle Lake and huckleberries are added incentives.

From Mountain Loop Hwy east of Granite Falls, turn north at MP 7.1 on Green Mt. Rd. (USFS Rd. 41). Stay left at a fork in 1.8 mile (pavement ends) and continue another 15.4 long miles on the main traveled road to the signed trailhead near Tupso Pass (*elevation: 3,100 feet*). From here, it's an initially steep, then easier, but rocky, wet, and rooty climb to Saddle Lake (**2.5 mi**; *elevation: 3,800 feet*). You'll get a peak at Three Fingers along the way. Just before passing the lake, an old unmaintained trail to the right leads west over Meadow Mt., then southeast (5.8 miles total) to a former Goat Flat trailhead also on USFS Rd. 41 west of Saddle Creek (that trailhead is 10.8 miles from Mountain Loop Hwy.). No camping is allowed within 200 feet of Saddle Lake, and no fires beyond this point. There are campsites 0.2 mile past the lake and at Goat Flats. Continue on the main trail as it climbs a ridge to meadows, tarns, huckleberries, and better views of Three Fingers, then the big view from Goat Flat (**4.8 mi**; *elevation: 5,000 feet*). Big Bear and Liberty Mts. are to the southeast, the Boulder River descends to the northwest, and Mt. Baker cuts the sky forty miles north. The meadows are colorful summer and fall. Goat herds were spotted here in the past.

The path continues another 1.5 miles along the south side of Tin Can Ridge to a small saddle overlooking the glacier (*elevation: 5,700 feet*). From this point, lingering steep snow requires an ice axe and possibly crampons (and the skills to use them). For experienced climbers, the route generally continues along the ridge, sometimes on its north side, to easier terrain, followed by steep rock scrambling and a series of ladders going straight up to the lookout, precariously perched on the 6,854-foot south summit (1-2 hours from the saddle). There's a sheer drop of 2,000 feet out the east window. It's easy to dawdle at Goat Flat and beyond, so allow time to scoot back before dark.

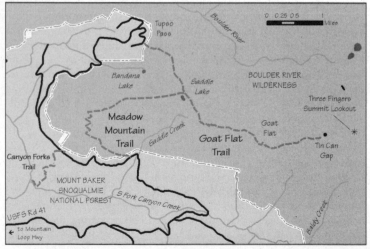

97. Greider Lakes

Distance: 4.2 miles round trip   Time: Allow 3 - 5 hours
Elevation gain: 1,300 feet   Season: June - October

*O*f the few maintained trails available in the Sultan River Basin, Greider Lakes is a good choice. While steep and a little rough in places (partially rebuilt in 1996), the two lakes it leads to offer fine scenic payoffs for the effort. A cliffy viewpoint high above Big Greider Lake used to add an adventurous side trip, but has become overgrown and difficult to follow. The elevation of both lakes is just under 3,000 feet which suggests an earlier season than many other Cascade hikes; however, a large avalanche slope between the two lakes makes the going unadvisable when there's still much snow above.

Find the trailhead near the east end of Spada Lake northeast of Sultan (road is open only from late April to late October). From U.S. Hwy. 2, turn north on the Sultan Basin Rd. at MP 23.1, just east of the town of Sultan. Follow this road (mostly paved) about 13.5 miles to Olney Pass and a fork in the road just past a registration pull-out where recreation users are invited to fill out a form. Note that the lake basin is closed at

Little Greider Lake.

189

night and no camping is allowed, except at backcountry sites near the lakes. Stay right at the fork and continue another seven miles to the obvious trailhead on the right (*elevation: 1,600 feet*). The trail leads past a rustic woodsy picnic area and a junction with a short loop trail around a pond (comes out 100 yards up the road from the trailhead). A giant hemlock tree on the right makes a whale of a nurse-log exhibit, perhaps sprouting from a big rotten log centuries ago. Stay right and wander up increasingly steeper trail past a waterfall, some big trees, and a mostly obscured view of Spada Lake below.

After about three dozen switchbacks, the path tops a shoulder and levels out. Little Greider Lake is just beyond (**2.0 mi**; *elevation: 2,900 feet*). The trail wanders past several campsites and crosses the outlet (Greider Creek) on a footbridge above a cool cascade. This is a good turn-around point for an easier trek. The path rounds the lake and crosses the broad avalanche slope before reentering woods near Big Greider Lake. Head left at an apparent junction for the short descent to the lake (more campsites), a half-mile past Little Greider.

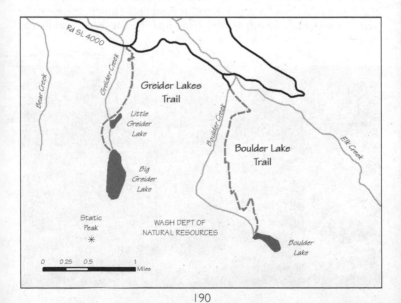

98. Boulder Lake

Distance: 7.6 miles round trip

Time: Allow 4 - 6 hours

Elevation gain: 2,100 feet

Season: June - October

The trail to Boulder Lake, perched in a cirque above Spada Lake, begins at a trailhead 1.3 miles beyond the trailhead for Greider Lakes (*see Hike 97 for directions; map, p. 190*). Expect a comparable climb over four steepish miles, some on old road bed. This scenic area certainly deserves better facilities for hiking. A new high-route loop trail to Greider Lakes (below Static Peak), for example, would make an outstanding trek, although the crags and walls would certainly offer some challenge to the trail engineers. Maybe someday.

From the trailhead (*elevation: 1,600 feet*), cross a bridge over Boulder Creek (**0.2 mi**) before reaching the end of the old logging road (**1.0 mi**). The trail soon enters a large and lumpy rock-slide with good views. Where the trail nears Boulder Creek again, pass a signed fragile area and puncheon across a wet meadow (**2.8 mi**), followed by the lake a mile beyond (**3.8 mi**; *elevation: 3,700 feet*). Good campsites with firepits are scattered above the lake and an outhouse is located behind, just over the crest of a small hill.

Boulder Lake.

NORTH CASCADES—
99. Bridal Veil Falls & Lake Serene
Distance: 4.2 - 8.0 miles round trip   Time: Allow 4 - 7 hours
Elevation gain: 1,000 - 1,900 feet   Season: May - October

The popular hike past Bridal Veil Falls to Lake Serene south of Index was reconstructed in the late 1990s and remains one of the best choices for an early or late season mountain adventure in the Skykomish watershed. Of course, summer is fine too, just a little more populated. Beauteous waterfalls and a pretty lake in a rugged setting make it worth the grunt in all but the worst weather. To reach the trailhead, turn south off U.S. Hwy. 2 at MP 35.2 onto Mt. Index Rd., just before the bridge over the South Fork Skykomish River. Stay right in a quarter-mile and find the big parking area on the left just ahead (*elevation: 600 feet*).

The route follows an old logging road for a long mile, partly by way of an easement across private timber land, to a blocked road on the left (a former access). The road shrinks to a trail shortly beyond this point,

and soon reaches a junction (**1.7 mi**). Here, a short spur on the right climbs to the base of Bridal Veil Falls, a worthy 0.4-mile sidetrip. Use caution at the falls—the rock is slick! There's a plenty good view from a reasonable vantage point, so no need to push the safety margin. Kids should be kept close.

The main trail continues to Bridal Veil Creek, crossing on a bridge with the roaring falls high above. A series of switchbacks and steps gain nearly

Bridal Veil Falls.

Lake Serene.

1,000 feet over the next mile before the way bears west on easier grade for the final scenic traverse to the lake (**3.6 mi**; *elevation: 2,500 feet*). Lake Serene can hold ice even in July, but the trail is generally snow-free by May. The massive rock walls and pinnacles of Mt. Index rise to the south and west. The lakeshore is fragile, thus no camping or fires are allowed. The hike offers great views of nearby peaks and the South Fork Skykomish River valley below, including Sunset Falls to the northeast.

Heybrook Ridge and a decoration of high voltage transmission lines (*see Hike 57*) divide the South Fork from the North. To avoid the crowds, try going on a weekday or a not-so-sunny weekend.

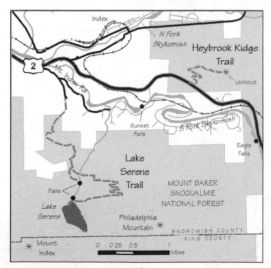

NORTH CASCADES—
100. Barclay Lake

Distance: 4.0 - 7.6 miles round trip   Time: Allow 2 - 6 hours
Elevation gain: 300 - 1,700 feet   Season: May - October

*O*ne of the highest rock faces in the Cascade Range, the north wall of Mt. Baring rises an abrupt 3,000 feet above the south shore of Barclay Lake east of Index. The view, needless to say, is impressive, but so are the crowds on a sunny summer weekend when forty cars or more can jam the trailhead. Go early, or pick a weekday in cooler weather to avoid the throngs. Then expect a pleasant two-mile hike through mature forest to a placid mountain lake. A few western hemlock giants line the trail. In a setting like this it's easy to forget that much of the watershed has been hammered by clearcut logging. Nevertheless, the wildlands rising above Barclay Lake are still pristine and form the southern extent of the new Wild Sky Wilderness (*see p. 24*).

From U.S. Hwy. 2 a few miles east of Index (MP 41.1) turn north onto USFS Road 6024 and drive just over four miles to the trailhead at the road end (*elevation: 2,200 feet*). Mt. Baring is the big peak straight ahead; across the valley are Gunn and Merchant Peaks. The trail is gentle and in generally good shape all the way to the lake, and even a little enchanted with all the puncheon to walk between mossy rocks and slopes.

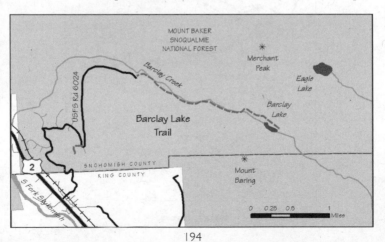

*Mt. Baring over
Barclay Lake.*

The trail crosses Barclay Creek on a footlog (**1.4 mi**) and soon reaches the west end of the lake (**2.0 mi**; *elevation: 2,500 feet*). The trail continues along the north shore, passing several campsites and wide open views of Mt. Baring. The face was climbed in 1960, but it took a tragedy to pull it off (several years earlier a climber fell while descending after an unsuccessful attempt). Later in summer, the water level drops to expose narrow beaches rimming the lake.

From near the east end of Barclay Lake (**2.3 mi**), a rough unmaintained trail heads left and steeply up the mountainside to two other lakes 1,400 feet above. The rough path can be difficult to follow in places; after climbing through woods followed by a brushy talus slope, watch for a fork where the path seems to go up a gully, but stay right to find the trail in woods nearby. Tiny Stone Lake is just ahead, and Eagle Lake, set in a broad subalpine-like basin (extensive wetlands known as Paradise Meadow), is not far beyond, less than two miles from Barclay Lake. Mountain views are really no better here than at Barclay, but the lakes add a scenic extension for those looking to burn off a few more grams of breakfast.

NORTH CASCADES—
101. Lake Elizabeth

Distance: 0.7 mile loop (or more)   Time: Allow 1 - 2 hours
Elevation gain: Minimal   Season: May - November

The easy loop trail around lovely Lake Elizabeth is not officially in Snohomish County, but is accessed from U.S. Hwy. 2 and a logging road ten miles east of Index. The little lake is somewhat isolated at the headwaters of Money Creek, in a narrow valley shared by headwaters of the Tolt River to the west. Oddly, the designated Tolt Watershed boundary splits the lake in two (according to the Mt. Si Green Trails™ map). The trail is generally suitable for kids and seniors, although it can be muddy in spots and a bit overgrown if not recently maintained. It winds 0.7 mile through open forest and lush meadows bordering the lake. The drive in can be rough at times and it's possible you may have to walk the road for a mile or two due to occasional washouts.

From U.S. Hwy. 2 at MP 45.9 turn south at the sign for Money Creek Campground, just before a tunnel. Continue past the campground, cross the railroad tracks, then go right onto Miller River Road (USFS Rd. 6410) a mile from the highway. Immediately take another right on Rd. 6420 (signed for Lake Elizabeth) and drive this about

seven miles to the lake and trailhead on the right (*elevation: 2,900 feet*). On the drive in there is a nice view of the high meadows and snowfields of Goat Basin just inside the Alpine Lakes Wilderness Area. A slide area about two miles short of the lake can be trouble early in the year if maintenance crews haven't made the rounds here yet. Expect rough road through this section (possibly four-wheel-drive). The trail around the lake seems worthy of a serious upgrade, perhaps to a wheelchair accessible standard.

Lake Elizabeth.

NORTH CASCADES—

102. Blanca Lake

Distance: 8.0 - 11.0 miles round trip   Time: Allow 6 - 10 hours
Elevation gain: 3,300 - 4,000 feet   Season: July - October

Blanca Lake, the largest high-elevation lake in Snohomish County, and one of the North Cascades' most spectacular (and surreal), lies in a deep glacier-carved basin on the southern edge of the Monte Cristo Range. The chalky-green water contains the suspended dust of granite that is continually being carved away by the Columbia Glacier not far above the lake. The glacier is unique as well. Flanked by Columbia Peak on the west, Monte Cristo Peak to the northeast, and Kyes Peak to the east, it is nearly a mile long and a half-mile wide, which makes it exceptionally large for a south-facing glacier at this elevation and latitude. Like most glaciers in the North Cascades it is in retreat—an expected response to climate change. The hike to the lake, though strenuous, offers magnanimous views of big trees, water, rock, and ice.

To reach the trailhead, leave U.S. Hwy. 2 at MP 49.5 and follow the Beckler River Rd (USFS Rd 65) 15.7 miles to USFS Rd. 63; turn right, then in two more miles stay left to find the trailhead just up the hill (*elevation: 1,900 feet*). In mid-2007 flood damage blocked the road 1.3 miles from the trailhead, but the road was walkable and repairs were planned. The first half-mile of trail follows a good tread through an old clearcut, then steepens before entering old-growth forest with many large Douglas fir and western hemlock trees six feet or more in diameter. After three dozen switchbacks, the trail enters the Henry M. Jackson Wilderness at the crest of a ridge (**3.0 mi**). Glacier Peak is visible to the northeast. A slight descent leads past tiny Virgin Lake cupped in a saddle near 4,600 feet. Blanca Lake is less than a mile farther but nearly 600 feet downhill on rougher trail. Never-

Blanca Lake.

theless, this colorfully intriguing gem (**3.9 mi**; *elevation: 4,000 feet*) is well worth the descent and the steep climb on the return. When the water isn't too high, one can cross a log jam at the lake outlet (Troublesome Creek) and follow a rough path along the west (left) shore of the lake. More adventurous hikers can scramble up the basin to a closer view of the Columbia Glacier and the peaks that cradle it. Travel on the glacier, of course, requires climbing gear and mountaineering skills. Waterfalls tumble into the basin. Note that routefinding can be tricky in early season when the upper portions of the trail are under snow.

103. North Fork Skykomish River

Distance: 6.4 - 18.0 miles round trip   Time: Allow 3 - 10 hours

Elevation gain: 500 - 3,100 feet   Season: May - November

The trail off the end of the North Fork Skykomish Rd. northeast of Index offers a pleasant stroll in old-growth forest, as well as one leg of several extended and more strenuous loop options. If a more relaxing time in the woods is the objective, consider an easy up-and-back hike in the North Fork valley. From the main trailhead, one can also choose a moderate four-mile hike to Curry Gap along the Quartz Creek Trail, or an easy 0.2-mile walk to the river bridge on the West Cady Ridge Trail, which also offers a potential 17.6-mile loop (*see Hike 104*). Note that a secondary trailhead for the walk up the river valley may require a 1.5-mile road walk to the former North Fork trailhead. This road is badly eroded but may be four-wheel driveable.

From U.S. Hwy. 2 at MP 49.5, turn north on USFS Rd 65 (Beckler River) and continue 15.7 miles to a junction; turn right on Rd 63. The main trailhead is 4.5 miles ahead (*elevation: 2,500 feet*). The road was blocked by washouts 3.2 miles from this trailhead in 2007 but repairs were planned. Walk (or drive) the remaining rough road to the old North Fork trailhead and the signed trail that leads gently upslope to the left of a parking area. The path quickly enters an enchanted old-growth forest, passing large trees, and winding along several attractive puncheon boardwalks to a junction (**3.0 mi**; *or 1.5 miles if beginning at the old upper trailhead*). One can either continue ahead

North Fork Sky near the trailhead.

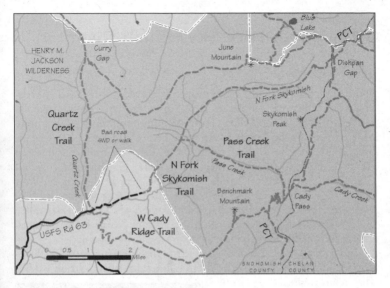

or turn right on the Pass Creek Trail, descending 0.2 mile to the river (*elevation: 3,000 feet*). There is no bridge and crossing may require a good footlog or wading, if the water's not too high (the river is often low enough to ford in summer). Don't attempt it if uncertain. There are good campsites above both banks. (The Pass Creek Trail climbs 1,300 feet in about four miles to meet the Pacific Crest Trail (PCT) near Cady Pass.) The North Fork Trail continues to a potentially difficult river crossing (**5.5 mi**) and campsite; turn back if the river's high. The trail rises more steeply to the PCT at Dishpan Gap (**8.8 mi**; *elevation: 5,600 feet*). Wander leftward as time allows for the bigger views.

Back at the main trailhead, Quartz Creek Trail heads north, quickly enters the Henry M. Jackson Wilderness, and climbs a moderate mile to a broad meadowy flat just above a noisy Quartz cascade. Turn around here for an easier walk, or continue to Curry Gap three miles ahead (*elevation: 3,900 feet*). The Monte Cristo Peaks, close by to the west, are largely obscured by forest. A trail drops from the pass to Cadet Creek, while another heads right to begin the long-ish ascent up Bald Eagle Mt. and extensive meadows beyond that are better suited to overnight trips.

104. West Cady Ridge & Benchmark Mt.

Distance: 6.4 - 14.4+ miles round trip   Time: Allow 1 - 12 hours
Elevation gain: 1,700 - 3,600 feet   Season: July - October

West Cady Ridge offers an excellent, moderately strenuous day-hike to open meadows and great views of the Cascade Crest region above the North Fork Skykomish River. Plan on at least a 3.2-mile one-way hike to good views, or continue another four miles to the summit of Benchmark Mt. for an ambitious, delightsome 14.4-mile roundtrip. Or, make it an 17.6-mile loop by way of the Pass Creek Trail and a ford across the North Fork Skykomish River. There are also good camping options. Note that the ridge trail is popular with equestrians but generally isn't crowded. Do carry plenty of water.

See Hike 103 for directions to the main trailhead near the end of USFS Road 63 (access via USFS Rd 65 from US Hwy. 2 at MP 49.5). The trail leaves the south side of the main parking area (*elevation: 2,500 feet*) and ambles through nice woods to a scenic bridge crossing of the North Fork (**0.2 mi**). From here it's a moderately steep climb—steeper as you go—to alpine meadows at the ridge crest above (**3.2 mi**; *elevation: 4,200 feet*). Columbia Peak dominates the skyline to the northwest. Sloan Peak's sharp horn looms to the right. A high point is soon reached which

Glacier Peak from Benchmark Mountain.

makes a good turn-around for a moderate dayhike (**4.0 mi**; *elevation: 4,800 feet*). Mt. Rainier rises to the south-southwest.

From here, the trail descends 200 feet in forest before climbing again in meadows past a horse camp and muddy tarns, then another campsite near a junction with the trail to the summit of Benchmark Mt. (**6.9 mi**). The summit (**7.2 mi**; *elevation: 5,816 feet*) is generous, offering a great view of Glacier Peak, Mt. Baker, Mt. Stuart, the Monte Cristo peaks, and the Wild Sky Wilderness.

For the big 17.6-mile loop, either return to the junction and turn left, or follow a good, short trail from the summit down the east side of Benchmark to the maintained trail in upper Pass Creek basin (a small stream may exist nearby a few hundred feet below the summit). The trail reaches a junction with the PCT about 1.5 miles from the previous junction just west of Benchmark. Head left 1.6 miles to the Pass Creek Trail (camping available) and descend this trail four miles to a ford of the North Fork Skykomish—not normally a problem by mid-summer in dry weather. If there's even the slightest doubt about fording the river, reverse the circuit so you don't end up stuck near the end of the trip. Intersect the North Fork Trail in another 0.2 mile and head left three miles to the start (*see also Hike 103*).

NORTH CASCADES—
105. Evergreen Mountain Lookout
Distance: 3.0 - 15.0 miles round trip   Time: Allow 2 - 9 hours
Elevation gain: 1,300 - 3,000 feet   Season: July - October

The trail to the nicely refurbished Evergreen Mountain Lookout north of Skykomish is only 1.5 miles long, but it's a steep 1,300-foot gain, at first in trees, then meadow, with sufficient visuals to keep you trudging upward. Access to the lookout, however, is restricted to over-night rentals (sleeps four) which can be reserved online or by phone.

In late 2006, flood damage closed the road 8.3 miles from the trailhead, so check with the Forest Service for current status (may be bikeable). If open, leave U.S. Hwy. 2 just east of Skykomish (MP 49.5), turning north on the Beckler River Rd. (USFS Rd. 65). Drive this 12.7 miles to a five-way junction at Jack Pass. Turn right on Rd. 6550, then

Sunset from the Evergreen Mountain lookout.

left in 1.1 miles on Rd. 6554, a skinny but generally good road that should have your passengers clawing at the dash and arm rests. Note any wide spots in case you need to pull over to let someone pass. This winding road leads 8.8 miles across burned and logged slopes and up a few switchbacks to a parking area just past the trail sign (*elevation: 4,300 feet*). The hike is straight-forward, but steep, up through an old clearcut then woods before reaching a saddle and viewy meadows. Continue up the ridge to the summit lookout at 5,587 feet. The view is excellent: Monte Cristo peaks to the north (Columbia, Kyes, and Sloan are prominent), Glacier Peak, the Cascade Crest, Alpine Lakes Wilderness and Mt. Stuart to the south and southeast, Mt. Rainier and Beckler River to the south-southwest, and Mt. Baring, Townsend Mt., and Merchant and Gunn Peaks to the west-southwest. Go midweek in late July and early August for less people and more flowers, including lush drifts of lupine, paintbrush, tiger lilies, asters, and valerian. Kudos to the volunteers who helped restore the lookout.

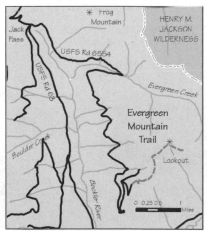

NORTH CASCADES—
106. Sunrise Mountain & Scorpion Mt.

Distance: 4.2 - 9.0 miles round trip   Time: Allow 3 - 6 hours
Elevation gain: 1,500 - 2,500 feet   Season: June - October

This relatively short hike, also known as Johnson Ridge, offers quick access to the high country east of the Beckler River near the southeast corner of Snohomish County. Good views, mid-summer wildflowers, and fall color provide sufficient appeal to make the trek anytime it isn't buried in winter snowpack. From U.S. Hwy 2 near MP 49.5 turn north on Beckler River Rd. (USFS Rd. 65) and follow this about seven miles to the end of pavement and Rd. 6520. Turn right and drive another 2.7 miles to a fork; stay left to reach the trailhead in another four miles (*elevation: 3,600 feet*).

The path leads up a very steep grade (an old road) to a flat area and a trail in small trees (**0.8 mi**), then forest. Reach a meadow view in 0.4 mile more before ascending to the top of Sunrise Mt. (**2.1 mi**; *elevation 5,100 feet*) and a view of Glacier Peak. The trail descends eastward about 300 feet then regains the elevation as it generally follows Johnson Ridge in meadows below the summit of Scorpion Mt. (**3.9 mi**). A skinny path leads up the ridgecrest to the top (*elevation: 5,400 feet*) with good views of Mt. Fernow (south-southwest), other nearby peaks, and little Joan Lake below. The main trail descends 400 feet in a half-mile to the lake.

Glacier Peak.

107. Iron Goat Trail

Distance: 1.0 - 7.0+ miles round trip   Time: Allow 1 - 4+ hours
Elevation gain: 0 - 700+ feet   Season: May - October

In King County, west of Stevens Pass, twelve miles of abandoned railroad grade with tunnels, switchbacks, and snowsheds have been converted to trail, mostly by volunteers. Over half the distance was open in 1997 and by mid-2007 all but the Windy Point Crossover Trail was complete. The crossover creates an excellent seven-mile loop that should be finished by 2008. The three-mile leg from Scenic to Martin Creek is barrier-free. There are three trailheads to choose from: Wellington, Martin Creek, and now Scenic. All include historic interpretive displays, restrooms, and barrier-free trail. Wellington offers a look at the west portal of the old tunnel below Stevens Pass and a large snowshed close by, accessible late spring through fall. Approaching from the west, turn around at Stevens Pass then return westbound to MP 64.3; turn right and follow the Old Cascade Hwy. 2.8 miles and go right again to the signed trailhead.

Down-valley, the excellent new interpretive site at Scenic may be the best start, just north of US Hwy 2 at MP 58.2. Or head up to Martin Creek (from MP 55, go 2.3 miles and turn left on USFS Rd. 6710 to find the trailhead in 1.4 miles). At Scenic, the path is paved initially but is somewhat hilly for wheelchairs. Quickly pass a junction with the new crossover trail that climbs steeply up the mountainside to Windy Point.

The pavement ends just ahead with compacted gravel beyond. Good trail maps and more are displayed at each trailhead. See also www.irongoat.org. A link to the Kelley Creek Trail is also in the works.

West portal of the Old Cascade Tunnel.

NORTH CASCADES—
108. Lakes Valhalla, Janus & the PCT

Distance: 5.0 - 8.0+ miles round trip   Time: Allow 3 - 6 hours
Elevation gain: 800 - 1,300 feet   Season: July - October

The longest trail in the state, the Pacific Crest Trail (PCT), is also one of the hardest to get to locally. It does not cross a single road in Snohomish County, as it winds around Glacier Peak and along the Cascade Crest. In most areas, except around Stevens Pass, an overnight backpack is required to really enjoy it. A number of spur trails, often eight miles or more in length, lead to the PCT from the east and west. To the north, the trail doesn't touch a road until High Bridge on the Stehekin River, twenty miles outside the county. However, the PCT does cross U.S. Hwy. 2 at Stevens Pass, and although the pass is a couple of miles south of the county line, the gravel road up Smith Brook just east of the pass offers the easiest approach to Snohomish County's portion of the PCT. Here, a one-mile spur trail leads to the east county line at Union Gap, and the official crest of the North Cascades. The Smith Brook trailhead is a good place to begin a multi-day backpack and also makes a great start for a dayhike.

Lake Valhalla.

Head east on U.S. Hwy. 2 to Stevens Pass, about 65 miles from Everett. Continue down the highway to a hidden left turn at MP 68.7, just beyond the point where the highway divides. Cross the westbound lanes (caution) to USFS Rd. 6700 and drive this road 2.7 miles to the trailhead on the left (*elevation: 4,200 feet*). The trail climbs moderately in forest on the short trek to Union Gap and the PCT (**1.0 mi**; *elevation: 4,700 feet*). Right goes to Lake Janus; left to Lake Valhalla. It's a bit under 2.5 miles and a 700-foot descent (plus a slight gain) in woods and meadow to pretty Lake Janus. Either continue north on the PCT another two to five miles for good views from the crest; or for an easier option with impressive views, stay left at the gap for Lake Valhalla.

The trail to Valhalla is surprisingly flat much of the way, with occasional views of Nason Ridge (east), Smith Brook valley, and Lichtenberg Mt. (south). After 1.5 miles the trail rises gradually to a saddle (**2.5 mi**; *elevation: 5,000 feet*) and an excellent lake vista just beyond. The lake is an easy descent in 0.3 mile from the saddle. Just before the saddle, a narrow path leads northwest less than a half-mile up a meadowy ridge with abundant mountain ash and even better views, including Mt. Stuart (south-southeast) and the jagged summits of the Alpine Lakes

Wilderness. It's feasible to continue to the summit of Mt. McCausland or to the ridge on the right for a good view of Glacier Peak to the north. From Lake Valhalla (**2.8 mi**; *elevation: 4,800 feet*), one could also continue on the PCT for about five miles back to Stevens Pass, if a ride can be arranged. From the lake, the trail climbs over a low ridge then descends about 1,000 feet in the next two miles before a long easy stretch overlooking Stevens Creek and U.S. Hwy. 2. The PCT trailhead is behind a large parking lot just east of the pass.

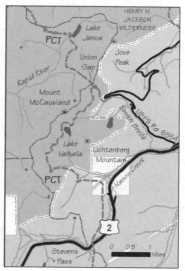

NORTH CASCADES—
109. Poe Mountain

Distance: 5.4 miles round trip   Time: Allow 4 - 6 hours
Elevation gain: 1,900 feet   Season: July - October

The Cascades Crest—the eastern boundary of Snohomish County—is remote and roadless country better enjoyed with a backpack on a multi-day adventure. Nevertheless, a few dayhikes into the area are also possible (*see Hikes 108 and 110*). For a good look at the high ground east of the crest, consider a moderately steep, but not too long, trudge up Poe Mountain above the Little Wenatchee River just over the line into Chelan County. See Hike 110 for directions to the White River bridge. Continue eight miles to USFS Rd 6504 (a mile past Soda Springs Campground) and head right 6.1 miles to the trailhead (*elevation: 4,200 feet; map, p. 210*).

A good path leads steeply to the wooded ridge (**0.7 mi**; *elevation 4,900 feet*), then ambles left staying close to the crest. Views steadily improve as you gain the higher meadows (passing one short section of poor trail). Skip the path leading up a false summit, and instead take a left fork that descends slightly in a narrow sloping meadow to a junction. Stay right and right again to reach Poe's summit (**2.7 mi**; *elevation: 6,015 feet*). A left at either fork leads 2.5 miles down to the Little Wenatchee River Trail (0.1 mile from that trailhead).

Glacier Peak from Poe Mountain.

NORTH CASCADES—
110. Cady Ridge & Dishpan Gap
Distance: 8.0 - 16.0 miles round trip   Time: Allow 6 - 12 hours
Elevation gain: 2,300 - 3,300 feet   Season: July - October

Some of the better high mountain scenery in the county is found along the Cascade crest, the natural divide that keeps western Washington west and eastern east. The Pacific Crest Trail (PCT) more or less follows this divide except for a wide swing west around Glacier Peak. The area is beautifully remote—not a single road crosses the crest anywhere in Snohomish County (Stevens Pass is south of the county line). As a result, hikes in the area are longer and generally better suited as overnighters. Nevertheless, several dayhikes are possible, including a 6.5-mile run up Cady Ridge from the Little Wenatchee River. There are also two options for longer loops via Cady Pass and the Little Wenatchee. Note that water is skimpy later in summer.

Head east on U.S. Hwy. 2 over Stevens Pass to the Lake Wenatchee turnoff at MP 84.5. Go north on SR 207 past Lake Wenatchee State Park (stay left at 4.3 miles), and cross the White River 6.5 miles beyond (becomes USFS Rd. 65). Sockeye salmon spawn here late summer and fall. Watch for Glacier Peak twenty miles up-valley—maybe the best view of the mountain from a paved road. It's about fifteen miles from here to the trailhead and the end of the road at Little Wenatchee Ford Campground (*elevation: 3,000 feet*), a three-hour drive from Everett.

East Cady Ridge.

Note that the last mile or so of road to the trailhead can be rough.

The trail makes a short, steep descent to cross the river on a stout bridge and soon reaches a junction (**0.5 mi**). The easier 5-mile hike to the Cascades crest at Cady Pass is via Cady Creek, nearly all in woods. Cady Ridge (right) is more scenic and the trail wastes no time gaining elevation—and views. Trees thin out as you approach the ridge. Huckleberries, lupine, and mountain ash lure you on to bigger meadows, and a great view of Glacier Peak to the north (**4.0 mi**; *elevation: 5,300 feet*)—a good turn-around point for an 8-mile day. Or, continue in meadows to the PCT (**6.5 mi**; *elevation: 5,300 feet*), then choose one of two 16-mile loops for the return.

Left leads a half-mile to Lake Sally Ann, charming and cold, then skirts below Skykomish Peak, touching the crest (and county line) before descending to Cady Pass at 4,300 feet, 3.5 miles from Sally Ann. West are the Monte Cristo Peaks; Sloan Peak is northwest. Descend Cady Creek Trail for the return. A second option heads right at the Cady Ridge/PCT junction and climbs 400 feet to Wards Pass in 0.6 mile. Another 0.9 mile of up and down leads to a four-way junction at Dishpan Gap (*elevation: 5,600 feet*). The North Fork Skykomish falls away to the left; June and Johnson Mountains beckon to the northwest. Stay right on the PCT 0.8 mile, fork right, then right again at Meander Meadow in 0.3 mile. This descends seven miles to the Little Wenatchee River trailhead.

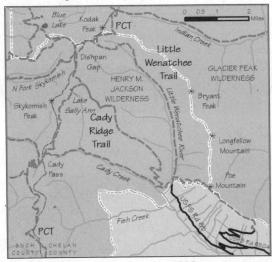

Llama trekker, Cady Ridge Trail.

Other Walks & Hikes

Not every trail in Snohomish County is listed in this guide. Space limitations, access problems, private property issues, safety concerns, changing conditions, and other factors make it difficult to include every foot of trail. Of the trails that aren't listed, many are "unofficial" paths, particularly in the lowland and foothills areas, and were likely excluded because they cross private land where public use is not always welcome. However, on state and private timber land, access is often allowed and old road grades offer a way to reach many destinations. A little detective work will reward more ambitious hikers with a variety of possibilities. But do get permission where necessary.

Historically, urban areas have been slow to develop their own trail systems, although things are picking up in that regard for some communities. Nevertheless, a strong argument can be made that there is a major deficiency of good hiking trails in most (but not all) populated areas of the county. At the same time, new trail systems are developing, in both urban and rural areas thanks to the good work of trails enthusiasts, volunteers, agency staff, and other concerned citizens.

On National Forest lands, where trail development (and trail eradication) unfolded over many decades, the situation is actually much better. Like many other areas in western Washington, Snohomish County enjoys a good number of trails and trail miles on federal lands in the North Cascades, despite the loss of countless miles from logging and road-building. In recent years, however, the number and miles of trails seem to have stabilized, more or less, and many of them are listed in this guide. Consult with the U.S. Forest Service for the latest information on these and other trails in the National Forest. And while you're at it, write your Congressional representative and demand better funding for trails. The Forest Service is willing to make needed improvements, but Congress has a way of routinely underfunding the trails budget.

As for other walks and hikes that wouldn't fit in this edition (for whatever reason) here are a few more to ponder:

COASTAL AREAS

Stillaguamish River Delta

Some dikes and levees along the lower Stillaguamish River and delta near Stanwood have obvious appeal for walking, but most are on private land without public access or with limited fishing and hunting access. It would be great to see more areas opened up for hiking, especially when the public contributes a major share of the financing needed for dike construction and maintenance. Opening up the dike from Big Ditch Slough back to Stanwood has been discussed as one of several attractive possibilities. A planned new riverfront park in Stanwood would improve access as well.

Tulalip Reservation & Other Tribal Lands

Of the several native tribes living in Snohomish County, only the Tulalip Tribe controls access to a large area of land and water. The Tulalip Reservation extends from I-5 west to Possession Sound and from the Snohomish River delta north to McKees Beach near Kayak Point. Non-natives should respect the tribe's sovereignty over these lands and seek out permission for access where necessary. Areas that are perhaps of most interest to hikers are the saltwater beaches near Priest Point, Mission Beach, Tulalip Bay (*see Hike 3*), and north along Port Susan's wild beaches at the base of steep bluffs 300 to 400 feet high.

Mission Beach

Mission Beach occupies a unique landform, a high, narrow, eroding, glacially-deposited peninsular bluff that defines the southwesterly shore of Tulalip Bay, west of Marysville. While public access is somewhat complicated by this thing called private property, it's feasible to walk a good chunk of the shoreline when the tide is more out than in. On the southwest side a piling sculpture of sorts frames the view. Hat Island is anchored straight away in the middle of Possession Sound, Port Gardner and the Everett waterfront are visible to the left, and the Mukilteo Ferry cuts across the water between. Lots of homes line the better beaches, with wilder shores between.

Snohomish River Delta

In addition to existing public trails around Spencer Island and along the river at Langus Park (*see Hike 36*), there are many more miles of unofficial trails, roads, and walkable dikes along the lower sloughs and main channel of the Snohomish River. Some are reasonably accessible; others are brushy or display super-sized no trespassing signs. Secure permission where necessary.

URBAN AREAS

Parks, Promenades, Etc.

Most urban parks of any size have at least minimal facilities for walking. If something less than a half-mile of path is all that exists at any particular park, it's probably been excluded from this guide. That's not to say that these little paths aren't worth walking. Urban waterfront areas, too, often include some kind of walkway or promenade between buildings and the water where a little nature experience might be combined with some window shopping or a winter tea break. Marinas are explorable also, although you might need a boat or a boater friend to get past the security gates.

Historic & Cultural Sites

Formal and informal sites of cultural or historic interest abound in Snohomish County, some with short walking paths, sidewalks, or parks nearby. Check maps, libraries, roadside markers, and the like, or find the original downtown core and residential districts of almost any community in the county for insights into our regional past. Everett, Edmonds, Stanwood, East Stanwood, Arlington, Snohomish (see Hike 14), Monroe, and Index are especially interesting. Easy strolling, say, from a little park to a bakery or museum and back, makes a good outing on all but the blusteriest days of the year. In fact, every small town in the county has something unique to offer, from antiques and used books to funky espresso stands and squeaky floor cafes. In Everett a hillside residential area of narrow winding streets, older homes, and nice views affords interesting wandering, too. Maybe start at Rucker Hill Park near the west end of 33rd St. Check with the Edmonds park department for brochures describing walks there focused on local art and history.

Pigeon Creeks

In south Everett's Howarth Park, a minor trail system accesses Pigeon Creek #2 and short paths meander along Pigeon Creek #1 at lower Forest Park, an unofficial trail network that may eventually become part of a larger system linking the parks and waterfront.

Boeing / Paine Field

This might have been listed as a hike, considering Boeing's official walking tour of the world's largest building—birthplace of the 747—takes over an hour and covers a third of a mile. Instead, call the tour folks (800-464-1476) and schedule a visit to this monster airplane palace on one of our scarce rainy days.

Mill Creek

Lots of urban paths meander through the planned community of Mill Creek, and most are public. Much exploring is feasible. See Hike 21 or just find a good map, then try Library Park off the Bothell-Everett Highway, or Heron Park on Village Green Dr. for two other possible starts.

Willis D. Tucker Park
See the park listing on p. 230 for directions to this new regional park which includes a substantial and growing trail network.

Burke-Gilman & Sammamish River Trails
Just across the line in King County, two major urban trails can be easily accessed from south Snohomish County, including the famed Burke-Gilman Trail that links north Lake Washington with downtown Seattle, and the equally popular Sammamish River Trail which passes through Bothell on its winding way to Redmond. The river trail is generally open to a variety of user groups from walkers and bikers to wheelchairs and roller blades, plus horses in some areas. Access this elaborate, paved, and busy trail system from parks on the north end of Lake Washington, or, from Bothell, turn south off Main St. on 102nd Ave. NE and cross the bridge to Sammamish River Park on the right. Blyth Park is a long block south and a few more west on W. Riverside Dr. This park offers a pleasant (when it's maintained) 0.7-mile loop in the woods.

Mother Nature's Window
Recently acquired by Snohomish County Parks, this 34-acre natural area on 100th St. near 55th Ave. in north Marysville is mostly forested and contains a bit of old growth and a few trails, but minimal facilities. After suffering from abuse for a time, it's been reclaimed and cleaned up by the neighborhood.

Other Urban Trails
Over time, new trails can be expected in urban and outlying areas as the population expands and the demand for new facilities increases. Coastal ravines from Everett to Edmonds (Big Gulch, Japanese Gulch, etc.) are prime locations for new trails. So unless overzealous budget-slashing politicians consistently get their way, this should mean new trail opportunities for everyone. Contact Snohomish County Parks and other local park offices on occasion to see what's in the works and how you might help safeguard the trails budget, or make new projects happen.

LOWLANDS & FOOTHILLS

River Dikes & Levees
Snohomish County, the City of Everett, and others have worked to establish trails along dikes and levees and more could be developed as the concerns of diking districts and landowners are addressed. Trail design techniques are avail-

able to address concerns ranging from public safety to the protection of dikes and related facilities from impacts by users. Such trails can also be temporarily closed during flood events or for regular maintenance. Again, considering the level of public investment in building and maintaining such facilities, it's only reasonable that public access to dikes and levees be accommodated wherever possible. Many areas along the Snohomish and Stillaguamish Rivers are especially attractive and physically accessible already. Older dikes on farmlands in some coastal areas also offer great trail potential. Get permission if required.

Portage Creek Nature Area

This 157-acre natural area near Arlington should only get better for walking (and birdwatching) over the next several years, although you might bring along the rubber boots, even in summer. A small network of trails along wetlands and a big mowed loop around a former pasture currently offer an hour's stroll. A bit of boardwalk near the wetlands would make a nice addition. Kudos to Gene Ammon for his conservation efforts here. The county acquired the property for the public in 1995 and 1996. The south access, including a barn with information about the area is off Cemetery Rd. (204th St.), a half-mile west of 67th Ave. The north access is off SR 530; head south on 59th Ave. 0.2 mile to a white gate and gravel entrance road on the right.

Stimson Hill

The hills northeast of Arlington include much publicly-managed land (DNR), largely dedicated to timber production, and sorely lacking in trail or vehicle access for the general public. Locked gates are the norm unless there's logging underway, which is not the time to be puttering around these places anyway. Stimson Hill used to be a regional favorite because of the great views opened up by clearcutting—which is not to say views are more important than trees. However, the gate on the main access road had six locks on it at one point. The trees, fortunately, are coming back and the views have moved to other clearcuts. Diehard forest walkers might try parking near (not in front of) gated roads off Cedarvale Rd., among others, and wandering old grades with a map and compass. Check with DNR for a map and for walkable (bikeable?) roads where the buzzsaws are dormant.

Frailey & Wheeler Mountains

Old roads and trails exist within large areas of public and private timberland in the hills between Arlington and Darrington, particularly on Frailey Mt. and Wheeler Mt. Clearcuts opened up some nice views in many areas, but newer cuts and ongoing reforestation mean the big panoramas have a way of moving around over time. Old logging grades still make for interesting expeditions to good views, a few big trees, water access, cascades, and various geologic nuances. Much of Frailey Mt., straddling the Snohomish-Skagit County line, is managed by DNR, while the U.S. Navy (Jim Creek Naval Radio Station) controls a principal access to Wheeler Mt. Changing road conditions and gate closures complicate exploration.

Perhaps the best place to reach Frailey Mt. is from the Lake Cavanaugh Rd. east of Arlington. Head east on SR 530 to MP 32.7 and turn left just before the river bridge, quickly crossing the Darrington Branch railroad grade (and future Whitehorse Trail). Pavement ends in 1.8 miles, followed by a great view of Whitehorse and Three Fingers Mountains. At 3.5 miles, a gated spur road on the left leaves a right-hand switchback. Park here and wander up the road leading to Frailey's long ridge. An elusive 2,666-foot summit lies about three miles west. Good views can be had of Lake Cavanaugh, Mt. Higgins, and Whitehorse Mt. There may be a number of spurs and overgrown roads.

As for Wheeler, you probably need to know someone connected to the Naval Station to get access as a sponsored guest, although security issues may further limit access. To find out, turn south from SR 530 at MP 25.6 onto Jim Creek Rd. and drive to the Navy guardshack seven miles ahead. The trailhead is just inside on the left. Miles of old logging roads and trails, generally open to hiking and mountain biking, wind around the hillsides to little lakes and views. If you don't have a connection and do have a fishing pole, you could previously access the trail to Twin Lakes several miles south of the gate, but only during fishing season. There are extensive wetlands and smaller lakes here as well, all draining into Cub Creek's narrow canyon. Hopefully the Navy will keep some areas public friendly. (It may be feasible to access Wheeler Mt. from the south via USFS Rd. 41, 4150, and long spur roads of uncertain status.)

White Chuck Bench

From a bluff above the confluence of the White Chuck and Sauk Rivers southeast of Darrington, an old trail runs 6.7 miles up the White Chuck through second-growth forest, flood plain, and old-growth forest north of the river. Low elevation means the trail, partly on an old logging railroad grade, would normally be accessible most of the year—even in winter if it's mild. But the big storm of October 2003 rendered it heavily damaged and inaccessible through 2007, although plans were in the works to repair access and the trail itself (check status with the Forest Service). Determined 'shwackers might still be able to make a day of it, but most will want to wait for repairs. Stream crossings can be a challenge during periods of higher runoff. Once reopened, big cedar trees and river and mountain views make the trip worthwhile even on a marginal day. The White Chuck River Rd. (still washed out in 2007) follows the opposite side of the river and ends at the White Chuck River Trailhead (not to be confused with White Chuck Bench). The "Bench" trail could be walked from either end, but the more interesting part is upriver.

To reach the downstream trailhead from Darrington, turn left off Mountain Loop Hwy at MP 44.8 onto USFS Rd. 22, and assuming the bridge is fixed, pass the river boat launch in 0.2 mile and take the next right. The trailhead is 0.3 mile up the hill on the right just around a bend (*elevation: 1,100 feet*). There are good views of Sloan and Bedal Peaks, Mt. Pugh, and White Chuck Mt. near the trailhead from atop a high eroded bluff. For the upriver trailhead, the previous access, White Chuck River Rd. (USFS Rd. 23), is likely blocked at a washout at 1.8 miles. It's about four miles from here to the former east parking area on the left, just after a bridge over the river. The Rat Trap Pass Rd. (USFS Rd. 27) may be the better access once it reopens (*see Hike 69*).

Crystal Creek is crossed a half-mile from the east end and is the trickier crossing, difficult or impossible at moderate to high water levels unless and until a new bridge is installed. Near Crystal Creek is an impressive view of Mt. Pugh. A little farther west, watch carefully for a glimpse of Glacier Peak upriver through the trees.

Hubbard Lake & South Fork Stillaguamish River

With the support of concerned citizens, Snohomish County acquired nearly 1,000 acres of land around Hubbard Lake and along the South Fork Stilly east of Granite Falls. The potential for park and trail development, as well as open space and habitat protection is excellent. The land, called Robe Canyon Historical Park, includes the Robe Canyon and Lime Kiln Trails (*see Hikes 53 & 54*), and an extensive gorge along the river. A new bridge is envisioned to span the river and complete the link between existing and future trail systems.

Spada Lake & Sultan Basin

The Spada Lake reservoir northeast of Sultan has a number of developed picnic sites and viewpoints with short walking paths, much of which is barrier-free. Several North Cascades hikes can be accessed from the area as well (*see Hikes 97 & 98*).

NORTH CASCADES

Niederprum Trail

The main climber's route up Whitehorse Mt. near Darrington, this trail is very steep and may be in rough shape if not recently maintained. It's a long haul to meadow views where climbers ascend and traverse to Lone Tree Pass and beyond. Due to steep rock and potentially dangerous snow slopes it's best to let the more experienced peak baggers ponder the higher ground. You may see them carrying ropes and other gear for the glacier crossing and summit climb high above. To find the trailhead, turn south off SR 530 on Mine Rd. and drive about 2.5 miles (road becomes USFS Rd. 2030); angle left between houses where pavement ends. The trail's on the right.

Huckleberry Mountain

Expect a long trudge (7 miles, 4,500-foot gain) on good and bad trail to alpine meadows overlooking Buck Creek, the Suiattle River, and a sky full of summits, Glacier Peak included—and, as the name suggests, some sweet edibles in season. Go east on Suiattle River Rd. (26) to MP 14.6 and a small parking area next to the trail. Water gets scarce up high later in summer. A camp is passed at three miles. Views are limited until near the ridge crest. Due to the low starting elevation, the trail is none too popular and fades in meadow below a high point. A fire lookout once stood on another high point to the west.

Sulphur Creek

The curious thing about this little hike is the "hot springs," which might better be described as "tepid puddles," elusive, strong-smelling from sulphurous gas, and otherwise uninviting. Unlike the iron-rich mineral water that once bubbled at Kennedy Hot Springs (*Hike 71*), the source and nature of this spring is, perhaps, more intimately linked with the Glacier Peak volcano, an easy crow-fly to the southeast. However, the trail up the creek passes through nice old-growth forest so let that be the main attraction. There may be a lot of downed trees. Find the trailhead west of the creek directly across from the Sulphur Creek Campground near the end of the Suiattle River Rd. (MP 22.5).

Circle Peak

If the roads are passable, the almost forgotten trail to a lookout site on Circle Peak, east of White Chuck Mt., is still a good choice for experienced trekkers with routefinding skills. Check the status of the Suiattle River bridge on USFS Rd. 25 that was knocked out in 2003; if it's been repaired follow it from MP 10 on the Suiattle River Rd. (USFS Rd. 26) for three-plus miles to Rd. 27. Stay right for two miles to a fork. One option is to go left on Rd. 2703, if passable, about six miles to its end and look for a boot track leading to the old trail in less than 100 yards (may be hard to find); woods and meadow lead to summit rocks in 2.5 miles. Or for a longer hike on good trail (perhaps seven miles one way) continue on Rd. 27 to the Crystal Lake trailhead (*see below*). Recent improvements were made to the old trail between Circle Peak and the Crystal Lake Trail, with the assumption that access would soon be restored.

Crystal Lake

Crystal and Meadow Lakes, near the west end of the Meadow Mt. Trail, are reachable as a long dayhike (*see Hike 69*), but a 3.5 to 5.0 mile road walk (each way) makes the area more appealing as an overnighter. If Crystal Lake is the objective, walk the old road bed (2710) about 1.7 miles to the fork before Crystal Creek. Left goes to the old Crystal Lake Trailhead in about 1.5 miles. Beyond, pass the old trail to Circle Peak (left), recently improved. The scenic lake is above the falls about 1.7 steep miles from the old trailhead. Or stay right at the earlier road junction for the longer approach via Meadow Lake. Near the end of that road (at five miles) head up the Meadow Mt. Trail for less than two miles to a junction. Right goes on to Meadow and Fire Mountains. Left leads down several hundred feet in under a mile to Meadow Lake. A rough boot track continued over a ridge a long mile to Crystal Lake. A complete loop of about 14 miles is feasible, but expect some brush and crummy trail.

Peek-A-Boo Lake

Southeast of Darrington, the old trail to Peek-A-Boo Lake switchbacks up a wooded ridge to a fragile meadow in two miles, then drops several hundred feet to the forested lake in another half-mile. A road washout on the approach (two miles from the trailhead) was hikable in 2007, but was expected to be repaired soon. From Mountain Loop Hwy at the confluence of the White Chuck and Sauk Rivers (MP 45), turn west on USFS Rd. 2080, stay right at a fork (sign), then right again on Rd. 2083 in 1.7 miles, and left on Rd. 2086 in another 1.7 miles. The trail's 1.3 miles beyond at a right-hand switchback. Mt. Pugh and White Chuck Mt. are visible on the drive up.

Cougar Creek

An old and beauteous trail now used mostly by climbers headed up Sloan Peak begins on the right a few miles up the North Fork Sauk River Rd. The problem, however, is The River. It must be crossed to get to the main trail leading to meadows north of Sloan. Fording anytime but at low water is either impossible or dangerous (it takes so little current to jam a body under a log or stump in the river . . .). Maybe let the more experienced mountain brutes bag this one. See Hike 77 for a more inviting alternative just over the ridge.

Old Government Trail

An easy, seldom used, 1.6-mile trail from Barlow Point Trail (*see Hike 79*) runs down-valley to near the Sunrise Mine Rd. east of Granite Falls. This is a remnant of a much older trail that paralleled the old Monte Cristo Railroad grade, and predates construction of the Mountain Loop Hwy.

Marten Creek

Marten Creek is a steep and not terribly interesting hike up an old grade off the Mountain Loop Hwy near MP 20.7 east of Granite Falls. The first mile is very steep and was built in the 1940s to access the Marten Creek Mines. The route passes the site of a Douglas fir "heredity experiment" begun in 1916. Seedlings from all over the Northwest were planted here to compare growth characteristics in the decades-long quest for the perfect timber tree. Signs explained the project and results. The trail eases off in Marten Creek's upper broad valley, then crosses the creek, before disappearing in brush less than three miles from the road. The old trail once continued another two miles and climbed 500 feet to Granite Pass on the way to Darrington. Expect some downed trees.

Canyon Lake

A three-mile road walk leads to a short path and a fishable lake on the southwest edge of the Boulder River Wilderness. Take Green Mt. Rd. (USFS Rd. 41) from Mountain Loop Hwy at MP 7.1, then stay right on Rd. 4110 in two miles, and right on Rd. 4111 in two miles more. The road is probably closed at 2.7 miles (or before), leaving at least three miles to the lake. Trail's on the left.

Lake Isabel

Isabel: a big mysterious lake in a remote area that, surprisingly, lacks a good trail. The easiest access is heavily used by 4WDs and ATVs, or "quads," that seem to have been given free reign by DNR to just about destroy the place. Remarkably, there is a reasonably good route to the lake that avoids much of the chaos, but it's circuitous, disconnected, and difficult to describe, with numerous opportunities to get off-route. For the intrepid footster with good routefinding skills, half the fun will be in piecing it together (start near Hogarty Creek). Good views, an old kiln, a mine shaft (not for entering), several nice waterfalls on May Creek, and a bit of old-growth forest are among the attractions. Perhaps some day volunteers will mark and upgrade this hiker's route, hopefully with a little support from DNR to install log barriers and signing to discourage the motorheads from ripping it up.

The less confusing route, largely shared by off-roaders, is described below, although it still requires some route-finding ability. Follow U.S. Hwy. 2 two miles east of Gold Bar to MP 30.1 and turn left on Reiter Rd. In 0.8 mile stay right at the intersection with May Creek Rd. In another mile, pass a gravel quarry on the right and a former quarry on the left where most of the off-roaders park. Just beyond, turn left on a DNR logging road which may or may not be driveable to transmission lines nearby. Drive, bike, or walk the rest of the road and stay right at a fork to reach May Creek a mile from Reiter Rd. Scamper across on rocks if the water isn't too high. From here the route follows an old railroad logging grade that gently climbs to the west then bends to the east. There are a number of other roads and trails intersecting this grade, so it's easy to become a missing person here. Memorize your progress for the hike back out. Generally, just stay on the main traveled route. A steep section higher up leads to a flat grade, and an upper creek crossing on stringer logs left over from a former bridge. A bit more steep and rocky roadbed leads to a sharp bend to the left and a flat open area. In another 100 yards or so, look for the old foot trail to the lake on the left (three-plus miles to here, a mile more to the lake). Follow easy but rough trail northward past big cedars and a campsite near the base of a big beautiful waterfall (it dries up in late summer). Follow a very steep and poor boot track almost straight up (with some root-assisted scrambling) to the lake, near campsites and an outlet stream with a gauge. Thoughtless campers sometimes trash the shore here, but the lake is otherwise wild and pristine. One can wander left, some on path, some not, to a second, westerly outlet. Expect slippery logs and rocks to clamber over.

Index Town Wall

The high rock walls rising above the town of Index are something of a rock climber's dream, but experienced hikers can find a couple short steep hikes of interest here as well. Trails are cliffy in places, hard to follow, and not maintained, and thus not for everyone. The area truly deserves something like a five-mile loop below the towering walls, up to an overlook or two, and perhaps a return by way of the North Fork Skykomish River. For now, try an easy stroll through town, a quiet road walk along the rushing river, or for experienced scramblers, a steep, hand-over-hand ascent to Lookout Point, 900 feet above the valley.

Leave U.S. Hwy 2 at MP 35.7 and go one mile north to Index and cross the bridge. Stop at the city park and look directly up the street to the big cliffs. Scan upwards and you may see Old Glory waving among the trees at Lookout Point, near the top of a triangle-shaped rock face. Enjoy a saunter around town or along the river, or for Lookout Point, walk ahead to Index Ave. and turn left. Just before the railroad tracks, head right 0.1 mile (if publicly accessible) to an inconspicuous climbers' path and a skinny wooden bridge. A boot track climbs to the base of high walls and among ledges to a steep wooded gully in less than a mile (turn back if uncertain). Very steep clambering among trees leads to Lookout Point at the top of the gully. A few more steep steps upward then leftward brings you to a large granite platform, flagpole, and the words "Lookout Point 1922" etched in giant letters in the rock. The town of Index lies far below. Be cautious on the descent, avoid cliffs, and don't lose the route.

An easier way to see the big walls up close is to follow the paved road a mile downriver to a short dirt road leading right to a parking area. A climber's path crosses the tracks (caution!), heads right 0.1 mile to an old quarry where you can ogle the climbers for a bit on just about any sunny day in summer. Beyond, switchbacks lead up steep forest and rightward before ending at the base of an impressive rock wall.

Curry Gap & Bald Eagle Mt.

Bald Eagle Mt. Trail above the North Fork Skykomish River, is doable in a day, but limited views make the trek somewhat less appealing than nearby alternatives like Blanca Lake and West Cady Ridge (*see Hikes 102 and 104*). From the Quartz Creek Trailhead figure four miles to Curry Gap and three more to Bald Eagle Mt., where an opening affords views to the north. The route is of more interest as an overnighter and can be continued as a two to four-day loop via June Mt., Blue Lake, the North Fork Trail, Pass Creek, or West Cady Ridge.

Pacific Crest Trail

If you happen to find your calendar open for four to six months from spring through early fall, consider a little 2,650-mile jaunt from Mexico to Canada via the Pacific Crest Trail (PCT). If you only have a week or two to spare, take a serious look at doing the chunk of it that runs along the east boundary of Snohomish County—the Cascade Crest. The trek from Stevens Pass north to Cloudy Pass and the Suiattle River, or on to Rainy Pass or Canada's Manning Park makes an extraordinary outing that, for obvious reasons, attracts a lot of bipedal pack luggers and a few super-light, high-tech feet beaters every

year. If you're in shape and you happen to catch mostly good weather along the way, it can be a trip of a lifetime. If not, well, there's always next year. Several of the dayhikes listed in this guide offer access to the PCT (*see Hikes 64, 65, 71, 74, 103, 104, 108, and 110*). If a longer hike is the plan, check on trail conditions and refer to one of many guidebooks available that detail the trek. Because of high elevations and lingering snowpacks, late July through September is typically the best time for an extended hike on the local segment of the PCT.

Image Lake and GlacierPeak.

Buck Creek Pass

Really an overnight backpack, the 20-mile roundtrip to Buck Creek Pass is more than most people will attempt in a day. The pass is on the east county line at the Cascade Crest where easy summit hikes offer great panoramas. Views of Glacier Peak and neighboring summits are exceptional. The trailhead is at the end of the Chiwawa River Rd. (USFS Rd. 62) in Chelan County, north of Lake Wenatchee. The Liberty Cap Trail to High Pass makes a great sidetrip.

Cloudy Pass

Another long access to the crest region of Snohomish County's far east begins at Holden Village above Lake Chelan (to reserve space on the ten-mile shuttle to the village from the Lady of the Lake ferry, see www.holdenvillage.org). Again, this is really overnight backpacking country, but excellent day hikes east of the crest are available. A ten-mile trudge up Railroad Creek past Hart and Lyman Lakes to Cloudy Pass is a North Cascades classic. Scurry up a knoll for the grand views. Or, to experience some of the best of the Glacier Peak Wilderness, continue across to Suiattle Pass and the PCT, Agnes Creek, Image Lake, Miners Ridge, or a descent of the Suiattle River (*Hike 64*).

Public Parks

Almost every community in Snohomish County has at least one park of some kind, and though some may be on the meager end of the excitability spectrum, many others are surely worth a visit. Some of the nicer ones are listed below. The availability of walking paths is noted. If good parks and trails are lacking in your community, call the mayor to see what you can do to help rectify things.

In 1997 the county started charging fees to park or launch a boat at Kayak Point, Wyatt, and Flowing Lake Parks. Check with the county park department for details. A similar fee-based system at state parks was thankfully discontinued in early 2006. Those who can least afford such fees should not be excluded from the joy and enrichment that come from our parks and trails. And where fee-based camping is provided, cyclists and walk-ins who don't generate car-related impacts and expense on the park system should always be given a better rate.

Parks listings are loosely organized from north to south. A few non-park sites, like the Sultan Basin Recreation Area, are included because of obvious recreation value.

COASTAL AREAS

Kayak Point Park

Adjacent to some of the prettiest marine shoreline in the county, Kayak Point County Park northwest of Marysville is a good starting point for a bit of beach wandering (*see Hike 2 for directions*). The 670-acre park was acquired from ARCO in 1972 after the company shifted its refinery plans north to Cherry Point in Whatcom County. For a $5 parking fee (2007), the park offers camping, picnicking, a barrier-free fishing pier, scenic paths, fine sunsets, and great views of Port Susan, Camano Island, and the Olympic Mountains. Expect to share the place with many other folks late spring through early fall. You might even catch a glimpse of a whale, though don't go expecting that on your first visit. Bring binoculars to better the odds. A public golf course adjoins the park to the east.

North & South View Parks

These two pocket parks on the north Everett waterfront are on a narrow strip of land between the water and Marine View Dr. and just southwest of the Maulsby Swamp. A good paved path links them together (*see Hike 15*).

Marine Park

On the Everett waterfront, Marine Park offers water access to Jetty Island, Port Gardner, Possession Sound, and the Snohomish River. Short walking paths, small floats, a fishing pier, lawns, sea sculptures, and viewing areas warrant at least a brief visit. Expect a lot of traffic at the major multi-laned boat launch (a couple of slots are reserved for non-motorized craft). The city runs a free summer foot ferry to Jetty Island from here, and a private ferry links with Hat Island (no public facilities). The park is at the west end of 10th St. off Marine View Dr. (*see also Hike 15*).

Jetty Island Park

On the Everett waterfront, Jetty Island is a 210-acre, two mile-long landform created by modern *homo sapiens* from harbor dredge spoils dug from Port Gardner waterways. Yet the island offers a surprising respite from city life a stone's throw away, and includes a two-plus-mile beach, an interpretive nature trail, barking sea lions on occasion (fall and winter), and sometimes even warm saltwater for swimming. A foot ferry shuttles island goers to and from the Jetty in summer (*see Hike 4*).

Howarth Park

This big little park off Mukilteo Blvd. has tennis courts, a playground, nice woods, bluff trails, views, and picnicking. A high footbridge leads across railroad tracks to a viewing platform and a fine gravel and sandy beach below (*see*

Hike 5). The bridge can be reached from the main park area above or from the Pigeon Creek #2 parking area below. Howarth Park is about 1.5 miles southwest of Forest Park. The eastern park entrance off Olympic Blvd. is closed at night. The west entrance is near Seahurst Ave. and Mukilteo Blvd.

Harborview Park

For an excellent, unobstructed view of Possession Sound, the Everett waterfront, Mt. Baker, the Olympics, and Whidbey, Camano, and Hat Islands, try this little view park between Everett and Mukilteo, a half-mile west of Howarth Park. There's interest in acquiring a trail down the bluff to Darlington Beach to access 4,600 feet of public shoreline near the mouth of Merrill Creek. Stay tuned.

Lighthouse Park

Next to the Mukilteo ferry terminal, this inconspicuous 18-acre former state park has 1,500 feet of walkable public shore (*see Hike 6*), interpretive exhibits, a fishing pier, picnicking, and ferry-watching, once you get past a gigantic parking lot used by island commuters. This is also Point Elliot, one of western Washington's most important historic sites. It was here that 2,000-plus members of native tribes in the region gathered in 1855 to witness the signing of the Elliot Point Treaty by 82 Indian leaders. This lone act essentially gave all of Northwest Washington to non-native settlers in exchange for peace, a few small reservations for some of the tribes, and a promise for equal access to traditional fishing and hunting grounds. Many non-natives groaned about the latter for generations. A skimpy sign near the restrooms commemorates this immense historic event. A historic lighthouse, the U.S. Coast Guard Lightstation Mukilteo, built in 1905, stands to the north (open for tours on spring and summer weekends). The lighthouse was restored in 1987.

Picnic Point Park

This 54-acre county park has 1,200 feet of walkable public shore, most of it sandy beach, although the beach connects with a much more extensive and walkable beach at lower tides running northward to Mukilteo and south to Edmonds and beyond (*see Hikes 6 and 7*). The park was donated to the county for park purposes and has been developed with paths, viewing areas, a pedestrian overpass across the railroad tracks, a picnic area, and portable restrooms. The park is at the west end of Picnic Point Rd. between Edmonds and Mukilteo, and can be reached via Highway 99 and Shelby Rd. which becomes Picnic Point Rd. The park opens early and closes at dusk.

Meadowdale Beach Park

Just north of Edmonds is this 105-acre park with one major trail to the beach (*see Hike 9*), lots of nice woods, and 800 feet of public beach. The main highlight of the park and natural area is the 1.2-mile trail to the beach. A small play area and Lunds Gulch Creek are other attractions. The park is off 156th St. SW about a mile west of 52nd Ave. W.

Brackett's Landing

This beachfront city park is adjacent to the Edmonds ferry terminal and is a popular spot to watch shipping traffic and the ferry come and go. Interpretive facilities, benches, nice walkways, a good chunk of public beach, a small jetty, and views of Mt. Baker to the north as well as Whidbey Island, Kitsap Peninsula, and the Olympics. Scuba divers frequent the area and an underwater park has been established around an artificial reef. Outside cold showers are also available. The park spans both sides of the ferry terminal and makes a good starting point for a beach walk to the north (*see Hike 7*). Or, wander south to Olympic Beach (*Hike 8*) and the long fishing pier where a great poster shows you how to properly fillet a fish. Then head east up Main St. to the historic downtown area near 5th Ave.

Marina Beach Park

Another small but nice city park in Edmonds exists south of the ferry terminal at the end of Admiral Way. The park has lots of grass, a play area, picnic tables, barbeque grills, a nice beach, walking paths, a pet area, and historic features. The site was originally named Point Edmund by the Wilkes expedition in the mid-1800s. The park is well connected to the rest of Edmonds' pedestrian-friendly waterfront by a bridge (*see Hike 8*).

Richmond Beach Park

Richmond Beach Park, less than a mile south of the county line, offers excellent picnicking (several shelters), short walking paths, a scenic play area, sandy beach, and a great view of the Olympic Mountains. Beach wandering, by way of the footbridge across the railroad tracks, is best when tides are below five feet or so—and preferably on the way down, not up. Much of the park, formerly a sand and gravel pit, is ADA-accessible, although a steep ramp leading to the beach itself may preclude wheelchair access to some otherwise nice amenities (*see Hike 10*). From Richmond Beach Rd. west of SR 99, turn south onto 20th Ave. NW and drive a couple of blocks to the well-marked park entrance.

URBAN AREAS

Twin Rivers Park

This 55-acre county park in Arlington at the confluence of the North and South Forks of the Stillaguamish River has ballfields, a new course for "disc golf," and several paths in woods by the river (*see Hike 31*). The park is on the left near the river as you head north out of town on the SR 530 bridge. Downriver, the City manages another much smaller park with a play area, Haller Park, near the Centennial Trail bridge over the Stilly, where extensive gravel bars are generally accessible in summer.

Church Creek Park

Ballfields, picnic and play areas, forest, walking paths, and lawns can be found at this attractive city park in Stanwood on 72nd Ave. NW north of SR 532. The author's brothers built a great little trail here in the early 1970s.

Mother Nature's Window

This 34-acre county park in Marysville has woods and trails (*see p. 215*).

Jennings Nature Park

This large city park has it all: rolling lawns, play and picnic areas, a duck pond, extensive wetlands, a creek, woods, walking paths, a ballfield, a Master Gardener demonstration garden, a big cannon, historic buildings, and more. Considering the serious crowd factor on a nice weekend, one gets the impression Marysville may be short of parks. At other times, it's a pleasant place to wander, hold hands, watch birds, or read books. (*See Hike 12 for directions.*)

Harborview Park

This Marysville Park has a big lawn, a play area, and 0.5-mile paved walking path that feels (and is) disconnected, with a good view across open fields. From Sunnyside Blvd. head west on 52nd St. NE to find the park in a few blocks.

Foothills Park

Find this quiet little city park with rolling lawns, trees, and a 0.5-mile loop trail on 58th St. NE, a few blocks west of 67th Ave. in Marysville.

North Pointe Park

A short path, nicely built, surrounds a portion of this Marysville park, although it really should be extended into a loop. Find the park two blocks south of Grove St. on 70th St. NE.

Lake Stevens Area

Perhaps the nicest park on Lake Stevens is Lundeen County Park at the north end of the lake. Though small, it offers a nice view of the water plus a swimming beach, barrier-free fishing dock, play and picnic areas, a basketball court, and minor wetland interpretation. From SR 9, head east 0.8 mile on Lundeen Parkway (signed to City Center); the park is on the right. Other parks on the north end of the lake include the City Swimming Beach west of the city center, and North Cove Park next to the police station downtown. Wyatt County Park and its popular boat launch and swimming beach are on the lower west shore of the lake off S. Davies Rd. Another small swimming access is on Lake Stevens Road just north of 3rd St. NE.

Legion Memorial Park
Land donated to the city by the American Legion in 1932 led to the development of this multi-faceted 4-acre park with walking paths, play areas, tennis courts, ballfields, a golf course, a small arboretum, horticultural center, garden compost demonstration site, a meeting hall, and good views of Everett's industrial waterfront and beyond. See Hike 15 for a good waterfront loop that can begin at this park.

Wiggums Hollow Park
This Everett City park near 10th and Poplar has short paths, a ballfield, play and picnic areas, and lawns—a good place to while-away an hour or two.

Hannabrook Park
Located in Everett at 5815 Brookridge Blvd. (south of Mukilteo Blvd.), this 6-acre park has trails, picnicking, and play areas.

Johnston-Kelly Park
The kids at View Ridge Elementary School have helped develop and maintain this 1.8-acre nature park with trails since 1993. The park is on Basswood, south of Mukilteo Blvd near 47th St. SW, near the southwest corner of Forest Park.

Forest Park
It seems amazing to think it now, but Forest Park once supported a zoo with exotic animals from around the world, including elephants, bears, and kangaroos. Now only a petting zoo of familiar domesticated farm animals exists, a transition that seems entirely appropriate given humanity's increasing concern for the welfare of our planet's endangered wildlife. The park's current 111 acres includes play areas, forested walking paths (*see Hike 16*), lawn areas, a public swimming pool, tennis courts, horseshoes, a ballfield, picnicking, the historic Floral Hall (a lovely old log building on the National Historic Register), plus a separate 60-acre chunk of park land on Pigeon Creek #1 with more trails, views, and 3,000 feet of saltwater shoreline. Jackson Elementary School kids have worked for years to reestablish a healthy salmon run in the creek. An interpretive trail along the entire length of Pigeon Creek has been proposed. From Evergreen Way, follow 41st St. west (becomes Mukilteo Blvd.) a few blocks to find the park just around the bend on the left. Across from the second entrance is the gated Pigeon Creek Rd. that leads to the lower 60 acres and the beach in 0.8 mile.

Walter E. Hall & Kasch Memorial Parks

These two adjacent south Everett parks are not of much interest to walkers, but they do offer limited play and picnic areas in addition to all the busy ballfields and golf course that occupy most of the parks' 200 acres. There's some interesting history here: Hall was built over a landfill, and Kasch used to be a Bomarc missile site. Reach the former from W. Casino Rd. west of Evergreen Way, and the latter from Airport Rd. to the west.

Rotary Riverfront Park

This 11-acre park in the Lowell area of south Everett is a recent addition on the lower Snohomish River near the former home and lumber mill of E.D. Smith, founder of Lowell in 1861. The park includes a river boat launch and trailhead parking for the Lowell Riverfront Trail (*see Hike 37*). There are also nice views of the river, the Mt. Baker volcano, and other peaks of the North Cascades.

92nd Street Park

On the east side of the Mukilteo Speedway and south of 92nd St. SW is an attractive park with large rolling lawns, forest, and two small wetlands, as well as play and picnic areas and nearly a half-mile of trails in trees and sun.

Thornton A. Sullivan Park

This is the popular 110-acre Everett city park on Silver Lake in south Everett (on Silver Lake Rd. off 19th Ave. SE). The park includes a swimming beach, small boat rentals, picnic and play areas, and a nature path across Silver Lake Rd. (*see Hike 18*). Look for a wild sea monster in the trees north of the beach behind Camp Patterson. The park gets really busy in summer.

Hauge Homestead Park

This small but pleasant park with a dock and access to Silver Lake is located at the corner of 19th Ave. SE and Silver Lake Rd. Find short paved paths (*see Hike 18*), picnic and play areas, and possible launching of a canoe or kayak.

McCollum Park

What used to be a county landfill is now 77-acre McCollum Park, one of the western county's more attractive regional parks. There are play and picnic areas, a swimming pool, ballfields, and walking trails in the woods (*see Hike 19*), as well as a BMX racetrack and a WSU Cooperative Extension facility next door. The Adopt-A-Stream folks have developed an educational facility here as well. McCollum Park, the county's first, is south of 128th St. a few blocks east of I-5. The North Creek Trail to Mill Creek also begins here (*Hike 21*).

Willis D. Tucker Park

This new regional park features ballfields, play areas, administrative offices for the county parks division, natural areas, and an emerging trail system that should reach several miles in length once completed. From I-5 head east on 128th (becomes 132nd) for four miles and turn right on Snohomish-Cascade Dr. Turn left at a stop sign (Puget) to find the entrance just ahead.

Logan Park

The author's first home in Washington (1967) was directly across the street from this former gravel pit, and we had just as much fun there as kids do today. Only now, instead of building miniature roads and dams in the sand and dirt, you can enjoy a ballfield, play area, and walking path on five acres. The park is in Brier at the intersection of Logan Rd. and Locust Way.

Martha Lake Park

The county park on Martha Lake is small (6 acres) and a little noisy—not from users but from traffic on 164th St. SE. In fact, the park can be less busy at times other parks are crowded, despite several hundred feet of attractive natural shoreline. The park is nicely developed with paths, boardwalks, docks, play and picnic areas, and a swimming beach. Early morning visits spring through fall may be best when traffic isn't so obnoxious. Turn north off 164th St. onto East Shore Dr. and find the park just ahead on the left.

Meadowdale Playfield

An urban park and sports complex in Lynnwood, Meadowdale Playfield has ballfields, picnic and play areas, a duck pond, rock sculpture, and a mile of mostly paved paths (*see Hike 23*).

Southwest County Park

Another large (120 acres) and largely undeveloped county park in the Edmonds area, this site includes a lot of nice forest and a fairly good, but limited trail system, and no other facilities (*see Hike 24 for details*). Park on Olympic View Dr. near 180th St.

H. O. Hutt Park

This small (7 acre) natural area in Edmonds contains an attractive grove of Douglas fir trees, but no facilities. A short walking path leads past two giant firs. The trailhead is on 187th St. SW, just east of 94th Ave. W. Parking is problematic. From Olympic View Dr., head up the hill at 190th Pl. SW.

Sierra Park

The interesting thing about this small Edmonds park off 80th Ave. W and 190th St. SW is the short Path for the Blind (*see Hike 26*). There are also a small arboretum, picnic area, play area, basketball court, and ballfield here.

Seaview Park

A few blocks north of Sierra Park on 80th Ave. at 186th St., find lawns, a ballfield, play and picnic areas, and short paths.

Lynndale Park

Lynndale Park off Olympic View Dr. is a surprising spot on 37 acres near a confluence of power lines. Despite the obvious electrical downside, there are significant amenities here, including pleasant picnic sites in the woods, picnic shelters, play areas, an amphitheater, tennis courts, a ballfield, basketball courts, an orienteering course, and a fine little trail system, some of which is paved and barrier-free (*see Hike 25*). Access the park from Olympic View Dr., near 73rd Ave. W.

Daleway Park

This long and skinny park in Lynnwood has play and picnic areas, a kids' spray pool (in summer), basketball courts, horseshoe pits, some nice woods, and a 0.2-mile trail running the length of the park. Access it from 64th Ave. W, a few blocks north of 196th St. SW.

Scriber Lake Park & Wilcox Park

One of Lynnwood's few natural gems, Scriber Lake is a veritable paradise among the steel and concrete of southwest Snohomish County's immoderately crowded landscape. A lovely path circles the lake (*see Hike 28*), and a diversity of birds and small mammals have scratched out a living here. The paths, wetlands, a marshy lake, woods, benches, and blinds for birdwatching are the principal amenities. Wilcox Park to the north across 196th St. SW is developed with the more urban-traditional play and picnic areas among nice trees. The parks are not linked but can be mutually accessed via the crosswalk at the Scriber Lake Rd. traffic light. Reach Scriber Lake by car from 198th St.; Wilcox park from 196th St. and Walnut Way.

Edmonds City Park

From the outside, the city park at Edmonds doesn't look particularly inviting, but on the inside it's nicely landscaped, well maintained, and loaded with family funster amenities. Picnic and play areas, a wading pool, a gazebo, barrier-free walking paths, a ballfield, nice trees, and lots of rich lawn should keep the kids adequately entertained. Park on 3rd Ave. north of Pine St. near downtown Edmonds. Open dawn to dusk.

Maplewood, Yost Memorial & Pine Ridge Parks

Three nicely wooded parks in Edmonds offer southwest county residents a choice of destinations for walking and picnicking in a natural setting close to home (*see Hike 29*). The larger of the three, Yost Memorial Park, covers 48 acres and offers play and picnic areas as well, plus an outdoor public swimming pool, tennis courts, and a limited trail system in a wooded ravine. From downtown Edmonds take Walnut St. up the hill (east) several blocks to the park entrance. The smallest, Maplewood, is a newer facility with short paths, a play area, and semi-private picnic spots among trees and lawn. Find the elusive entrance at the end of 89th Pl., north of 200th St. SW. Pine Ridge Park, at 24 acres, is less developed and serves more as a natural area protecting Goodhope Pond and surrounding wetlands. Several short paths lead to views of water and wildlife. Access this area from 83rd Ave. W., three blocks south of 200th St. SW.

Esperance Park

This 6-acre park with ballfields, picnicking, and walking paths is located next to Edmonds Elementary School at 222nd St. SW and 80th Ave. W.

Echo Lake Park

This park is located just inside King County south of N. 200th St., east of Aurora Ave. N. and provides lake access, lawns, benches, picnicking, and hosts a portion of the Interurban Trail. A two-mile gap in this regional trail is being completed from Echo Lake to the current trail terminus in south Lynnwood.

Silver Creek Park & May's Pond

At ten acres and close to power lines, Silver Creek Park south of Mill Creek has some nice amenities, including a half-mile walking trail with bridges among woods, wetlands, and a small pond. Enhancements to the creek have been made to help recover salmon habitat. There are limited picnicking and play areas in the park, located off 20th Dr. SE south of 180th St. SE and east of SR 527. May's Pond is close by, north of 180th St. and behind a swimming pool. There are a few short paths and a play area here as well.

Rhody Ridge Botanical Garden

This site southwest of Mill Creek is not a conventional park for picnicking or kids' play, but was graciously donated to the county for the benefit of people who want to experience (and maybe learn from) a well-kept, privately established arboretum. Access is by appointment only with the resident caretakers. Check with county park staff or the website for information.

North Creek Park

This fine nature park south of Mill Creek was developed by the county off 183rd St. SE a half-mile west of SR 527. The park has good picnic facilities, a viewpoint, and an extensive, albeit incomplete, boardwalk trail system through wetlands (*see Hike 38*). Expect good birding and wildlife viewing in winter and spring. Park opens early, closes at dusk.

Evergreen Playfield

South of 220th St. SW on 56th Ave. W. in Mountlake Terrace, this facility is mostly made of ballfields, with picnic/play areas and tennis courts. A good paved trail winds around the edges under conifers.

Jack Long Park

Find this three-acre woodsy park with play and picnic areas in Mountlake Terrace on 58th Ave. W. south of 220th St. SW.

Terrace Creek Park

Also in Mountlake Terrace is this woodsy, 52-acre park and natural area with play and picnic areas, a pool, a unique "golf course" for disc throwers (tee off and sail it to a basket hundreds of feet away), plus a wide, easy trail running the length of the park (*see Hike 30*). Access the park and trail off 48th Ave. W., near 233rd St. SW.

Brier Park

Find this modest-sized city park with lots of lawn, ballfields, play and picnic areas, and walking paths on the north side of 228th St. SE between Poplar Way and Brier City Hall.

Horizon View Park

With ball courts, play and picnic areas, and pleasant paths, this six-acre park is located on 47th Ave. NE south from 201st Pl. in Lake Forest Park just south of the county line.

Blyth Park

Also just inside King County is Bothell's Blyth Park on 37 acres with forest, lawns, play and picnic facilities, and a 0.7-mile interpretive walking trail close to the Sammamish River. The popular Sammamish River Trail runs through the park. From downtown Bothell turn south off Main St. onto 102nd Ave. NE, cross the river, and turn right on W. Riverside Dr. to reach Blyth Park.

Paradise Valley Conservation Area

This site was not open to the public in 2006, although future plans call for trails, historic preservation, interpretive and educational facilities, and other amenities in the coming years. The 663-acre property is located on Paradise Lake Rd. near the King County line, in the headwaters of Bear Creek, an important salmon tributary of the Sammamish River. Homesteaded by the Lloyd family in 1898 and farmed for generations, the family knew it was a real treasure and agreed to sell it for preservation purposes in 2000 at well below its appraised value. Check with Snohomish County Parks for more information.

Pilchuck Park

For a simple picnic break on the Pilchuck River in Snohomish, Pilchuck Park off 2nd St. and Cypress Ave. is a maybe. The park includes play/picnic areas, tennis courts and ballfields and a paved (and uninteresting) pedestrian path around them, plus a big soccer field complex to the south.

Ferguson & Hill Parks

Nice woods with paths, play and picnic areas, and access to Blackman Lake are found at these two lakeside Snohomish Parks east of SR 9 and Ave. D and north of 13th St. An unsightly and seemingly unnecessary cyclone fence detracts from Hill Park's otherwise pleasant setting.

LOWLANDS & FOOTHILLS

Wenberg State Park

Wenberg is a heavily visited, semi-urban state park on just 46 acres on the east side of Lake Goodwin. The 550-acre lake is scenic if you can see it between all the people and the boats. For some quiet, visit on a crummy day or in the off-season (November through March). From the Smokey Point exit on I-5 north of Marysville, head west on SR 531 2.3 miles, turning right at a stop sign, then left at the park sign almost five miles from I-5. The park entrance is on the right in another 1.5 miles. Good picnicking (with grills), beach sunning, swimming, motor and non-motor boating, and camping are available. A few short paths wind along the shore and through Doug-fir and red-cedar forest.

Lake Goodwin Community Park

This new 12-acre county park is located on the north shore of Lake Goodwin and includes picnicking, swimming, and walking paths. Access the park from Lakewood Rd. five miles west of Smokey Point (I-5 Exit 206).

Gissberg Twin Lakes Park

Next to I-5 north of Marysville is this green but predictably noisy county park of 54 acres enclosing two artificial lakes that formed after the state excavated a zillion truckloads of fill to construct I-5. Besides fishing, swimming, and picnic potential, an easy, pleasant walk in the grass circles both lakes (*see Hike 33*). Find them west of the freeway, 0.7 mile south of SR 531 (Smokey Point exit).

Portage Creek Wildlife Area

A county park and nature reserve southwest of Arlington with fields, wetlands, and trails (*see p. 215*) comprise this important lowland wildlife area.

River Meadows Park

East of Arlington this excellent riverfront park on about 145 acres was once a dairy, and a native Stillaguamish settlement before that. The county park fronts the South Fork Stilly for a mile and contains mixed forest, lovely fields (grass and wildflower meadows), the site of an historic homestead, picnic areas, tent camping, and six miles of easy walking paths (*see Hike 32*). From SR 530, a half-mile north of the South Fork bridge at Arlington, turn right on Jordan Rd. Stay right in a mile and continue another three miles to the park entrance on the right. Closes at dusk.

Jordan Bridge
To reach this mini-park and suspension footbridge over the South Fork Still-aguamish River, take SR 530 a half-mile north of the South Fork Stilly bridge in Arlington and turn right on Jordan Rd. Stay right at a junction in one mile and drive another six miles to the footbridge and parking area on the right. A 0.6-acre parcel on the Stilly was donated to the county in 1974 to preserve this famous landmark, since rebuilt. Stairs lead to a little beach below the bridge.

Squire Creek Park
This 28-acre, nicely wooded county park is mostly of interest to campers and there's a good fishing access to Squire Creek. No link to the Whitehorse Trail in 2007. The park is off SR 530 at MP 42.4, about 4 miles west of Darrington.

Frank Mason Park
Near Granite Falls, this 17-acre park has frontage on a ten acre lake, Lake Gardner, near the west end of town next to SR 92. Follow Crooked Mile Rd. to the park and its fishing dock, picnic area, and paths.

Backman Park
This small fishing access on the Sauk River is about 2.6 miles south of Darrington on the Mountain Loop Hwy. Turn left on Clear Creek Rd. just before the Backman Creek bridge. Park is 0.4 mile ahead on the right. No facilities.

Langus Park
Acquired from DNR, 96-acre Langus Park was named for an avid park supporter. The park and a 2.8-mile paved trail along the river and slough were dedicated in 1991 (*see Hike 36*). Future trail extensions are possible. Also considered is a rather ambitious footbridge to be hung underneath the I-5 Snohomish River overpass to link Langus Park to the rest of Everett's emerging riverfront trail system. The land was originally inhabited by native people.

Spencer Island & Steamboat Slough
Spencer Island, part of the Snohomish River delta in north Everett, is a haven for both wildlife and recreation. Snohomish County owns the southern portion, while the Washington Department of Fish and Wildlife owns the lion's

share on the north end. The island attracts hunters and photographers, and both come here often, both looking for a good shot. Despite the apparent conflict, the area has become a birdwatcher's paradise in winter and spring. A fairly extensive trail system also exists (*see Hike 36 for details*).

Bob Heirman Wildlife Park at Thomas Eddy

A beautiful 344-acre natural area fronting the Snohomish River south of Snohomish with a good trail to river banks and bars. Also a small lake and wetlands, plus picnic facilities. Hiking only (*see Hike 39*); no dogs allowed. Access is off the Connelly Rd. east of SR 9.

Lord Hill Regional Park

In 1879, Mitchell Lord homesteaded on this anomalously high hill near the confluence of the Snohomish and Skykomish Rivers west of Monroe. By the 1930s the whole dern thing had been logged off and the DNR started pulling the second-growth fifty years later. Quite fortunately, Snohomish County Parks managed to rescue about 1,300 acres of the hill, including some maturing forest, substantial river frontage, several ponds, and the not-quite-towering Devil's Butte area for a major regional park. An extensive trail system, much of it open to horses and bikes, has been developed (*see Hike 40 for details and directions*). No camping or fires allowed. The park opens early, closes at dusk.

Lake Roesiger Park

This small county park on 38 acres has a swimming beach, dock, picnic tables, lawn, a short trail in the woods (that really should be extended toward the lake and made into an attractive loop), and limited camping. The park is off Lake Roesiger Rd. a mile north of West Shore Rd. Park closes at dusk.

Flowing Lake Park

Located on the north shore of Flowing Lake east of Snohomish, this 33-acre rural wooded park (with fee access) includes a swimming beach, fishing dock, boat launch, play areas, good picnic sites, walking paths, and a nice campground. From U.S. Hwy. 2 near Snohomish, exit to 88th St. SE, cross the highway and continue 0.8 mile to 131st Ave. SE; turn left. In 1.3 miles go right on Three Lakes Rd. Drive another 2.5 miles to 171st Ave. SE; go left 1.2 miles, then right on 48th St. SE (park signs). The county park entrance is 0.5 mile ahead.

Sultan Basin Recreation Area (Spada Lake)

Northeast of Sultan in the Cascade foothills is Spada Lake, a large reservoir that serves as a major component of the Everett water system, serving two thirds of the county population. To protect water quality, public use of the lake and watershed is strictly regulated. From late April to late October one can access a number of improved sites during daylight hours only. Camping is not allowed, except at backcountry sites near Boulder and Greider Lakes (*see Hikes 97 & 98*). Boating is okay, but not internal combustion motors, nor inflatables like tubes and rafts. Fishing with bait and swimming are also prohibited.

From U.S. Hwy. 2 just east of Sultan head north on the Sultan Basin Rd. 13.5 miles to an information/registration area at Olney Pass. The road forks just ahead. A right reaches the South Fork site (picnicking, boat launch) in 3.2 miles; the South Shore site (boat launch) in 5.3 miles; the Nighthawk site (excellent picnic area, a half-mile of walking paths, and boat launch) in 5.8 miles; and the Bear Creek Overlook in 6.3 miles with an excellent view of the lake from the east. The Greider Lake Trailhead is a mile farther. From the fork near Olney Pass, a left leads to Culmback Dam, a viewpoint, and the North Shore picnic site, but this road may be closed for security short of the dam, which impedes access to barrier-free paths, picnic sites, and a great view of the lake from the north.

Wallace Falls State Park
A very popular (i.e. crowded) place in summer, this fine state park offers limited tent camping and picnicking, but is best known for the spectacular falls on the Wallace River (*see Hike 56*). The famous falls are conspicuous from U.S. Hwy. 2 near Gold Bar. Follow the signs to the park from U.S. Hwy. 2 near MP 28. Best flows are after a fall storm or in late spring. The park closes at dusk.

Wallace River Roadside Park
On the south side of SR 2 west of Startup is this small picnic area with frontage on the little river with the big waterfall a few miles upstream (*see Hike 56*).

NORTH CASCADES

USFS Wilderness Areas
Considering there are more than 630,000 acres of federal land in Snohomish County—nearly all of it in the national forest, including one of the most dramatic mountain landscapes in the lower-forty-eight states—there sure ought to be a slug of designated wilderness here. Right? Fortunately, there is. That doesn't mean that all of the fragile places worth protecting have been saved, but great strides have been made over the past several decades to ensure future generations have more than a slim chance to experience much of what we can today.

Three wilderness areas have been established in the region, including the Glacier Peak Wilderness, one of the first such areas set aside anywhere in the nation (1960). Over 570,000 acres are protected in an area covering parts of

Snohomish, Skagit, and Chelan Counties. The area is entirely dominated by the state's fourth-highest volcano, *DaKobed*, or Glacier Peak, rising almost two miles above sea level. Two other wilderness areas were designated by Congress in 1984—the Boulder River and Henry M. Jackson. The latter covers 103,000 acres, mostly in Snohomish County and includes the peaks and glaciers of the Monte Cristo area. The Boulder River Wilderness includes 49,000 acres and has Whitehorse and Three Fingers Mountains at its heart. Hopefully, a new Wild Sky Wilderness near Index will become a reality in 2007.

All these wilderness areas contain extensive trail systems, especially Glacier Peak with over 450 miles worth. Henry M. Jackson has about 50 miles of trails, and Boulder River holds 25 miles. Yet all three wilderness areas contain plenty of places that are so wild and rugged and trail-less that no one ever visits. Check with your local climber, hunter, or fisher friend for hints on where to go to avoid humanity altogether. But beware: this is no playground for the inexperienced. Hazards are many, and more than a handful haven't come out alive. Consider a comprehensive mountaineering course if this sort of thing sounds appealing. It just might save (if not change) your life.

Viewpoints & Water Access

Officially, few designated viewpoints exist in Snohomish County, yet there are still hundreds of places where there is a unique or scenic vista of something natural worth looking at: a bay, a lake or river, a waterfall or cascade, a canyon or gorge, a mountain, a glacier, a tree or a forest, an area frequented by wildlife, an uncommon ecosystem, a pretty place to snap a picture. Such places are not always located at a convenient roadside pullout, or a park, or on the brink of a steep precipice, although a few are and that makes them handy. So, while the author was making the rounds in Snohomish County checking out the trails, some of the more interesting vistas were noted. Approximate locations are noted on the facing page.

Also, there happen to be dozens of public fishing access areas in lakes and rivers that are managed by the Washington Department of Fish and Wildlife (WDFW), of which few people are even aware. Many of these were also noted. For fishers and non-fishers alike, access areas on lakes—waters that belong to us all, by the way—make great spots to launch a canoe or kayak. Even the smallest lakes can brighten an otherwise dull day when the mountains are snowed in and woods walks just aren't on the menu. Nearly all areas have at least a portable privy. However, use of these sites requires a fishing license or vehicle use permit ($10.95 for the latter in 2007; good for 12 months). Obtain one through WDFW or your local sporting goods store.

Selected viewpoints and water access areas around the county are listed below. A "⚓" symbol indicates water access suitable for launching a hand-carried boat. Assume that a conservation license is required for all WDFW sites. Incidentally, this is not a boater's guide. **It is the reader's responsibility to learn and practice boater safety, which includes, among other things, wearing an approved life jacket** (duh...). Cold water, wind, and changing weather are particular dangers. Currents in rivers, and both tides and currents in the Sound present additional hazards. If you're new to canoes, kayaks, or rowboats learn the ropes from someone who knows. Boldness is useless when your boat, or worse, you, are suddenly sinking to the bottom.

Here are almost eighty sites to check out.

THE COAST

Big Ditch Slough ⚑
See Hike 1 for directions to this pleasant viewpoint and walk north of Stanwood along Skagit Bay and within the Skagit Wildlife Recreation Area. Views include the bay, Camano, Whidbey, Fir, and Fidalgo Islands, plus Mt. Baker, and the Twin Sisters Range. A variety of birds and other wildlife inhabit this coastal floodplain, a major habitat area that is ecologically linked not just to the bay, but to the extensive estuary and delta of the Skagit River. Nice sunsets, but closed after dark. (WDFW site.)

Kayak Point ⚑
A good fishing/viewing pier at Kayak Point County Park plus a fine beach are great for a lengthy morning wander or a sentimental sunset stroll. Views are west toward Port Susan and Camano Island. Bring binoculars for birdlife and marine mammals. You could even see a whale. (*See Hike 2 for directions.*)

Tulalip Bay ⚑
On the Tulalip Reservation west of Marysville, one can access the water and enjoy a view of the bay at Tulalip Bay Marina, as well learn some history of the place by way of an interpretive walk near the water (*see Hike 3*). From I-5 take Marine Dr. to 64th St., go left, then right on Totem Beach Rd. to the marina entrance on the left.

Mission Beach
Across the spit from Tulalip Bay is a good view of Possession Sound and Hat Island from Mission Beach Rd. From Marine Dr. take 64th St. 0.4 mile, turn left. Look to the left at a sharp bend just past the cemetery.

Legion Memorial & Grand Avenue Parks
To reach Everett's modest-sized Legion Memorial Park, follow Grand Ave. north from downtown, passing the late Sen. Scoop Jackson's home and Grand Ave. Park at 17th St. (*see Hike 15*) with a nice view of the Navy Homeport and marina. A footbridge to the waterfront has been considered here and is certainly warranted. Continue north to find Legion Memorial Park at 2nd St. Westward off Alverson Blvd. are great views of Port Gardner, Possession Sound, the Snohomish River delta, Hat, Whidbey, and Camano Islands, the Olympic Mountains, and Mt. Baker. A large wetland below, Maulsby Swamp, offers a glimpse of what some of the natural coastline may have once looked liked.

North & South View Parks
These are two parks with a paved path connecting them to the north Everett waterfront on Port Gardner (*see Hike 15*).

Marine Park 🌴

Water access to Jetty Island is a highlight at Everett's Marine Park, but short walking paths, a small fishing pier, and viewing areas are worth a visit. Whidbey and Hat Islands are to the west, Point Elliot and Mukilteo to the southwest. The park is off Marine View Dr. at the west end of 10th St.

Howarth Park & Pigeon Creek

Howarth Park offers several good viewpoints, one from the park road above the bluff overlooking Port Gardner and the Everett waterfront. Scamper down and across the grass to reach a path along the bluff and a link to the pedestrian overpass over the railroad tracks. From this bridge there is a great view up and down the coast (a good spot for binoculars or a spotting scope). The same bridge can be accessed from the Pigeon Creek parking lot below (off Olympic Blvd.; may be closed). Mukilteo and the Whidbey Island ferry are visible across Possession Sound to the southwest, Port Gardner, the Everett waterfront, Navy Homeport, and the Mt. Baker volcano (on the horizon) to the northeast, and Whidbey and Camano Islands to the northwest. (*See also Hike 5.*)

Harborview Park

This is a great viewpoint between Everett and Mukilteo, with a wide panorama of islands, Possession Sound, the Everett waterfront, and Mt. Baker.

Everett harbor from Harborview Park.

Lighthouse Park (Mukilteo) 🌴

Adjacent to the ferry terminal, this former state park offers access to some good walkable beach (*see Hike 6*), as well as views across Possession Sound to Whidbey Island and beyond. It is also a good place to watch the ferry come and go while you develop ideas for the perfect Northwest mystery novel. Be sure to read the interpretive signs; this place has some important history. Also, look for a small public float and walkway next to the ferry dock.

Picnic Point

The county park at Picnic Point offers good access to the waterfront between Edmonds and Mukilteo and is a convenient starting point for beach walks (*see Hike 7*). A footbridge over the railroad tracks accommodates partial views of the coastline, but walk down to the beach to better enjoy this attractive shore. Whidbey Island is to the northwest, and the Kitsap Peninsula sprawls west to southwest.

Meadowdale Beach

See Meadowdale Beach Park (*and Hike 9*) for access to the beach by way of a long path through the park. About a half-mile south of the park one can also access the beach from a tiny parking area off 162nd St. SW. Lack of parking means it's probably hopeless to try on nice weekends (be friendly and don't block the neighbors). There is a Cascadia Marine Trail campsite here also.

Edmonds Area Viewpoints

Several good viewpoints have been developed around Edmonds, including the Stamm Overlook north of town on Olympic View Dr. across from High St., with two benches, flowers, a tiny parking area, great view of sunsets and the Olympics, and two trees (a fir and a cedar) that seem to have eloped. Another overlook with a similar view is a few blocks south on Ocean Ave. From Olympic View Dr. turn west onto Cherry St., then right on Sound View, left on Water St., and left on Ocean (parking at south end). Note that trains move through the area fast and frequently. A few blocks south is a viewpoint on Sunset Ave. reached via Edmonds St. Edmonds historic district is a delight also. Walk up Edmonds St. to 5th Ave. and take a right. (*See also Hike 8.*) Look for the Edmonds (or Union) Marsh interpretive trail south of Dayton, east of the tracks.

Richmond Beach 🌴

Although it's just across the border in King County, Richmond Beach's beach is definitely worth a visit for any southern Snohomish Countian. On a cool clear winter morning the view of the Olympics is exceptional. If the tide is more out than in, there's good beach to walk as well. (*See Hike 10 for directions.*)

Urban Areas

Stillaguamish Riverfront Park & Trail (Stanwood)

A new park and trail system along the lower Stillaguamish River in Stanwood has been on the drawing board for years, and funding remains the primary obstacle. Hopefully, the project will also lead to improved hiker access to river dikes within and beyond the city limits, including Port Susan, West Pass, and Skagit Bay. A new train station and a "city trail" linking the historic portions of East and West Stanwood are part of the grand plan. State and federal agencies need to fork over some cash (grants) for the town's worthy vision.

Jennings Nature Park

This Marysville park has good views of the Allen Creek wetlands. It's worth carrying binoculars and a bird book in spring (*see Hike 12*).

Lake Stevens 🌲

Although Snohomish County lacks any "really large" lakes like the ones found in surrounding counties, there is one "fairly sizeable" one, Lake Stevens, which most locals are familiar with. In the past when the lake was a little more remote from urban civilization, the area developed as a resort community, and for many, a weekend or summer hideaway. Now, of course, there is nowhere

North Cove Park, Lake Stevens.

to hide. Most waterfront property that could be developed has been, and as growth and development in the region continue to explode more or less out of control, Lake Stevens is rapidly being absorbed into the greater megalopolis. All is not yet lost, however. To get a good look at what's left, try Lundeen Park on the north shore, or North Cove Park next to the city center. A public boat launch is nearby just off Main St.

Langus Riverfront Park 🌴
Across the Snohomish River from north Everett, this park includes an extensive path, boat launch, and good views of the river (*see Hike 36*).

Viola Oursler Viewpoint, Riverside & Summit Parks
A fomal viewpoint in north Everett looks out across Smith, Spencer, and Ebey Islands, I-5, and the Snohomish River floodplain to the North Cascades. On the horizon left to right, Whitehorse Mt., Three Fingers, and Mt. Pilchuck are most prominent. Crane your neck to see Mt. Baker to the north. The Viola Oursler Viewpoint is on E. Marine View Dr. near 7th St. Find a similar view from Summit Park next to I-5 (Summit Ave. and 20th St.). Riverside Park (Everett Ave. at E. Grand Ave.) is partly obstructed, an okay spot to sit, but no view of the river.

Rotary Riverfront Park 🌴 (Lowell)
Try this little park on the Snohomish River southeast of Everett for a good look at the river, nearby wetlands, wildlife, and prominent peaks of the North Cascades, including Mt. Baker above the smooth moving water. The Lowell Riverfront Trail is also accessed here (*see Hike 37 for directions*).

Silver Lake 🌴
See Thornton A. Sullivan Park (*and Hike 18*) for details and directions to Everett's largest lake. A good view from walkways and floats can be found along the east shore and at Hauge Homestead Park. Paddling a canoe or kayak in the off-season might be worthwhile; motor boats over 10 horsepower and 8 mph are banned all year.

Lake Stickney 🌴
A small and pretty lake with a fair bit of natural shoreline still intact is Lake Stickney in the 'burbs south of Everett. From SR 99 a mile north of Mukilteo Speedway, head east on Gibson Rd. a few blocks to 17th Ave. W. Turn right and find the WDFW public fishing access just around a bend. Like most small lakes, Stickney is better as an easy paddle than as a stop on a Sunday drive.

Lake Serene 🌴
A pretty little lake in the middle of suburbia, Lake Serene may still not be

worth driving far to look at, but it does beckon an easy paddle by canoe or kayak in the off-season. Look for Canadian honkers and mallards, plus pink and white lily pads blooming in spring. The WDFW public fishing access is off Serene Way at 140th St. SW, which can be reached via Highway 99 and Shelby Rd. Park across from the fire station. No internal combustion motors are allowed.

Martha Lake 🌴

This modest-sized lake is heavily developed but worth an early morning visit when noise from nearby traffic is less intrusive. Briefly stroll the south shore, relax on the dock, or launch a canoe or kayak from Martha Lake Park off East Shore Dr. just north of 164th St. SE. A WDFW public fishing access and boat ramp is adjacent to the north.

Scriber Lake

A nice path, floating walkway, interesting seating accommodations, and duck blinds for wildlife viewing are key features to be explored at this attractive lake and natural area in the heart of Lynnwood (*see Hike 28 for details*).

Lake Ballinger 🌴

One of the larger lakes in the county, Lake Ballinger is probably best known for the public golf course built on its northerly shore. But there is also a public fishing access, dock, and a little swimming beach off Lakeview Dr. near 236th St. SW. Boating is allowed but internal combustion motors are not. The park is a city of Mountlake Terrace facility. It may be best to avoid the area in nice summer weather, unless it's crowds you crave.

Blackman Lake 🌴

When in Snohomish, take a look at Blackman Lake either at Ferguson Park east of Bickford Ave. just south of SR 9, or Hill Park off Lake View Ave. north of 13th St. There are simple woodsy urban parks here with picnicking, play area, and two small fishing docks. Hill, unfortunately, is stuck behind an unsightly chainlink fence. Perhaps there's an explanation? Paddlers can access the lake easily from Ave. A north of 13th St. No motorboats allowed.

Al Borlin Park (Buck Island)

On the east side of Monroe between the Skykomish River and Woods Creek is Buck Island and Al Borlin Park. The park is within a wooded floodplain, so facilities are limited to picnic areas, river access, and a great little trail system that links with Lewis Street Park on higher ground to the west (*see Hike 41 for details and directions*). The park opens early and closes at dusk.

LOWLANDS & FOOTHILLS

Lake Ketchum 🎣
Northeast of Stanwood is this small public access point managed by WDFW. The little lake is rather developed so don't go looking for anything spectacular here. Residents are working with state and county officials to improve water quality, reduce algae and unwanted vegetation, and restore ecological, scenic, and recreational values to the lake. From I-5 exit 215, find 300th St. NW and head west three miles to 76th Ave. NW; turn right. In less than a mile, turn left on S. Lake Ketchum Rd. Park on the right in a half-mile.

Sunday Lake 🎣
Here is a pretty little mostly developed lake near I-5 with a small dock and float, suitable for one or two people dying to stare at ducks and cattails—really, what life in the Northwest oughtta be. No internal combustion motors are allowed, so it's a friendly place to launch a canoe or kayak for a twenty-minute paddle in the off-season (forget it May through September). From SR 532 1/4 mile west of I-5, turn south onto E. Sunday Lake Rd. Look for the WDFW public fishing sign on the left in 0.9 mile. Closed after dark.

Pilchuck Creek
Two miles west of SR 9 on Stanwood-Bryant Rd. just east of the bridge over Pilchuck Creek is a small parking area and popular summer swimming hole, with gravel bars, woods, and a nice bit of water. Take a look on the way through.

Lake Armstrong 🎣
An attractive little lake where motorboats are banned, Lake Armstrong is enjoyable by rowboat, canoe, or kayak. Drive a mile north of Arlington on SR 9 to a narrow steep paved road angling to the right uphill, signed for the lake. Drive this around a bend, crossing the Centennial Trail and passing the 1994 Wildlife Farm of the Year (on left). In 0.6 mile turn left on E. Lake Armstrong Rd. and find the WDFW parking area on the left in 0.4 mile. The return to SR 9 can be tricky and is best avoided during commute hours.

Riley Lake 🎣
Find this marshy lake east of Arlington off SR 530 (MP 25.6). Drive Jim Creek Rd. six miles and go left on Lake Riley Rd. two miles to the lake and fishing access (stay left at a fork). Transmission lines and houses diminish the appeal, although it is pleasantly quiet. Internal combustion motors are not allowed.

Lake Cavanaugh Road
For a good view of the North Fork Stillaguamish valley, take SR 530 east from Arlington to MP 32.7 and turn left on the Lake Cavanaugh Rd., just before

the river bridge. Narrow pavement ends in two miles but good gravel continues over the east end of Frailey Mt. another four miles to Lake Cavanaugh in Skagit County. At 2.5 miles from SR 530 there is a great view of the valley from a bump next to a road cut. Look past the beer cans and shotgun shells to the Boulder River valley (feeds the Stilly), Three Fingers, and Whitehorse Mt. to the southeast. Mt. Higgins is to the east. A wide spot just beyond offers more room to park and almost as good a view.

Stillaguamish River 🎏

For a look at the lower Stillaguamish River in the county's rural nordland, try I-5 exit 210 and head west on Jackson Gulch Rd. 1.4 miles to Pioneer Highway (historic Silvana is a mile to the south). Turn right and immediately left on Norman Rd. and follow this 2.5 miles to a sharp right bend in the road with shoulder parking and a guardrail next to the river. There are good views up and down with Whitehorse Mountain, Three Fingers, Mt. Pilchuck, wooded terraces, and surrounding farms adding to the scene. Another wooded spot to gander is farther west. Continue north and west on the Norman Rd. 2.3 miles to Marine Drive and head straight across to find a WDFW fishing access area on the left just ahead. In Silvana another access is on the north side of Pioneer Highway at Hevly Rd. A planned new riverfront park in Stanwood may improve access as well. Closer to I-5, you can reach the gravel bar upstream of the freeway bridge by heading west from I-5 on SR 530 to 7th Ave. NE. Turn right here and follow this dead-end road under I-5 to a wide paved shoulder just beyond. It's a 0.2-mile walk on a grassy road to the bar.

The river's two major forks are also relatively easy to view. The North Fork Stilly roughly parallels SR 531 between Arlington and Darrington (*see Hikes 31 and 43*). At MP 38.8, an information sign explains why this river is famous among flyfishers. Zane Grey fished near here in 1918. The South Fork is especially scenic along the Mountain Loop Hwy east of Granite Falls. The falls, of course, is one of the better spots, but several trails and campgrounds offer views and easy access as well (*see Hikes 52, 53, 54, and 55*). The forks converge at Twin Rivers Park in Arlington.

North Mt. Lookout & Nels Bruseth Memorial Garden

A good view of the Sauk and S. Fork Stilly valleys and surrounding mountains is found at the old lookout site atop North Mt. near Darrington (*Hike 45*). Across from the ranger station, check out Nels Bruseth Memorial Garden.

Jordan Bridge

An intriguing suspension footbridge over the South Fork Stillaguamish River is between Arlington and Granite Falls, accessed via Jordan Rd. Nice views up and down the river are worth a look. Stairs lead to a beach under the bridge.

Granite Falls

There are only a few waterfalls in Snohomish County that you can drive to year-round, and Granite Falls, from which the nearby timber town takes its name, is a good one despite marginal facilities for the public. From downtown Granite Falls, follow the Mountain Loop Hwy north about 1.8 miles out of town to a small WDFW parking area on the left just before crossing the bridge over the South Fork Stilly. Even at low flows the falls are noisy and inviting—thundering when higher runoff races by in fall and spring. The drop is not great, but the view is good. Walk the obvious wide path (road bed) about 150 yards to stairs and either continue or drop down the steps to complete a short loop of about 0.2 mile. The big concrete structure below is a fish ladder to help ocean-going salmon and steelhead make their way up-river to spawn (no fishing allowed here). The river cuts an impressive gorge with high rock cliffs on the opposite shore. The rock can be slippery close to this tumult, so best to obey the signs. Big cedars and Douglas fir trees line the banks above the falls. With some creativity and minimal funding, the falls could be improved to a first-class viewing area. As it is, the signs, fencing, and concrete clash with the gem nature put here. But go see it anyway.

Cedar Stump

For those who have never seen a really big tree, the old cedar stump at the northbound I-5 rest area near Arlington (MP 207) is worth a gander, perhaps to spur a little consideration of what an incredible forest once existed in the region. In less than a century and a half, we humans have managed to destroy 90 percent of the old forests of Washington, although some still argue that we've locked up too much remaining forest in parks and wilderness. Hardly.

Seven Lakes 🌲

If it's not summery out, a visit to one or more of these little lakes northwest of Marysville makes a suitable mini-adventure when there's absolutely nothing else to do, or if you just want to see more of what this county is made of. The seven-plus lakes are scattered around Lake Goodwin (*see Wenberg State Park for directions*). Paddlers might enjoy them in almost any kind of weather. If it's too nice, though, expect lots of folks with similar ideas. There are public boat launches and WDFW fishing access areas, and/or swimming at almost all lakes in the area. A good county map will help you find them. Better ones include Goodwin (the biggest lake, has a county park and a state park with camping, etc.), Crabapple (access on the north side, attractive, small, no motor boats allowed), Ki (access from SR 531 shoulder on the north side, slow motor boats permitted), Shoecraft (access west side, water-skiing in the middle of the lake), Martha (north side access, pleasant), and Howard (west end access, no motors). Except for Goodwin, facilities are limited, though most have at least an outhouse.

Lake Cassidy 🐟

Of interest to canoeists and kayakers is this pleasant lake three miles north of Lake Stevens. Lake Cassidy has lots of marshy shore and wetlands nearby, within a developing rural setting. County Parks owns a big wildlife reserve on the north end, plus a new float adjacent to the Centennial Trail (*Hike 35*). A WDFW public fishing access is just south of where Lake Cassidy Rd. (60th St. NE) meets S. Lake Cassidy Rd., 0.6 mile east of SR 9. Park across the road.

Lake Bosworth 🐟

A small WDFW fishing access exists at the north end of Lake Bosworth, a modest-sized lake with lots of homes and some undeveloped shoreline. Motor-powered boats are prohibited, so it's good for a paddle. From the flashing red light in Granite Falls, head south on Granite Ave. (becomes Robe Menzel Rd.) and drive about three miles to a junction with Bosworth Rd.; stay right up the hill. In 0.8 mile, just after a sharp bend, turn right on E. Lake Bosworth Dr. and find the fishing access in a mile, off the end of this road.

Snohomish River 🐟

The County's namesake river, and one of the region's three principal river systems, is (surprise!) the Snohomish. The river collects runoff from the Skykomish and Snoqualmie Rivers which merge to form the Snohomish two miles southwest of Monroe. Good vantage points of the lower river are at several parks and public fishing access areas. The estuary at Port Gardner in North Everett is best viewed from W. Marine View Dr. (*see Hike 15*), and from SR 529. Upriver, try Langus Park (*Hike 36*), Lowell Riverfront Park (*Hike 37*), Riverview Rd., downtown Snohomish (*Hike 14*), Thomas Eddy (*Hike 39*), Lord Hill (*Hike 40*), and Shorts School Rd., three miles south of Snohomish. For a good look at the river's broad floodplain try Summit Park in North Everett at Summit Ave. and 20th St. The best place to view the Snoqualmie River, of course, is at Snoqualmie Falls in King County. A placid stretch above the confluence is visible from the WDFW public fishing access near the junction of High Bridge Rd. and Crescent Lake Rd.

Pilchuck River

Access areas can be found two miles east of Lake Stevens on Russell Rd. and at the Pilchuck Ballfields in Snohomish just east of Maple Ave. on 86th St. SE.

Lake Roesiger 🐟

With all its little woodsy bays and points, Lake Roesiger was once one of the more attractive lakes in the county. But like so many other lovely natural waterfronts in western Washington, humans and their houses, yards, and contrivances have encroached on the water's edge on all sides, vastly replacing the natural shoreline with a chaotic collage of development. Multitudes of boats, docks, floats, and portable comforts crowd the banks. And now that "water cycles" are the rage and singing birds are passé, even the quiet is missing from the lake most of the summer. All that said, Lake Roesiger still intrigues. At the right time of day or year (water skiing is banned late September through late May), there remains something to see and breathe here. Try Lake Roesiger County Park off the Lake Roesiger Rd. on the southeast shore, or the WDFW boat launch and fishing access at the south end (off Middle Shore Rd.), a mile south of the park.

Spada Lake 🌴

Spada Lake, a large reservoir in the foothills northeast of Sultan, is the main water supply for two-thirds of the Snohomish County population. The lake was created with the completion of Culmback Dam, a rock and clay structure, in 1965. The dam was raised 62 feet in 1984, doubling the size of the lake, and a hydroelectric project was constructed by Snohomish County PUD. Recreation amenities—mitigation for the dam and power project—were completed in 1990. Public use of the area is highly restricted to day use only (late April to late October). There are excellent picnicking facilities, limited walking paths, and good viewpoints, mostly barrier-free. For more information, try the PUD at 877-783-1000. From U.S. Hwy. 2 at the east edge of Sultan, head north on the Sultan Basin Rd. about 13.5 miles to an information/registration area and a road fork. Stay right to find Bear Creek Overlook on the left in about six miles. A short steep path offers a great vantage point for photos and sunsets. The roads are unpaved but well maintained. Lake Chaplain to the west is also part of the Everett water system but is not open to public use.

Flowing Lake 🌴

Flowing Lake is a modest-sized lake northeast of Snohomish with an attractive county park (daily fee) on the north end. Boating, fishing, swimming, camping, and short walks are all available. The lake can also be reached from the WDFW fishing access at the south end (turn right, or south, off Three Lakes Rd., then a quick left on Spada Rd., a left on Storm Lake Rd., and left again on Wonderland Rd.).

Storm & Panther Lakes 🌴

Two smaller lakes near Flowing Lake, Storm and Panther Lakes, are also worth a paddle. Storm Lake's WDFW site is just a block east of the southern access to Flowing Lake (above). To reach Panther Lake's public fishing access turn north off Three Lakes Rd. onto 163rd Ave. NE, then left in a mile on Panther

Lake Rd. The WDFW access is just ahead on the right. Panther is a pretty lake with woods and a marshy shore, and not too developed. Internal combustion motors are not allowed at either lake.

Chain Lake & Wagner Lake 🌴

A very pretty little lake with a mostly natural and marshy shore is Chain Lake, hidden in a little valley a few miles north of Monroe. A WDFW public fishing access is a half-mile east of Trombley Rd. on Chain Lake Rd. Wagner Lake, not far to the southeast, is also quite attractive and holds evidence of the area's robust logging history. The WDFW access is on the east side of Wagner Rd. about 0.7 mile north of Woods Creek Rd. Internal combustion motors are prohibited.

Crescent Lake 🌴

This is a small, pretty lake with a mostly natural shoreline and WDFW public fishing access. From SR 203 south of Monroe head west to Crescent Lake Rd. and a parking area on the right before reaching the Snoqualmie River bridge. Mt. Rainier is visible to the south.

North Creek Park

A county park south of Mill Creek with a nice view of large wetlands, North Creek Park has a good boardwalk trail (*see Hike 38*).

Echo & Lost Lakes 🌴

Two small lakes near the King County line east of Bothell can be reached at WDFW public fishing access points, though like most smaller lakes, Echo and Lost are of more interest to fishers and boaters than sightseers. Echo Lake is mostly developed. To reach it turn south off SR 522 onto Echo Lake Rd. and drive 2.8 miles to the fishing access on the right. For Lost Lake, back up a mile to Lost Lake Rd. and turn east to find the lake access a short mile beyond. Lost is smaller but less developed and somewhat appealing. Farther west, a larger lake, Crystal, can be found off Crystal Lake Rd. Unfortunately, this lake is effectively locked up by private development.

Wallace Falls

The best view of this high—and highly impressive—waterfall is from the trail that leaves Wallace Falls State Park (*see Hike 55*), although it's also quite visible from U.S. Hwy. 2 near Gold Bar. While you're in the area, maybe check out the Wallace River Salmon Hatchery, a mile west of Gold Bar.

Index Town Wall

High rock walls rise abruptly above the town of Index (*see p. 221*).

THE NORTH CASCADES

Suiattle River

Many good views of this broad swift river can be had from Suiattle River Rd. (USFS Rd. 26) which leaves SR 530 seven miles north of Darrington. From its Suiattle Glacier headwaters, this designated Wild and Scenic River winds half-way around Glacier Peak, collecting meltwater from more than three-fourths of its glaciers. At various points along the river, some of the area's dominant peaks are visible, including Whitehorse and White Chuck Mt. (prominent to the south near MP 7). Look for a few tributary waterfalls high above the road, including a nice one to the north at 4.0 miles. The road accesses several trails listed in this guide and ends at 23 miles, near Sulphur Creek Campground. The Suiattle River joins the Sauk near SR 530 and the Sauk feeds the Skagit River at Rockport near SR 20.

Green Mountain Road

The drive to many mountain trailheads, though at times rough, is often scenic, thanks to old-growth forest (and view-penetrating clearcuts), waterfalls, cliffs, occasional vistas, wildlife, and wildflowers. Green Mt. Rd. is one possibility (*see Hike 61 for directions*).

Mountain Loop National Scenic Byway

This famed highway is a 50-mile long, mostly-paved road connecting Granite Falls and Darrington by way of Barlow Pass and the South Fork Stillaguamish and South Fork Sauk River valleys. Development began in the 1890s, first spurred by mining, and later, logging. Today, numerous trails, views, camp-grounds, picnic areas, and historic sites can be accessed here; however, winter snows near Barlow Pass prevent year-round access. The road is usually open from May until November; and from Granite Falls only to Deer Creek Rd. in winter; beyond is a popular snowmobile area (Deer Creek Rd. is closed to mo-torized vehicles mid-December through March). Fourteen miles of road north of the pass are unpaved, well graded, but dusty in summer, with some single-lane roadway and turnouts. Check with the Darrington Ranger Station or the Verlot Public Service Center for current conditions and a good travelers' guide to the route. Note that the drive is famous and busy on summer weekends.

Whitehorse Mt. & Three Fingers

Even the locals will tell you that the most spectacular thing about the little logging town of Darrington is the backdrop: 6,852-foot Whitehorse Mt. The peak, visible from much of the western part of the county, rises abruptly just a mile from a town that's barely 500 feet above sea level. This remarkable glacier-carved mountain is steep and impressive from all sides, although the long steep

View from the White Chuck Mt. Viewpoint, south of Darrington.

glacier on the north makes it particularly gorgeous from the Darrington area. The mountain is visible from many roads in and out of town. Try a turnout at MP 45 on SR 530 where an open field offers a great wide-open view of both Whitehorse Mt. and Jumbo Mt. behind and to the left. If drivable, USFS Roads 28 and 2810 up North Mt. just north of the Darrington Ranger Station offer excellent views of these and other neighboring peaks. The triple summit of Three Fingers is also prominent from many areas of western Snohomish County, including I 5 north of Everett, SR 530 east of Arlington (around MP 34), and SR 92 heading into Granite Falls. From these distances, in good light and with ordinary binoculars, you should be able to make out the old fire lookout atop the south summit.

White Chuck Mt. & Mt. Pugh

Good mountain views exist at a number of turnouts along the Mountain Loop Hwy. between Darrington and Granite Falls. The White Chuck Mt. viewpoint at MP 44.1 is a good picnic stop, small and scenic with a wheelchair-accessible restroom (bullet holes courtesy of the Northwest's gun-totin'-bottle-chuckin'-sign-shootin'-backwoods-pick-up-truckers). White Chuck is the obvious big one across the Sauk River. Nice. Downriver are the layered summits of Mt. Higgins, and Jumbo Mt. to the left. Around MP 46 and 47, among other places, are good views of Mt. Pugh, also visible from SR 530 west of Darrington. The north side of White Chuck Mt. is prominent from the Suiattle River Rd. near MP 7.

Glacier Peak, Mt. Baker & Mt. Rainier

The highest bit of terra firma in Snohomish County is the 10,541-foot summit of DaKobed, the "Great Parent," or as most of us know it, Glacier Peak, Washington's fourth highest—and least active—volcano. Its last significant eruption was about 12,000 years ago, when a huge mudflow reached pre-Darrington. The summit is only a few feet shy of standing two vertical miles above sea level, yet it is almost entirely invisible over vast areas of the county. Mt. Baker to the north and Mt. Rainier to the south are far more conspicuous from many locations, not just because they are higher (Mt. Baker is 10,781 feet and Mt. Rainier is 14,440 feet), but because they don't sit behind crowds of high rugged peaks like Glacier Peak does, say, when viewed from the Everett area. While Glacier Peak is closer to Everett than its two neighbors, it is buried much deeper in the Cascades than the others. Still, it can be seen up close from a number of trails in the mountains, and with a careful eye, from a distance as well (*for the former, try Hikes 63, 65, 70, 71, 74, and 110*). One can also catch a glimpse of Glacier Peak from SR 530 west of Darrington near MP 42 and 43. The volcano is just right of White Chuck Mt. and left of Mt. Pugh.

For the distant view, wait for mid to late summer or fall when most of the snow has melted off the lower peaks and then try to pick out the more conspicuously snowy (icy) one in the background. The mountain is visible at several points along I-5, but also try Home Acres Rd. a half-mile south of U.S. Hwy. 2, where Glacier Peak appears only a few degrees right of Mt. Pilchuck. If you're fanatic about it, you'll find all three volcanoes visible from a single point. From the east side, there's a good view from a paved road northwest of Lake Wenatchee (*see Hike 110*). It should be added that from a few select locations, Mt. St. Helens, well over a hundred miles to the south, is also visible, but barely. In a geology class at Everett Community College in 1980, we all walked out to the parking lot to watch the plume from an eruption.

Squire Creek Wall

This immense 2,500-foot granite wall plus the east face of Three Fingers are visible from near the end of USFS Rd. 2040. (*See Hike 67 note regarding access.*)

Clear Creek & Asbestos Creek Falls

Clear Creek is one of many attractive, cascading streams crossed by the Mountain Loop Hwy. When all you feel like doing is watching water go by, pack up the lawn chair and head for Clear Creek Campground near Darrington. Look for a view of the creek's little gorge close by (*see Hike 46*). Or head up Clear Creek Rd. (USFS Rd. 2060), across from the campground entrance, to check out the creek's interesting watershed. The road can be rough at times. At three miles, park on the left just before the shallow creek flowing over the roadway

(Asbestos Creek). A long series of falls, partly visible, but mostly not, tumbles down the east wall of Jumbo Mt. The name may be uninviting, but the view isn't. Unfortunately, the view doesn't get any better than right from the road due to vista-blocking vegetation higher up the slope. If the stream and road are passable, drive another 2.6 miles to a junction. Right leads 0.5 mile to a view of two high rock walls and the east trailhead for Squire Creek Pass (*see Hike 68*). Left goes to a bridge over Clear Creek in 0.2 mile and more views of more walls, partly obstructed by trees. A washout blocks progress in another 0.8 mile where there's a nice mountain view of the peaks south of Three Fingers. This old road leads about three miles to the north trail for Deer Creek Pass.

Sauk River

The Sauk River, a fork of the Wild and Scenic Skagit River, begins in the heart of Snohomish County's North Cascades. The North and South Forks, plus the White Chuck and Suiattle River tributaries downstream, drain much of the Glacier Peak and Henry M. Jackson Wilderness Areas. Good views of the Sauk are found along the Old Sauk, Beaver Lake, North Fork Falls, and North Fork Sauk Trails (*see Hikes 47, 48, 50, and 74*), and at many Forest Service campgrounds and pull-outs along the Mountain Loop Hwy north of Barlow Pass. The old Monte Cristo Rd. (*see Hike 80*) parallels the South Fork for three miles. The South Fork takes a steep scenic drop just below Monte Cristo Lake, 2.5 miles north of the pass, and is impressive at high water. Near MP 19 is a good view of Sheep Mt. towering above the road. Whitewater boaters congregate near the confluence of the Sauk and White Chuck Rivers and often put in at a launch off USFS Rd. 22 about 0.2 mile off the Mountain Loop Hwy (from Darrington turn left at MP 44.8). One can also check out the White Chuck River at a bridge on USFS Rd. 23, 5.5 miles east of Mountain Loop Hwy.

North Fork Sauk Falls

An impressive waterfall anytime of the year, this is a definite stop for hikers exploring the Mountain Loop Hwy. region. The viewpoint is at the end of a moderately steep 0.2-mile trail that switchbacks down into a canyon. There's a sheer drop-off at the trail end so younger kids may need to be roped in close. (*See Hike 50 for directions.*)

Monte Cristo Lake

In a broad floodplain of the South Fork Sauk River about 2.4 miles north of Barlow Pass lies Monte Cristo Lake, worth a quick visit in the spring or fall. Myrtle Lake is across the road at a bend. At a turnout near the lower end of the lake (marked by a modest cedar tree next to the road) look for a short path leading to a small sandy bank on the lake. The river begins a steep drop just below this point.

Verlot Public Service Center

This unusual viewpoint is included because of the giant tree section on exhibit and other interpretive exhibits, plus an opportunity to learn to identify local trees, shrubs and flowers (ask for the walking tour brochure at the Service Center). The site is east of Granite Falls next to the South Fork Stillaguamish River near MP 11 on the Mountain Loop Hwy. Short walks, barrier-free restrooms, and camping are available nearby, and information on the National Forest and Wilderness Areas can be found at the center, formerly the Verlot Ranger Station. The big Douglas fir tree across the road was at least nine feet in diameter and over 700 years old before it was cut in 1969. Various events through history are marked along the rings, since we know that one new tree ring is added to a live tree each year. Amazingly, the tree was already about six feet across when Balboa sighted the Pacific Ocean in 1513. Millions of big trees have been logged in western Washington since the first mills were established in the mid-1800s. Now only a relative few remain.

Mt. Pilchuck

Not only does western Snohomish County afford good views of Mt. Pilchuck, one of the region's more prominent landmarks, but the drive up the mountain (summer and fall) offers even more impressive views of the county. From Mountain Loop Hwy (MP 12) turn south on USFS Rd. 42, then stay left and follow this sometimes rough, sometimes good road seven miles to a big parking area and viewpoint near the former ski area. Then try to figure out what's what (a good topographical map helps). For the splendid panorama from the summit, try the Mt. Pilchuck Trail (*see Hike 95*).

Gold Basin Mill Pond & Hemple Creek Picnic Area

The upper valley of the South Fork Stillaguamish River is rich in timber and mining history, and the mill pond at Gold Basin is one of many historic sites that are easily accessible by car or on foot. Hemple Creek Picnic Area (with room for a lot of picnics, including some barrier-free) is nearby across the highway. From Granite Falls drive the Mountain Loop Hwy to MP 13.5 and find the signed parking area on the right, across from Gold Basin Campground. A short paved interpretive walk (wheelchair accessible) leads to a few remnants of the early 1900s sawmill and nice views of the mill pond. The impoundment formed behind a small dam and was used for log storage until the mill folded in 1913. The scenic pond has been enhanced to support young coho salmon. Hemple Creek Picnic Area, next to the campground (to the west), contains a small interpretive display and is a good place to frolic in the river when the water's down. The area is accessible nearly year-round.

Bear Lake

The trail to Pinnacle Lake (*see Hike 92*) quickly reaches Bear Lake, affording a nice view of the wooded lakeshore with minimal effort.

Lake Evan 🌴

A very short walk from the Boardman Lake Trailhead leads to this little mountain lake surrounded by old-growth forest (*see Hike 90*).

Dick Sperry Picnic Area & Sperry-Iverson Mine

Look for this nice lunch spot on the South Fork Stilly east of Granite Falls on the Mountain Loop Hwy. (MP 21.1). Upriver, the broad west face of Stillaguamish Peak is prominent. The Sperry-Iverson Mine (closed) can be seen across the highway 200 yards farther east, and a short path (may be overgrown) leads up a wooded hillside to Sperry's old cabin site. Just up the highway is a turnout near the site of a three-mile aerial tram that carried gold and silver ore over Marble Pass. In another half-mile is the old mining town of Silverton.

Coal Lake Road Overlook

Photographers seeking an easy vantage point for a rugged mountain scene might try turning north off the Mountain Loop Hwy at MP 25.9, east of Granite Falls. Drive up the Coal Lake Rd. 2.7 miles to a big turnout on the left side. The view of the South Fork Stillaguamish valley is excellent. Fall is especially nice when there is more color and the chance of a little fresh snow dusting the summits. Hall Peak and Big Four Mt. are to the south, with Sperry and Vesper Peaks behind and left. The road continues to Coal Lake and nearby trails (*see Hikes 86 and 87*).

Coal Lake 🌴

From the Coal Lake Rd. overlook (see above) continue up the road to the Coal Lake parking area (*see Hike 86*) and wander the short trail to a good view of another lovely montane lake. Watch for pikas whistling warnings in the rocks.

Big Four Ice Caves

For awesome views of some big peaks of the North Cascades, head for the new Big Four Ice Caves Trailhead. (*See Hike 55 for directions and a description of the easy hike to the ice caves.*) Big Four Mt., a real neck-craner, and Hall Peak's big spire dominate the skyline. If you don't care to hike a mile up to the cave viewpoint at the base of Big Four, try the level half-mile paved path and boardwalk nature loop with a visit to the Stilly River footbridge mid-way (barrier-free to bridge and possibly beyond). Big avalanches thunder down the mountain's precipitous slopes in winter and spring, producing the snow and ice accumulation in which the caves form. They are unsafe to enter, by the way. Early season, avalanche danger is still very high so the trail may be closed past the river bridge. The peak is named for a snowpatch high above that resembles the number "4" in summer (there's also a leaning "7" above it, and sometimes a "witch on a broom" to the right, best seen from the Coal Lake Rd. junction, where a keen eye might make out a sounding "sperm whale"). The area is generally inaccessible from January into April, sometimes longer, because of deep snows that close the Mountain Loop Hwy.

Sunrise Mine Road

One of the more dramatic close-up views of impressive North Cascades peaks and waterfalls can be found at the end of the Sunrise Mine Rd. 2.6 miles southeast of the Big Four Ice Caves. East of Granite Falls, turn south off the Mountain Loop Hwy at MP 28.8. Best times to visit are late spring through fall. Waterfalls run their highest in the spring and early summer. Even in cloudy weather, the views of stark, vertical rock walls may be worth a visit. From the road-end (at 2.2 miles), visible peaks include Del Campo Peak (the steeply layered summit directly up the valley), Morning Star Peak (closer to the right), and Sperry Peak (a towering pyramid to the southwest). Lewis Peak is visible just before the road-end, left of Del Campo. On the drive in, the spires of Big Four Mt. and Hall Peak are sublimely inexplicable. For a good strenuous summer hike in the area try Headlee Pass (*see Hike 83*).

Skykomish River

To check out the lower reaches of the Skykomish River (a state-designated Scenic River) try Monroe's Buck Island (*see Hike 41*), and these WDFW fishing access areas: on the north side of the river west of Lewis St. in Monroe; on the north side of Ben Howard Rd. two miles east of SR 203; north of U.S. Hwy. 2 on the west side of Sultan (picnicking), and on the south side of the river east of 311th Aveune SE at Sultan. A short reach of the Snoqualmie River which joins the Skykomish southwest of Monroe is also accessible. Look for a WDFW public fishing access near the junction of High Bridge Rd. and Crescent Lake Rd. west of SR 203. The latter will take you south to the famous falls in King County, still a half-hour drive from here.

One of the more famous stretches of whitewater in the state is Boulder Drop, about two miles west of Index. Pull off on the north shoulder of U.S. Hwy. 2 east of MP 34 where you can see the river near the top of the drop. Fleets of rafts and kayaks float this area in spring and summer, an exhilarating run, to be sure. For a chance at a spur of the moment, half-day ride (for a fee, of course), look for a guide early morning at the Big Eddy River Access on U.S. Hwy. 2 about 3.5 miles downriver (MP 30.5). It's a common meeting place and takeout for commercial raft trips on the Sky.

The North and South Forks of the Skykomish converge just below Index

North Fork Skykomish River.

near the U.S. Hwy. 2 bridge west of town. The North Fork parallels USFS Rd. 63 (or vice-versa) with good views at the old bridge into Index a mile north of the highway; just past Howard Creek (if open) at MP 9.1—turn left on USFS Rd. 6330 and immediately cross a bridge over the North Fork; park at the other end then walk out on the bridge for good views up and down the river, plus Mt. Index and the high rock wall leading right to Mt. Persis; farther up the North Fork Rd., there are several scenic stretches of bouldery, cascading whitewater. More serious and skilled adventurers might look around the Bear Creek confluence for more river views; *see also Hike 103*. Back at the forks, a future 1,300-acre state park (Forks of the Sky) has been reserved that includes substantial riverfront and some of the high cliffs of Index Town Wall.

The South Fork begins near the town of Skykomish (in King County) with the merging of the Beckler and Tye Rivers east of town. Waterfalls make these rivers intriguing, especially the Tye at Deception Creek (*see Hike 60*), and the South Fork between Index and Baring where three significant waterfalls are somewhat tucked out of sight. Public access improvements to all three are non-existent (this really ought not to be so). Sunset Falls is a spectacular sliding cascade that drops to a wide bend in the river 1.5 miles up the Mt. Index Rd. from U.S. Hwy. 2. Another 1.3 miles up is Canyon Falls, just below an arched bridge. Here, the river seems to be sucked into a dark hole in the Earth, reappearing as foam in a gash below. Poking around these falls is not only potentially dangerous (no facilities), access is complicated by extensive private development. The Mt. Index Rd. beyond the Lake Serene trailhead (*see Hike 99*) is intended for residents and guests only and big signs warn that your presence is unwelcome. Lacking a good connection, try Eagle Falls farther upriver, but only when you're headed east on U.S. Hwy. 2. Pull off at a turnout at MP 39 and follow a short rough path to a view of this falls.

Mt. Index & Mt. Baring

From many areas of southwest Snohomish County one can look to the Cascades and easily spot several sharp peaks and a deep gash in the skyline where Mt. Index, Baring Mt., Gunn and Merchant Peaks, and their neighbors rise like sentinels over the Skykomish River. The peaks are visible at various locations along U.S. Hwy. 2 east of Everett. Mt. Index is prominent east of Gold Bar and most impressive near the town of (where else) Index. This peak's near vertical north face is a Cascades' classic mountaineering objective. Behind the town to the west is Town Wall, a rock climber's paradise whenever the rain quits. To get closer to Mt. Index, try the moderately steep hike to Lake Serene (*Hike 99*). Heybrook Ridge offers a good view, too, and it's only half the effort (*Hike 57*). Mt. Index and the wall of cliffs leading to Mt. Persis to the northwest produce an impressive scene from the North Fork Rd. at about MP 3.5.

Equally impressive is Mt. Baring, farther east and across the river valley from Mt. Index. From the west, Baring stands out like some kind of petrified rocket launcher, though far more beautiful. While there is a good view of the peak just east of MP 36 on U.S. Hwy. 2 (straight down the highway), the best view from a road is at the end of USFS Rd. 6024 where the trail to Barclay Lake begins (*see Hike 100*). Things get dramatic a bit over three miles from the highway, beginning with the impressive southwestern rampart of Merchant and Gunn Peaks on the left (clearcuts below), followed by a good view of Baring's precipitous upper wall just beyond. The north face, nearly 3,000 feet high, is one of the highest cliffs in the Cascades. At mile four near the Barclay Lake trailhead a big waterfall slices the slopes of craggy Merchant Peak.

Deception Falls

Although Deception Falls is across the line into King County, it is a favorite stopping point on the drive to Stevens Pass. Several falls on the Tye River and Deception Creek are an easy stroll away and partly barrier-free (*see Hike 60*).

Stevens Pass

Also just outside the county, Stevens Pass is where the railroad and U.S. Hwy. 2 breach the crest of the North Cascades. There are no towering peaks here, but the drive over the 4,000-foot pass is scenic and popular year-round. A ski area operates in the winter, and the PCT crosses the highway here as well (*see Hikes 108 and 110*).

Public Campgrounds

Local, state, and especially federal land management agencies provide abundant camping opportunities in a variety of settings, usually for a fee (often $10 to $15 per site). Many sites fill up in summer. Camping by reservation is often required as the demand for campsites increases in late spring and summer. Many sites, however, remain first-come, first-served.

Free camping is sometimes available in the off-season. Most federal sites close altogether since there is not enough staff to pick up the trash, pump the toilets, or scare off mindless vandals—scourge of the wilderness—who torch outhouses and blow bullet holes through anything that clinks. Despite the problems, agency staff and campground hosts should be commended for the work they do to keep a struggling but good system alive. Some sites have potable water and chopped firewood in season. Nevertheless, always carry jugs of drinking water, and pack out your garbage and recyclables. Douse fires completely, just like the bear says. Burning plastic and aluminum trash in firepits is uncool and toxic.

In addition to all the campgrounds found along Mountain Loop Hwy, and the Skykomish and Suiattle Rivers, the Forest Service maintains several smaller group facilities, by reservation only. Informal camping occurs along many roads and rivers but this freebie alternative is often too damaging to vegetation, soils, and water quality to be recommended (even where it's legal). These might also be the places where the familiar phrase "watch your step" was originally coined.

For more information, contact the agency or concessionaire. To make a reservation at a national forest site, try **www.recreation.gov** or call 877-444-6777. These contacts were valid in 2007, but could change in the future. You can also get camping information from a local USFS office. Reservations are not usually required October through March. Reservations at most state parks can be made by calling 888-226-7688. Again, this is generally unnecessary fall through early spring.

CITY & COUNTY CAMPGROUNDS

Kayak Point Park
The county operates a decent campground with some barrier-free sites at Kayak Point Park above the beach south of Stanwood (*see Hike 2 for directions*).

River Meadows Park
Limited walk-in tent camping is available at this county park on the South Fork Stillaguamish River (*see Hike 32*).

Squire Creek Park & Campground
To find this attractive county facility, turn north off of SR 530 about 4 miles west of Darrington (park sign). Beautiful Douglas fir and sword fern forest on 28 acres next to Squire Creek. Many relatively private sites for tents and RVs, plus group camping with a large picnic shelter.

Ferguson Park Campground (Snohomish)
A small, urban campground on Blackman Lake in Snohomish is run by the city. Find it next to a busy shopping complex east of Bickford Ave. south of SR 9. Named for E. C. Ferguson, founder of the city in 1859.

Flowing Lake County Park
A nicely wooded park with good campsites, some barrier-free, just above the lake (*see p. 236 for directions*).

Lake Roesiger Park
The county operates a small campground in the woods at Lake Roesiger Park, across the road from the lake (*see p. 236*).

WASHINGTON STATE CAMPGROUNDS

Wenberg State Park
On Lake Goodwin northwest of Marysville, a few dozen sites and a lot of boats on the lake (*see p. 234 for directions*).

Mt. Pilchuck State Park
A few nice tent sites in the trees near the Mt. Pilchuck Trailhead (*see Hike 95 for directions*).

Wallace Falls State Park
North of Gold Bar, there are only a few tent sites at this park famous for the three-mile hike to the falls (*see Hike 56 for details*).

NATIONAL FOREST CAMPGROUNDS

In addition to the sites listed below, several group campgrounds are open by reservation only, including Beaver Creek, Coal Creek, Esswine, Marten Creek, Tulalip, and Wiley Creek. All are on the Mountain Loop Hwy east of Verlot. In the off-season, call the local office if you need to know which areas are open, or stop at Darrington or Verlot on the way.

Buck Creek Campground

An attractive, remote, modest-sized campground in big trees on a rushing creek above the Suiattle River Rd. at MP 15.3 (*see also Hike 49*).

Sulphur Creek Campground

About 30 sites at the confluence of Sulphur Creek and the Suiattle River, off USFS Rd. 26 at MP 22.5. Stand near the creek and your olfactory may just pick up a hint of sulphur, derived from the hot springs (i.e. warm puddles) a mile up the trail. The popular Suiattle River Trailhead (*Hike 64*) is also just up the road, so expect some traffic.

French Creek Campground

A primitive campground with a handful of sites a mile up the road to Boulder River Trail (*see Hike 44*) off SR 530.

Clear Creek Campground

A small area in trees next to the Sauk River, close to the road and close to Darrington. Frog Lake Trail (*Hike 46*) is across the road.

Sloan Creek Campground

In a nice remote location next to North Fork Sauk River and Trail (*Hike 74*) with easy access to big trees.

Bedal Campground

Attractive remote setting at the confluence of the North and South Forks Sauk River, 18 miles from Darrington. Some barrier-free sites. Many trails in the area, including North Fork Falls (*Hike 50*).

Turlo Campground

Westernmost USFS campground on Mountain Loop Hwy, at Verlot, 11 miles from Granite Falls. Perched in nice woods on the South Fork Stilly.

Verlot Campground

A nice early and late season campground with about two dozen sites, next to the river just upstream from Turlo. An easy trail links both campgrounds with the Verlot Public Service Center.

Gold Basin Campground

What once was a town is now a large campground with almost 100 sites (some barrier-free), including a number at the edge of the South Fork Stilly. Some walk-in tent sites are in mature forest. Playfield, coin showers, and amphitheater, too. A path leads across the highway to the mill pond historic site. East of Granite Falls at MP 13.5 on the Mountain Loop Hwy.

Boardman Creek Campground

On the river in hardwood forest, a small tent-only area at MP 16.9 on the Mountain Loop Hwy.

Red Bridge Campground

Smallish area east of Boardman on the Mountain Loop Hwy at MP 18.4. Private sites with good river access.

Monte Cristo Campground

A small walk-in (or bike-in) area near the old townsite, a four-mile hike from Barlow Pass along the old road; located on the left before crossing the creek-sized river (*see also Hike 80*).

Troublesome Creek Campground

Nice sites in forest near the creek and North Fork Skykomish River northeast of Index. A good nature trail nearby with two footbridges over the creek (*see Hike 59*).

San Juan Campground

A smaller site on the river two miles east of Troublesome Creek.

Money Creek Campground

Just south of U.S. Hwy. 2 near MP 46. Very nice sites in big trees along the rushing river, plus a good picnic area. Railroad tracks are nearby.

Miller River Campground

In King County, two miles south of Money Creek CG.

Beckler River Campground

Nice area on a small river, not quite two miles north of U.S. Hwy. 2 on USFS Rd. 65.

Hiking Organizations & Agencies

ALL EMERGENCIES CALL 911 (including search & rescue)

ORGANIZATIONS
Adopt-A-Stream Foundation, www.streamkeeper.org
American Hiking Society, www.americanhiking.org
Cascade Land Conservancy, www.cascadeland.org
Everett Mountaineers, www.everettmountaineers.org
Friends of Lord Hill, www.friendsoflordhill.org
Iron Goat Trail, www.irongoat.org
Monte Cristo Preservation Association, www.whidbey.com/mcpa
North Cascades Conservation Council, www.northcascades.org
NW Hikers Forum, www.nwhikers.net
Pacific Crest Trail Association, www.pcta.org
People for Puget Sound, www.pugetsound.org
Pilchuck Audubon Society, www.pilchuckaudubon.org
Sierra Club, Cascade Chapter, www.cascade.sierraclub.org
Stilliguamish Citizens Alliance, www.robecanyon.org
Volunteers for Outdoor Washington, www.trailvolunteers.org
Washington Native Plant Society, www.wnps.org
Washington Trails Association, www.wta.org
Wild Washington Campaign, www.wildwashington.org
The Wilderness Society, www.tws.org

CITY & COUNTY GOVERNMENT
Edmonds Parks & Recreation, (425) 771-0230
Everett Parks & Recreation, (425) 257-8300
Lynnwood Parks & Recreation, (425) 771-4030
Snohomish Co. Parks & Rec., (425) 388-6600

STATE GOVERNMENT
WA State Parks & Recreation, (360) 902-8844, or (800) 233-0321
  - Campsite reservations, most state parks, (888) 226-7688

WA Department of Natural Resources (DNR), Northwest Region
General info, (360) 856-3500, or (800) 527-3305
Report a forest fire, (800) 562-6010
WA Department of Fish & Wildlife, Regional Office, (425) 775-1311
- Vehicle use permit, www.fishhunt.dfw.wa.gov
WA Department of Transportation, (360) 705-7000
- Mountain Pass Report, (800) 695-7623
- WA State Ferries, (888) 808-7977, www.wsdot.wa.gov/ferries

FEDERAL GOVERNMENT
Mt. Baker-Snoqualmie National Forest, (425) 775-9702, or (800) 627-0062
- Recreation Information Center, multi-agency, (206) 470-4060
- Campsite reservations, (877) 444-6777, www.recreation.gov
- Northwest Forest Pass, www.fs.fed.us/r6/mbs/passes
Darrington Ranger Station, (360) 436-1155
Verlot Public Service Center, (360) 691-7791
Skykomish Ranger District, (360) 677-2414
Wenatchee River Ranger District, (509) 548-6977

OTHER USEFUL CONTACTS
Avalanche Hazard Information, (206) 526-6677; www.nwac.noaa.gov
National Weather Service Forecast, www.wrh.noaa.gov/sew

LAW ENFORCEMENT AGENCIES
All emergencies, CALL 911
Everett Police Department, (425) 257-8400
Snohomish County Sheriff, (425) 388-3393, main line
Search & rescue staff, (425) 388-3328
WA State Patrol, (360) 658-2588 (Marysville)

Index

269

About the author...
A resident of northwest Washington since 1967, Ken Wilcox is an avid explorer of the sprawling North Cascades. When he isn't hiking trails and climbing mountains—habits that ought to last a lifetime—Ken works as a writer and consultant for environmental and recreation projects. He is author of *Hiking Whatcom County* (2006) and *Hiking the San Juan Islands* (2001) and lives in Bellingham.

Hiker's Log

Date	Trail	Miles	Notes

Hiker's Log

Date	Trail	Miles	Notes